INTELLIGENCE AND HUMAN ABILITIES

Psychological research into human intelligence and abilities presents us with a number of difficult questions:

- Are human abilities explained by a single core intelligence or by multiple intelligences?
- How should abilities be assessed? With abstract tests, or with practical problems similar to those encountered in life, school and work?
- Do ability tests predict how a person will behave? If so, can they predict whether a person will succeed at school and at work?

Intelligence and Human Abilities critically evaluates research evidence from the past 100 years to consider these and other issues. It shows that, despite the apparent contradictions in this research, the evidence in fact supports one coherent model, a fact which has clear implications for researchers, educators and test-users.

This clear and engaging text provides an up-to-date evaluation of what the empirical evidence tells us about the number, nature and origins of human abilities. It will be essential reading for students and practitioners of psychology and education, and also for users of ability tests such as applied psychologists and personnel managers.

Colin Cooper was until recently a Senior Lecturer in the School of Psychology at Queen's University Belfast, UK.

INTELLIGENCE AND HUMAN ABILITIES

Structure, Origins and Applications

Colin Cooper

Routledge
Taylor & Francis Group

LONDON AND NEW YORK

First published 2015
by Routledge
2 Park Square, Milton Park, Abingdon, Oxon, OX14 4RN

and by Routledge
711 Third Avenue, New York, NY 10017

Routledge is an imprint of the Taylor & Francis Group, an informa business

© 2015 Taylor and Francis

Library of Congress Cataloging-in-Publication Data
Cooper, Colin, 1954–
  Intelligence and abilities / Colin Cooper.
    pages cm
  Includes bibliographical references and index.
 1. Intellect.   2. Ability.   3. Human behavior.   I. Title.
  BF431.C666 2015
  153.9—dc23
  2014040645

ISBN: 978-1-84872-066-4 (hbk)
ISBN: 978-1-84872-067-1 (pbk)
ISBN: 978-1-315-73558-0 (ebk)

Typeset in Joanna
by Apex Covantage, LLC

Printed and bound by CPI Group (UK) Ltd, Croydon, CR0 4YY

To Wesley

CONTENTS

PREFACE

Since the predecessor to this book, *Intelligence and Abilities*, was published, research in human abilities has blossomed. Emotional intelligence and practical intelligence have become popular concepts, and multiple intelligence theory offers an alternative to older conceptions of abilities. The study of working memory and its relationship to intelligence has also become somewhat controversial, with some arguing that the two concepts are identical and others claiming that they are distinct, though correlated. In each case, it is necessary to consider these theories carefully to determine whether they supplement or replace older models of cognition and ability. The field of cognitive epidemiology simply did not exist when *Intelligence and Abilities* was written. Cognitive epidemiology considers the link between childhood intelligence and cognition, health and physical functioning in old age, and offers some fascinating insights into what can (and cannot) be predicted from a simple ability test administered in childhood, although disentangling the influence of social factors from intelligence necessarily complicates these analyses.

There has also been steady research in more traditional areas such as the links between intelligence and performance at school and work. Such studies have moved away from simple correlational analyses, and it is now possible to test quite complex models of cause and effect that consider the role of both social class and cognition. Laboratory studies can also help us to understand the social and biological origins of abilities. For example, sophisticated methods of data analysis allow for more meaningful analysis of reaction time data to elucidate whether intelligence is linked to speed of information processing. It has also become possible to determine whether the same genes that influence some mental abilities are also involved in other aspects of performance: school achievement, for example—a finding whose implications need to be carefully considered if such relationships are found. Modern brain-scanning techniques can show how brain structure and brain activity are linked to cognitive abilities, and there has been a commensurate interest in exploring how the home environment and the unique environment that each individual develops for themselves is linked to their cognitive abilities.

Theories tend to come and go in psychology. For example, few researchers now work within the frameworks of Hull's learning theory, Brunswik's functionalism or Sheldon's constitutional psychology, even though each was enormously influential in its day. In contrast, models of human abilities have stood the test of time rather well. Some theories are still the focus of considerable research activity a century after they were first proposed, although the focus has swung from "how should we best conceptualise individual differences in thinking ability" to "why do different individuals develop different abilities, and what are the implications of this". The longevity of research into human cognitive abilities is probably because the main findings have proved easy to replicate, effect sizes tend to be large, and ability tests frequently have surprisingly large correlations with real-life behavior, which make them valuable tools for applied psychologists. This book considers the wealth of old and new literature, and tries to draw balanced conclusions about what abilities are, what influences them, and whether they predict real-world performance purely because scores on ability tests are linked to social class and background. The results are sometimes surprising.

1

INTRODUCTION

The psychology of ability is a branch of psychology that examines how and why people differ from one another—as opposed to other areas of the discipline that regard such "individual differences" as nuisances, to be ignored (or controlled for statistically) in psychology experiments. For example, social psychologists study variables that influence prejudice in the population, and do not trouble to consider whether or why some individuals are more prejudiced against minority groups than others. Cognitive psychologists try to draw inferences about neural mechanisms by studying how various features of stimuli influence response time; they are rarely interested in whether or why some individuals perform more quickly or slowly than the norm in all experimental conditions. Thus Cronbach (1957) identified two distinct disciplines of psychology. One comprises areas such as social, developmental, cognitive, physiological and behavioural psychology—branches that try to understand the broad laws that govern how people in general behave under various conditions. The second branch is that of individual differences, clinical and (sometimes) occupational psychology, which focus on how and why people differ from one another. And whilst there have been moves to reconcile these two approaches through experimental designs that consider both types of experimental treatment and individual differences, such studies still remain the exception rather than the rule.

Individual Differences

The psychology of individual differences is traditionally divided into four main areas: first, the psychology of motivation, which tries to explain what drives people to behave in certain ways; second, mood/emotion, which considers feelings (one area where there is genuine integration between individual differences and cognitive psychology thanks to workers such as Bower, 1981); and third, personality psychology, which tries to explain both what people do and the way that they do it through 'personal styles', such as anxiety or sociability. Finally, there is the psychology of abilities, which examines how well individuals perform tasks that involve thinking or problem solving, attempts to understand how many "talents" are necessary to explain individual differences in problem-solving behaviour, and seeks to understand why and how individual differences in these abilities emerge in the first place. Underpinning these four areas is the science of psychometrics (literally "measurement of the soul"), which is a branch of statistics dealing with the measurement of motivation, mood, personality and abilities, and other issues (e.g., bias) arising from psychological testing.

The Meaning of 'Ability'

It is first necessary to try to define the subject matter of this book: to set out what is meant by terms such as 'mental ability' and 'intelligence'. There is no shortage of definitions in the literature, but many of these are unenlightening: the great and the good from the world of psychology were invited to define what they understood by intelligence at a symposium in 1921 (Thorndike, 1921) and, as usual when psychologists are gathered together, the range of definitions was enormous, running from the rather unhelpful behaviourist view that "intelligence is what is measured by intelligence tests" to "ability to learn", or "capacity for abstract thinking". Sternberg and Salter (1982) offer a thoughtful historical discussion of what is meant by terms such as 'intelligence', 'mental ability' and 'aptitude', but let us try to build our own definition.

Abilities, in the broad sense, are any behaviours that can sensibly be evaluated. They will include typing, knowledge of steam locomotives, sprinting (and other sporting activities), reading a map, swindling people, cooking, managing one's finances, designing bridges, thinking up a plausible excuse to obtain an extension for a piece of coursework, growing onions, helping a depressed person, solving anagrams, diagnosing a fault in a piece of machinery or writing a creative essay. The key point is that it would be possible to assess the effectiveness of individual people who take part in these activities, either by

- monitoring behaviour (e.g., the number of words typed per minute, annual cost of rectifying design faults found in bridges, size/taste/yield of onions, time taken to run 400 metres, success at obtaining extensions), or by
- asking someone to evaluate their own or someone else's behaviour, for example, by giving a student a mark for the creative essay, asking depressed individuals to rate the quality of their therapy, or asking the therapist to rate the degree of improvement that their course of therapy has brought about. Where these subjective ratings are used to assess performance, it is particularly important to ensure that they are accurate: that is, that the measures have high 'reliability' and 'validity'.

It seems reasonable to suppose that two things affect how well a person can perform on any task that they are given: their level of ability, and the difficulty of the task. If we give people exactly the same tasks to perform, this controls for the effects of task difficulty. Therefore the only reason that one person performs better than another on a particular task measuring memory for faces (for example) has to be because they have a better memory for faces: they are more able at that task. We can at least rank-order people in terms of their performance on a particular task, and use this as an estimate of their ability.

In practice, we know that people may produce slightly different scores if they are given a second version of the task on a different occasion, and a branch of statistics known as psychometrics has grown up to address this and similar measurement issues. Without going into the details, it can be shown that given well-designed, appropriately lengthy tasks to perform, it is possible to assess a person's level of ability fairly accurately—and that abilities are fairly stable over time. For example, Ian Deary at Edinburgh compared the scores of 11-year-olds who completed a reasoning test with the scores that were obtained when the same people took the same test again 66 years later. The correlation between performance at age 11 and performance at age 77 was approximately 0.73, indicating that the scores are extremely stable over time (Deary, Whalley, Lemmon, Crawford & Starr, 2000). Children who reason well end up as adults who reason well: children who are weak at reasoning generally turn into adults who are weak at reasoning.

Characteristics such as this—behaviours that are fairly stable over time—are known as traits. Traits are usually divided into two categories. Personality traits describe a person's *style* of behaviour: for example, some people are anxious, whilst others are calm and relaxed; some people are sociable, whereas others prefer their own company and do not hanker after outside stimulation. Ability traits, on the other hand, reflect how well a person can *do* things—and this book considers how and why some people perform better than others at tasks that involve thinking. For example, it considers how well people can reason, remember things, visualise things, and so on.

From this, it may seem that all one needs to do in order to study abilities is devise a few tasks, measure how well people perform on them, and report the results. There are several reasons why this simple-minded approach will not suffice. The remainder of this chapter explores why this is so, and it gives a flavour of some of the types of tasks that psychologists typically study.

It is implicit in this definition that not everyone has the same level of a particular ability. All humans do some things—such as regulating our body temperature—pretty much equally effectively, or else we would die. Almost all of us are capable of performing activities such as manoeuvring our way through a busy crowd without jostling other people without even appreciating how complicated this feat is. Almost all of us may be able to infer a person's emotional state by combining a number of quite subtle cues without always noticing how and why we do so: slow, quiet speech delivered in a monotone coupled with a lack of emotion and little eye contact might lead us to infer sadness or depression, whilst rapid speech and much body movement may suggest that a person is anxious, for example. Indeed, psychologists and computer scientists often only appreciate how complex activities are when it is found that computers find them difficult or impossible to perform.

Mental and Other Abilities

Readers may feel some unease at this point since the list of abilities given above seems to be far more extensive than one might expect in a psychology text. Surely this book is not going to turn into a treatise on onion growing? And indeed it is conventional (though not, I believe, necessarily a good thing) to narrow down the field of abilities.

Each of the abilities in the above list can be regarded as reflecting a different mixture of at least four things:

(a) Task-specific knowledge or training. By definition, this will not generalise to other things: if I spend years becoming proficient at playing the bagpipes, the skills I acquire will not mean that I can pick up a violin for the first time and play it expertly.

(b) Physical prowess. All tasks require some sort of physical response, even if it is just clicking a mouse or saying a word. However some tasks rely on coordination, strength or agility (for example) for their successful completion.

(c) Emotional skills. Excessive anxiety can affect performance at many tasks: managing this might be important. Emotional skills will also be important when dealing with other people—e.g., leadership at work, or counselling.

(d) Thought processes. Unlike (a), these might generalise from task to task. For example, someone with an excellent long-term memory is likely to perform well at many subjects at school (where the emphasis is often on rote learning), or be a wonderful lawyer (learning case law) or accountant (tax and accounting regulations).

Though I have absolutely no data to back this up, I suspect that the extent to which each of these variables affects performance might be as shown in Table 1.1: the more stars, the larger the influence.

For example, if we assess typing performance by measuring speed and accuracy, experience at typing will have a huge influence. For experienced

Table 1.1 Possible influences of specific knowledge/training, physical prowess, emotion and mental abilities on various tasks

Task	Specific Knowledge/ Training	Physical Prowess	Emotion	Mental Abilities
Typing	****	**	*	*experienced typists ****beginners
Performance on a history test	****	*	*	****memory *reasoning
Football	****	***	****elite athletes *casual players	**
Success in getting a coursework extension	***	*	****	***
Solving a reasoning unlike anything previously encountered	*	*	**	****

typists, individual differences in mental abilities probably have little effect on performance, as the activity is "overlearned" or "automatised" and requires little or no conscious thought. The novice typist will however need to scan the keyboard looking for letters, and the speed with which they can do this will greatly influence their performance. Emotional skills are not really needed, and most people in the general population will have the physical ability to use a keyboard. So this is an example of an ability that largely reflects training and practice (in expert typists) plus some mental abilities (speed of scanning, for novices only).

Many of the assessments made at school reflect specific knowledge or training: a test of 'history attainment' is more likely to measure how well you can remember the content of a particular book or lecture notes rather than physical ability, or emotional skills. Mental abilities are probably not enormously important, although strategies for memorising material (perhaps using mnemonics or visualisation techniques) might well be useful, and some ability to understand language will also clearly be important. But the key point is that just because a person has a wonderful knowledge of 19th century history, we cannot tell whether that person knows anything at all about Ancient Rome—he or she may never have been taught it. This is the crucial difference between specific knowledge or training and mental abilities. Mental abilities are thinking skills that can generalise to a wide range of different tasks.

Much of the variation in sporting skills between people in the general population will be related to physical ability and practice/training/coaching, although for elite athletes, emotional skills become extremely important (Kremer, 2012) and cognitive strategies—for example, for analysing weaknesses in an opponent's game—will also matter. Talking to the depressed individual will require some emotional sensitivity (the effective therapist will positively ooze warmth, congruence and unconditional positive regard: Rogers, 1959), as might asking for a coursework extension, for which some creativity might be useful if the excuse is not 100% genuine. However, writing a creative essay (rather than one that is fact based), solving anagrams and reading a map are abilities that would seem to largely reflect thought processes, rather than any of the other three types of ability mentioned above, provided that we can assume that anyone who has been through the education system will be able to read and write.

I have laboured these issues a little because the distinction between task-specific training and cognitive skills is both important and frequently misunderstood. There seems to be little doubt in the public mind (and even in the minds of some psychologists who should know better) that the sorts of problems that psychologists study are closely linked to what people know, rather than how people think. Journalists interviewing me about the *Test the Nation* television programmes that administered a proper intelligence test to anyone who wanted to take it kept on talking about "the quiz" as if it was nothing more than a test of general knowledge.

There are very good reasons why the sorts of problems studied by psychologists *should not be closely related* to specific knowledge and training. If a person's performance on a task is influenced by both specific knowledge/skills and mental abilities (as with the history test example in Table 1.1), a person who has not had the opportunity to acquire the knowledge or skill-set will perform poorly. If we are interested in measuring individual differences in mental abilities, then we need to devise tasks where the influence of prior knowledge and training (and indeed physical and emotional skills) are minimal, so that a person's background or previous training does not influence their performance. This is why we use tasks that are quite different from those that people have ever encountered before, so that we can be fairly confident that the tasks measure thinking skills rather than specific knowledge or training. I give some examples of these tasks in Chapter 2. The downside of this is that critics sometimes argue that because the tasks do not closely resemble the sorts of problems that people encounter in real life, the sorts of abilities measured by psychologists are obviously irrelevant to how people behave in the real world. Whilst this could in theory be true, we shall see in Chapter 7 that this viewpoint is not supported by the evidence.

We therefore focus on just a small set of abilities—those that require a substantial degree of thought for their successful completion, and that assume no knowledge, physical or emotional skills other than those that everyone can be assumed to have gained as part of their education and development.

Although we all routinely perform amazing physiological and cognitive feats all the time, this book only considers abilities where people differ. This is necessary because it would otherwise have to cover the whole area of human physiology and psychology in order to cover everything that humans do. Instead, we focus on abilities that show a reasonable amount of variation within the "normal" population (i.e., performance at tasks where some people perform markedly better than others), rather than looking at tasks at which humans excel but that computers find difficult, or abilities that are found in groups with particular clinical diagnoses. For whilst abnormal behaviour is of great concern to clinical, forensic, educational and other applied psychologists, it is possible that the mechanisms that cause someone to show extreme difficulties in learning or using language (for example) may be of little relevance to how the other 99.9% of us behave. So this book focuses on abilities that vary within the general population, and not how the behaviour of people diagnosed with depression, schizophrenia, autism etc. differs from the norm.

Why Study Human Mental Abilities?

The psychology of mental ability is important for several reasons.

- It is interesting in its own right. There are plenty of folk-law stereotypes about abilities (e.g., the nutty professor who may be wonderful at nuclear physics but has no common sense, whatever that is). Some teachers have been exposed to the idea that there are at least 10 quite separate "intelligences"—and so each child will probably excel in at least one type of cognitive skill. Others claim that our genetic makeup has a massive influence on our mental abilities. Are any of these ideas correct? And what is it that makes people differ in their cognitive abilities?
- Western culture places considerable emphasis on individual differences in abilities (e.g., at school, or when applying for jobs). If we knew how these abilities originate and develop, then we could perhaps develop educational strategies to maximise each child's potential. For example, if it were found that stimulation during young childhood improved some mental abilities, governments could perhaps consider cognitive enhancement programmes for pre-school children.
- The assessment of abilities is one of psychology's greatest success stories. As will be seen in Chapter 7, ability tests are extremely useful in applied psychology, where they are estimated to have saved firms literally billions of dollars through allowing them to select applicants with the greatest potential for success (Kanfer, Ackerman & Goff, 1995). So once we have determined which abilities exist, what can we predict from a knowledge of a person's mental abilities? And is there any evidence that individual differences in mental abilities actually *cause* individual differences in everyday behaviour? Or do other variables (social class, perhaps) influence people's scores on ability tests?
- Psychologists try to predict behaviour. In order to do so, it is necessary to consider both individual differences (each individual's profile of abilities, personality and so on) and the situations, stimuli etc. to which they are exposed. For the reasons that were outlined earlier, researchers in cognitive psychology, developmental psychology and so on will probably want to control statistically for individual differences. Or rather, they *should* routinely do so, in order to perform more sensitive

statistical analyses: in practice most such researchers cling to the crazy belief that the people who take part in their experiments are identical, apart from random variations. We will show later that abilities correlate substantially with a huge range of variables (ranging from aspects of perception to reaction time and brain structure), and so researchers in all of these areas would be well advised to routinely measure intelligence and use it as a covariate.

Individual Differences vs. Experimental Psychology

Most branches of psychology (social psychology, physiological psychology, cognitive psychology, developmental psychology and so on) study how people typically behave when some independent variable is measured or manipulated. For example, a social psychologist might want to find out whether being a member of a minority group influences self-esteem. They might measure self-esteem in English people who live in England (where they are a majority) and also track down English people who have emigrated to Australia (where they form a minority)—and do the same for Australians resident in Australia and recently arrived in the United Kingdom. Then after some data analysis involving analysis of variance, they can decide whether being surrounded by members of a different culture has much effect on self-esteem.

A developmental psychologist might want to find out when children are generally able to see something from another person's perspective, and so might give groups of children who are within a month of their 4th, 5th or 6th birthday something like the "Sally-Anne Test" (Baron-Cohen, Leslie & Frith, 1985) that measures whether each child can recognise that other people may not know something of which the child is aware. Such data could be analysed using analysis of variance to determine whether there are differences between the three age groups.

Physiological psychologists may study how and why dopamine agonists (chemicals that affect the ease with which information is transmitted between some types of nerve cells in the brain) affect behaviour—for example, whether they influence addictive behaviour. Cognitive psychologists may study whether priming with a semantically related or structurally similar word affects the speed of recognition of a word: the examples are legion.

These experimental designs all have one thing in common. They test whether some thing (e.g., a drug, age, attitude, previous experience etc.) usually influences performance on some task. The key word here is 'usually', for the data from such experiments are almost always analysed by t-tests, analysis of variance and so on—statistical tests that are designed to test whether or not the difference in average scores obtained by two or more groups of people (or one group of people who are assessed on two or more occasions) are different. And because of this, they make one very large, very dangerous assumption. Cognitive, developmental social and most other psychologists assume that all people behave fairly similarly. This assumption is necessarily made because people's scores are averaged together. Any individual differences are ignored. I will show that this is unwise and that it will probably lead to analyses that are not as statistically powerful as they could be.

The Individual Differences Approach

Instead of studying how changing the nature of the task affects people's performance, individual difference psychologists look at whether some people perform consistently better than others at some cognitive tasks—and then develop models to work out why this might be, and what it implies. So instead of measuring whether being a member of a minority group influences self-esteem, an individual difference psychologist will be more interested in why some members of a minority group will experience high self-esteem, whilst others do not. In the cognitive psychology example, individual difference psychologists may focus their efforts on discovering whether some people perform consistently faster than others when identifying whether a group of letters spell a real word (either primed or unprimed). Are the people who respond fastest under the unprimed condition the same people who perform fastest under the primed condition? Do they also perform faster at tasks that do not involve language: for example, pressing a button as soon as a light comes on? This can give us some idea about whether some people are faster than others at all tasks, or whether some people have more efficient language-processing skills.

The key thing to notice is that we do not compare means (average scores from several people in several different experimental conditions) when performing this sort of analysis. Instead we just give several people a few different tasks to perform, and correlate their performance on these tasks. This shows whether a person's level of performance on one task is similar to their level of performance on another—even though the tasks may differ wildly in difficulty, or even be measured in different units. (For example, we could if we wanted to measure a person's reaction-time to one task in seconds, and their reaction-time to another task in hours. Or correlate these with height measured in metres or miles: correlations are not influenced at all by the scale of measurement.)

Thus whilst most psychologists focus on things that affect the behaviour of people in general, psychologists working with individual differences pose questions such as "why are children who have been brought together often so very different from each other", "how many distinct cognitive abilities are there" and so on: we focus on how people differ from each other, why these differences manifest themselves, and what their implications are. For example, occupational psychologists may want to measure individual differences in order to select candidates who are likely to perform best at some job.

Another related discipline (psychometrics) develops statistical theories to allow abilities and other aspects of individual differences to be assessed using tests, questionnaires and other methods. However apart from a brief mention of terms such as 'reliability' and 'validity' and an outline of factor analysis in Chapter 3, this book will not concern itself with the minutiae of how these abilities are assessed, or how the tests that are developed to do so are evaluated.

Cronbach's Message

At the start of this chapter, we mentioned Cronbach's (1957) sentiment that it is necessary to design experiments that take into account both independent variables and individual differences in order to understand or explain behaviour. In this section, I want to try to persuade psychologists from other disciplines that they really ought to consider administering ability tests. Why? An example may help.

Suppose that a teacher wants to discover whether some educational activity improves children's mathematical performance. She might randomly assign children to one of two groups: one group would take part in the educational activity every day for a month, whilst children in the control group would do something else for the same amount of time. She might then give all the children the same mathematics test; suppose that she also happens to give the children a reasoning test at the same time. She then analyses the mathematics data using a t-test or analysis of variance to compare the scores of the two groups. Here the independent variable is the type of activity performed, and the dependent variable is the score on the mathematics test. Table 1.2 shows some hypothetical data from just such an experiment. The first two columns show the reasoning and mathematics scores of the nine children in the control group, whilst the final two columns show these data for the eight children in the experimental group.

The average mathematics scores for the two groups are exactly the same, so a t-test will show no significant effect of treatment type. But the t-test

Table 1.2 Hypothetical scores of two groups of children on a task measuring mathematics ability (their logical reasoning scores are also shown)

Control Group		Educational Activity	
Logic	Mathematics	Logic	Mathematics
10	20	10	13
11	22	11	13
11	18	11	14
12	17	12	19
12	21	12	21
12	23	13	23
13	20	13	26
13	19	14	31
14	20		
Average	20.0		20.0

completely fails to identify a hugely significant effect in these data. You will find it useful to look at the numbers in Table 1.2 to see if you can spot what is happening.

On examining the data by eye, it is clear that the educational activity increases the mathematics performance of children who are good at logical reasoning, but it decreases the performance of children who are weak at reasoning (perhaps they just give up). It has little or no effect on children with moderate levels of logical reasoning. So although the educational activity does not affect the overall mean scores, it is clear that the experimental treatment (the type of activity undertaken) has a huge effect on the performance of children: it just does not affect them all in the same way. *This obvious result will be entirely missed by t-tests, analysis of variance and most other standard statistical tests.* There are statistical techniques that can reveal what is really going on in experiments like this (one is called 'analysis of covariance'), but unfortunately, these are rarely taught in university statistics courses, and so most experimental psychologists continue making the naïve assumption that the people who take part in their experiments are totally identical and that their intervention will therefore have pretty much the same effect on everyone. So whilst the psychology of individual differences is rather different from the rest of psychology, there is a strong argument for measuring various types of individual differences and incorporating such measures into traditional experimental designs.

The second reason why psychologists and researchers from other disciplines really ought to measure human cognitive abilities is a little more technical. Readers who loathe statistics can safely skip the remainder of this section.

A statistic such as t (in the t-test) or F (in analysis of variance) involves dividing a measure of the difference between the means of two or more groups by a measure of how much variation there is within the groups—the 'error term'. Part of the variation between people might be due to individual differences in abilities (or other traits). Some of it will just be random variation. Because F is computed by dividing the difference between the group means by the error term, it follows that the smaller the within-group variation, the larger F will be. And the larger F is (for a particular difference between means, sample-size and, number of groups) the more statistically significant it will be. The upshot of all this is that if we *measure* individual differences and perform analysis of covariance instead of analysis of variance the error term becomes smaller, F becomes larger, and we have more chance of finding a significant difference, if it exists. By measuring individual differences and treating them as a covariate (rather than having them enlarge the error term), we can increase the statistical power of the analysis—that is, boost the chances of correctly rejecting the null hypothesis. It therefore makes great sense to measure individual differences in mental abilities whenever one suspects that the dependent variable in an analysis of variance or t-test might be influenced by individual differences in mental ability.

For example, a researcher who wants to determine whether there is a gender difference in reaction time should consider whether any mental abilities are likely to influence reaction time (they do, as we shall see in Chapter 6). So she should seriously consider measuring that too, and treat it as a covariate in her analysis in order to perform a more powerful analysis. This essentially controls statistically for individual differences in ability: it allows the researcher to ask what the difference between the means would be *if everyone in the sample had the same level of mental ability*.

Whatever Happened to 'Intelligence'?

I have tried to talk about abilities in general rather than 'intelligence' or 'general ability' for three reasons. The first is that there might be no such thing as intelligence, and using the terms intelligence or general ability now would essentially prejudge the issues discussed in Chapters 3 and 4. For the notion of intelligence implies a sort of 'general cognitive aptitude',[1] which suggests that if individuals excel in one area (e.g., memory) they are also likely to excel in others (e.g., spatial skills, the use of language). Whilst this may be the case, it seems better to talk more generally in terms of 'abilities', of which 'general ability' 'general intelligence' or g may or may not be one until we have reviewed the evidence. The second reason is that intelligence seems to have acquired strong links with the classroom through the use of intelligence/ability tests to identify special learning needs. This is probably a bad thing in that it may suggest that intelligence is mainly concerned with knowledge acquisition at school—which it is not (primarily). The third reason is that the terms 'intelligent' or 'high IQ' have become value-laden. In the 1940s, terms such as 'moron', 'idiot' and 'cretin' were routinely used to describe certain levels of intellectual performance. We may have dropped these terms from polite conversation, but the negative overtones associated with low intelligence still linger on. There are plenty of callous monsters with high IQs, as the history books and personal experience testify, and it is all too easy to overvalue the importance of intelligence.

Overview of Other Chapters

This book focuses on the psychology of intelligence and ability, and it has three main aims. First of all, it describes what is known about the nature of abilities. It explores the main ways that people differ from each other. For example, is it the case that some people are good at solving all varieties of problems, whilst others struggle with everything? Or do we need to consider a number of quite distinct abilities such as language ability, visualisation and perhaps the much-publicised 'emotional intelligence'? We need to understand how many different mental abilities there are, and how they interrelate. This is sometimes known as the 'structural model', as it seeks to describe the basic nature of personality, mood, motivation or abilities.

We have already come across one structural model—the term intelligence implies that a person will have a similar level of performance on all abilities. However, one of the main concerns of individual difference psychologists is discovering the most accurate model to describe human abilities. For the number of tasks where individual differences in cognitive performance could be assessed (which is, you will recall, our putative definition of ability) is potentially very large indeed—almost infinite. There has to be some way of grouping these tasks together: to view performance on a number of these tasks as being influenced by a smaller number of basic abilities. For example, it might be the case that a single 'memory ability' influences how well a person can recall what he or she did on his or her 18th birthday, some foreign vocabulary they learned yesterday, and a 10-digit telephone number that was read out to them just a few seconds ago. But it is very, very dangerous just to assume this. Readers with a knowledge of cognitive psychology will be nodding their heads at this stage: episodic memory, long-term memory and working memory are thought to involve rather different cognitive and biological processes, and so it seems quite possible that someone with above-average working memory (for example) might not have a particularly good memory for life events. My point is that in order to decide which tasks are influenced by a particular psychological ability, one needs to analyse data. Just looking at the tasks is not enough, because similar-looking tasks might involve very different psychological processes.

Until the early 1970s, the main focus of research was into the structure of abilities. Very often, a statistical technique known as factor analysis was used to help make such decisions. However, technical (and other) problems with this method made the early results seem contradictory. Some research-ers claimed that just one ability influenced performance on all tasks; others found evidence for at least a dozen quite different abilities. Thus Chapter 3 of this book explores how factor analysis has been used to reveal the underly-ing structure of ability, and how there is now fairly good agreement about the underlying structure of abilities. Chapter 4 considers other structural theories: ways of conceptualising abilities that do not rely on factor analysis. Howard Gardner's (1993, 1983) theory of multiple intelligences draws on a number of sources of evidence (including the effects of brain damage and observation of the way in which different aspects of performance emerge together in developing children) to suggest an alternative to the factor-analytic findings. Interestingly enough, there is substantial overlap between Gardner's work and the models arising from factor analysis, even though they are based on quite different sources of data. Gardner would disagree vehemently with the above statement! Robert Sternberg (1985), on the other hand, uses a very broad definition of ability. He is interested not just in the sorts of cognitive tasks that are traditionally used in intelligence tests (tasks that are deliberately made abstract—decontextualised—so as to minimise the influence of life experiences on their difficulty), but also in 'practical intelligence' (the sorts of skills we all use in everyday life when dealing with people) and an 'experiential theory', which explains how we come to draw on previous experiences to perform complex sequences of mental opera-tions smoothly, easily and automatically. Emotional intelligence is currently a hugely popular concept: it attempts to determine whether (and why) some people may be better than others at recognising and dealing with their own and others' emotions. We look at the idea of emotional intelligence, the idea that being sensitive to one's own or other people's emotions is an impor-tant ability. Finally, Michael Howe (1988b, 1997) has made some interesting points about the whole nature of human abilities, arguing that is utterly wrong to regard abilities as being some properties of the individual that *cause* them to behave in certain ways. At best, Howe says, we can use the term 'abilities' to *describe* how people behave—never to explain it.

Then once some consensus was reached, the focus of research shifted to studying *why* people vary. For example, is it because of their family upbringing? Is it all down to how enriched the child's environment is during their early years of life? Could it be something to do with the way the neurons in the brain are interconnected or operate? Does schooling make us smarter? Does being smart make us perform better at school? Or is there no link at all between intelligence and education? Are there any differences in the brain structure or function of people with different levels of abilities? The second aim of this book (in Chapters 5–7) is to summarise and evaluate the literature in these areas. What is it that *causes* these individual differences to come about? Chapter 5 examines whether or not genetically similar individuals also have scores on ability tests that are highly similar, or whether it is the way in which children are brought up that determines their eventual levels of ability. The evidence shows that genetic influences are surprisingly large, and although the way children are brought up by their parents influences ability during childhood, the size of this decreases gradually to almost zero by late adolescence.

Given that abilities have a substantial genetic component, then it is logical to try to understand individual differences in ability using biological (rather than solely social, economic or political) models, since genes directly influence the biological makeup of the nervous system either directly or through interaction with environmental influences. Chapter 6 thus examines several experiments designed to show whether general ability is linked to brain structure and function, for example the speed and/or efficiency with which nerve cells in the brain transmit information. These vary from simple tasks measuring speed of perception and speed of responding to experiments that seek to determine whether any features of electrical activity recorded from the scalp are related to cognitive ability.

Finally, there is a considerable literature showing that performance on ability tests predicts real-life behaviour. Hence Chapter 7 explores some links between mental abilities and education, performance at work and health; for example, whether they will live a long or happy life, or whether they will succeed in their chosen career. Chapter 7 therefore examines how useful ability tests are for selecting individuals for various occupations—a topic that also has some theoretical importance, as some critics have suggested that the only thing that ability tests can measure is ability at taking ability tests! If test scores can be shown to correlate with real-life criteria (such as those related to education or job performance for example) then this objection can be safely ignored. Chapter 8 integrates the material from the previous chapters and briefly summarises what is known (and what is *not* yet known) about the psychology of abilities, and reflects on some myths and misunderstandings about human mental abilities.

This chapter has given a general idea of what abilities are, why psychologists try to measure them using tasks that seem rather different from anything that we normally encounter, and why psychologists from other branches of the discipline would be well-advised to consider measuring individual differences during the course of their research. Chapter 2 tries to make things a little more concrete by exploring how psychologists actually go about measuring individual differences in abilities—to give a flavour of the sorts of tasks that participants are asked to perform, and also outline some problems in measuring abilities.

Note

1   The exception being the work of Howard Gardner (discussed in Chapter 4) who speaks of 'multiple intelligences'.

2

WHAT ARE ABILITIES?

This chapter explores what psychologists generally mean by 'abilities' and considers how the study of individual differences in mental abilities differs from (but complements) cognitive psychology.

Individual Differences in Abilities

Abilities form one important branch of individual differences: there are others too, such as personality, mood and motivation that are beyond the scope of the present text. Of course there are many abilities other than those that involve thinking: sporting ability and skilled actions are two obvious examples. However this book does not consider individual differences in physical and sporting performance (e.g., swimming, sprinting, holding one's breath, driving, dancing, playing soccer, laying bricks). Although no one would deny that psychological factors may affect performance in all of these areas, for example in understanding how people anticipate where a football will land (Craig et al., 2009), it makes little sense to measure performance in groups of people who have not received equal amounts of experience and training on such tasks. So in practice, psychologists studying human abilities usually restrict themselves to measuring performance on tasks that are unfamiliar to people, so that prior experience training or practice cannot taint the results.

This book focuses on tasks that require thought or reasoning for their successful completion and that make rather few assumptions about previous knowledge or experience. In other words, it focuses on tasks that can be administered to almost anyone, rather than to special groups (such as elite athletes). Our aim is to study tasks (and groups of people) where the effects of these confounding variables is minimised. Thus when gathering data, careful thought must be given to the capabilities of the participant: for example, tasks assessing vocabulary when only some people are using their second or third language, or those requiring fine hand movements from an 80-year-old are likely to be fatally flawed.

Whether or not tests of "knowledge" should be considered as abilities is actually quite an interesting issue. Clearly tests that merely assess how well a person can remember rote-learned facts (French irregular verbs, Latin declensions, the periodic table, state capitals, health and safety legislation, car braking distances at various speeds) will only measure some ability if (a) everyone has had an equal opportunity to acquire the knowledge, and (b) motivation is not a factor. Thus measuring knowledge of French irregular verbs can only say something about a person's ability to learn facts if everyone has had the same opportunity to acquire that knowledge (by studying French), and everyone is similarly motivated to do well, and so will have put an equal amount of effort into learning the verbs.

This suggests that most tests of knowledge might be feeble measures of ability, because it is very hard to ensure that everyone is equally motivated to perform well. Thus an average score on the test could be obtained by a highly able student who has not put much time or effort into learning the material, a not-very-able student who has devoted huge effort to learning the material, or a student of average ability who has put an average amount of effort into learning the list of verbs. The influences of motivation and ability may well be confounded (impossible to separate).

However, psychology is (these days) an empirical science—one that is based on hard evidence, rather than speculation or personal experience. So rather than waste time debating and speculating about such issues—which can never lead to any firm conclusion—it is possible to test empirically whether scores on tests of knowledge can ever reflect abilities to a significant extent. (How? Just correlate people's scores on knowledge-based tests such as vocabulary with their scores on other tests that measure thought and reasoning but that do not require any prior knowledge.) One of my pet annoyances is that the general public often seems to believe that the conclusions that psychologists reach are a matter of personal opinion—and so many people believe that their own views and experiences are just as valid as the inferences drawn from careful experimentation and analysis.

That said, this book does not focus on tests of knowledge apart from that which people can be assumed to have gathered through the education system: for example, a basic vocabulary. This is because different people will have different interests, and so are likely to have acquired knowledge in different areas. I know next-to-nothing about popular music or films, but more than one might expect about computer programming and cooking, for example. Other people may know all about cars, newts, 14th century music or historic battles. So unless tests of general knowledge span a huge range of areas and therefore have a significant number of items measuring knowledge in every possible area in which people could have acquired knowledge, they are unlikely to be particularly useful as measures of ability.

Tasks, Scales and Tests

Throughout this book I have tried to make a distinction between 'tasks' and 'tests'. A task is a set of problems that look as if they all measure the same think—for example, 20 anagram problems, dreamt up over a cup of coffee. There is no guarantee that all of the items measure the same ability, nor that there are sufficient items in the task to measure anything with any accuracy. A scale, on the other hand, is a task that has some quality control associated with it. The amount of measurement error associated with a person's scores will be known. The appropriateness (difficulty, culture-fairness) of the items should have been established, and there may well be tables of norms to allow a person's score to be compared with those of the population to which they belong. Finally, a test is a collection of scales, and it is likely to be a commercial product: some are fiendishly expensive. Many tests involve combining scores on several scales—for example, combining scores on different ability scales to estimate a person's general intelligence, or combining scores on different memory scales to measure their memory skills. Tests and scales should have handbooks associated with them outlining what they measure, the age ranges for which they are appropriate, and instructions for administering, scoring, combining and interpreting the scales.

What Prior Knowledge Can We Assume?

In Western society at any rate, all children learn to talk and go to school where they are taught how to read, write and work with numbers. So we can probably assume that older children and adults have all received a basic level of specific training in these areas. Thus if we give adults an anagram to solve ('blue rot' becomes 'trouble') as everyone is familiar with the word 'trouble', their skill at rearranging the letters of blue rot should be a cognitive skill. An anagram where the answer is a less common word ('ale there' to 'ethereal', perhaps) is problematical. Young children or those who have not read widely may not have encountered the word ethereal, and so for them, the task would be impossibly difficult. The first item measures ability to solve anagrams, whilst the second one also measures vocabulary. As it could be argued that vocabulary might depend on the quality of education the child has received, the availability of books at home etc., the second item might be unfairly difficult for socially disadvantaged individuals.

The key point is that when designing items, care should be taken to ensure that the item content will be unfamiliar to all people who will take the test, otherwise performance on the item will reflect specific knowledge or training in addition to the ability that we want to assess. Each item should also require a bare minimum level of language skills, number skills, or general knowledge (unless the item is *designed* to measure language ability, etc.): the reason the item is hard should be because of the cognitive operations that participants are asked to perform, and not because some participants lack the knowledge or skills to recognise or generate the correct answer.

The Development of Tasks to Measure Cognitive Abilities

Ability tasks can be constructed using several different techniques (see for example Cooper, 2010 Ch. 18; Kline, 1986). For example, one way of constructing a vocabulary task would be to take a dictionary and draw a sample of words (each of which may have only one meaning) from it at random. It would also be necessary to *check* that each word has only one meaning and that words that are very obscure, very common, very technical or potentially offensive are removed. The correct definition (plus four incorrect ones) of 50 or so of these words could be given to a sample of people, who are asked to identify the one correct definition of each word. The task would generally be scored by giving one point for each correct answer. The beauty of using ability tasks such as these is that they are quick and easy to administer, and they do not rely on subjective assessments (as with marking essays).

If the above task consists of a large, broad sample of words from the language, then the total scores on should accurately reflect the extent of people's verbal comprehension. A task such as this must by definition measure what it claims to (it is 'valid') and if the number of items is large, and their difficulty is appropriate for the samples to whom it is administered, it will do so with little measurement error (it is 'reliable').

The Number of Items

Any written or orally administered task will usually consist of several items (normally at least 20 of them). For example, a person may be asked to think of something that tables, cats and triathlons have in common as the first item, then something that plants, books and large dining tables have in common, and so on. (I deliberately made these items quite hard—'legs' and 'leaves' are the answers.)

There are two reasons for having several items in a task. The first is that if just one item is used, each person can only score 0 (if they get the item wrong) or 1 on the task: with such a small range of scores, the test does not allow for very precise discrimination between people. Secondly, luck (or 'random error') will influence how a person responds to each item. For example, it is possible that someone with a stupendous vocabulary may not know the answer to a particular word in a vocabulary task, whereas if there are 20 items in the task, they are unlikely to be unlucky 20 times! Or if someone encounters a 'mental block' when answering an item (though they are usually very good at this sort of puzzle) increasing the number of items will allow their true ability to shine through. By devising tasks that consist of several items, the influence of random error will be reduced. On the other hand, you do not want to make participants bored or fatigued, so you would probably not want the test to last more than an hour at the very outside. Several psychometric techniques (e.g., the Spearman-Brown formula) provide sound, statistically based guidance as to how many items of a particular kind are needed to measure a concept accurately.

Standardisation

Standardisation and careful choice of items are the key to creating useful scales to assess abilities. For example, a 'standard' memory scale could involve participants reading a standard set of instructions, then being shown a particular set of 20 irregular shapes printed on a standard-sized sheet of paper for a standard amount of time—e.g., 90 seconds. They might then be required to sit quietly for a standard interval (e.g., 30 seconds), and then be given as long as they want to identify the 20 shapes they previously saw from a standard printed page of 50 shapes.

The crucial thing is that the experience should be the same for everyone, no matter where in the world they take the items, or who administers them. Then (and only then) we can be confident that the items are equally difficult for everyone. If people are given different sets of instructions, for example, some individuals might be unclear about what they are to do—and this may lead to their performance being underestimated. Likewise, if the sheet of shapes is shown for over 30 seconds, or if some people are not required to sit quietly for the full 30 seconds before attempting to recognise the shapes, their performance may be overestimated. The key thing about any scale used to measure abilities is that it has to be precisely defined in terms of content, and given to people in precisely controlled conditions to ensure that scores are comparable.

Assessing Performance

There also has to be a standard way of assessing performance on a task. For the task outlined above, it is fairly obvious: performance on the memory task should probably be assessed by counting the number of shapes correctly identified from the list. But what if someone marks all 50 shapes as having being present on the original sheet? If one point is given for each shape that is correctly identified, they would presumably score 20/20 correct—but will also have wrongly identified 30 of the shapes as having been present on the first list! The instructions should probably stress that people should mark only 20 of them, though the scoring scheme needs to specify what to do if someone ignores this. (For example, "mark only the first 20 responses".) Or wrong answers could be penalised (e.g., deducting one mark for every incorrect answer). The people who solve the items need to be told how they are scored, so that they can ensure that they can maximise their performance.

Sometimes it is hard to develop tasks to assess what seem to be important abilities. Genuine, real-world creativity is one example: the problem here is that people tend to have specialised interests, which makes it hard to compare their performance. How should you decide whether devising a proof of a mathematical theorem is more or less creative than writing a poem or composing a song, for example? Leadership is another. How could you compare the leadership performance of a bank manager in Bangkok with that of a garage manager in Ghana, given that they will be interacting with different groups of people, and trying to manage their teams to achieve different goals?

In addition, some tasks can be much harder that others to score. For example, how do you think you might you go about scoring a task designed to measure how accurately a person can sketch an object (e.g., a bicycle) from memory? There are some ways round these problems, but a discussion and evaluation of them is beyond the scope of this book. My reason for flagging these issues is to point out what the most frequently studied tasks generally look like, and to note the possibility that psychologists may focus on some types of task and ignore others just because it may be hard to assess performance at some types of task.

Having a Clear Idea What the Task Is Meant to Assess

When deciding which abilities to assess, it is important to ensure that the task designed to assess a particular ability does not depend on other skills or knowledge. For example, suppose that you want to measure how well an adult can identify the relationship between two things, and apply that rule to a third thing. "Dog is to puppy as cat is to . . .", for example. Here the person has to work out that a puppy is a young dog, and so can work out that the correct answer is the word for a young cat. This sort of item is normally designed to measure how well the person can identify what the rule is ("inductive reasoning"): it is this which makes the item hard.

What if the item was rephrased as "hare is to leveret as ferret is to . . ."? Although this looks similar to the previous example, it relies on a good vocabulary for its correct solution. Unless you happen to know (or can guess) that a leveret is a young hare, and you know that a kit is a young ferret, you cannot possibly answer this item correctly. In the previous example, it was the (simple) relationship between the words that made the item difficult, as it is practically certain that all adults would know the meaning of words such as "cat". In the second example, it is likely that only those with a good vocabulary plus good reasoning skills will be able to answer the item correctly. Writing items is a far more difficult job than it may at first appear.

Item Difficulty

If everyone who takes a series of items obtains the same score, then the task is clearly ineffective at identifying those who are highly able. In addition, if all of the items seem to be impossibly hard, participants are quite likely to give up trying and may just guess answers randomly. If the items are trivially easy, participants may become bored and so make silly mistakes, or else look too hard at the items trying to spot subtle nuances of meaning or tricks that do not exist. As children get better at solving just about all types of items as they get older, it is thus normal to develop separate tests for children of various age groups and adults, although some tests can be used with both adults and children (Glutting, Adams & Sheslow, 2000).

Cultural Sensitivity

It is also important that you have an understanding of the population for which the task is developed. If a task is designed to be used in several different cultures, great care has to be taken when writing items to ensure that all the concepts and vocabulary used are equally familiar. For example, if we were to rephrase the above example "dog is to puppy as alpaca is to _____", inhabitants of South America would probably find that item considerably easier than would the rest of us, just because they alone know the word for a young alpaca. Several debates in the literature concern the appropriateness of standard American English for children in socially deprived urban areas, and attempts have been made to devise puzzles that are relevant for children brought up in such surroundings. Here is a genuine example of a test item designed for use in such a setting.

> Hattie Mae Johnson is on the County. She has four children and her husband is now in jail for non-support, as he was unemployed and was not able to give her any money. Her welfare check is now $286 per month. Last night she went out with the highest player in town. If she got pregnant, then nine months from now how much more will her welfare check be? (a) $80, (b) $2, (c) $35, (d) $150, (e) $100.
>
> (Aiken, 1971, p. 107)

Such items do not solve the problem of social or cultural bias; the item is likely to be incomprehensible to a middle-class child or anyone outside the United States because they may not understand the meaning of some phrases and will probably not know how welfare benefits were computed many years ago, which is necessary in order to work out the correct answer. It is far better to reduce cultural bias using clear, carefully written sentences, and content that is likely to be familiar to everyone. Or better still, it may be possible to avoid language altogether, and measure some abilities just using shapes. "/ is to − as \ is to . . ."

However it may be difficult or impossible to eliminate all forms of cultural bias. In some cultures it is seen as bad-mannered to outperform someone else, which can influence the way in which individuals perform psychological tasks (Cox, Lobel & McLeod, 1991). This is likely to affect motivation to perform well on an ability test. Thus although some psychologists have attempted to draw inferences about the ability scores of different nations (Lynn, 2008), doing so is dangerous.

The Psychology of Abilities

Thus far, we have assumed that a person's ability can be defined as their level of performance on any standard task where their level or quality of performance can be assessed, although we have noted that we normally select the tasks so that they measure cognitive skills and are not unduly influenced by prior knowledge or experience. So according to this definition, performance when playing a novel computer game, finding one's way through a strange city without a map, recalling a list of nonsense words that were learnt earlier, and countless other things reflect abilities.

According to this logic, to understand a person's abilities, we just need to devise some tasks that tap a person's performance and draw up a list of the scores on each of these tasks for each person—a profile of their abilities. We could then interpret this profile by highlighting those tasks where the person performs appreciably better or worse than the rest of the people in the population: for example, noting that one person performs better than 90% of their peers when navigating through a strange city.

As explained in above, we would have to ensure that each person was given exactly the same tasks to perform, with the same instructions, time limits and so on. The important thing to appreciate is that so far we have defined abilities in terms of performance on tasks: we are suggesting that there are potentially as many different human abilities as there are tasks that people can perform. We can show this graphically in Figure 2.1

Each square represents a different task, and we assume that each person's level of performance on each task can be measured. The ovals represent abilities. These abilities are not directly observable: we can only infer that a person has a particular level of ability (e.g., ability to recall simple tunes after hearing them once) by measuring their performance on tasks (such as listening to several tunes, and attempting to recall each one). We argue that people vary

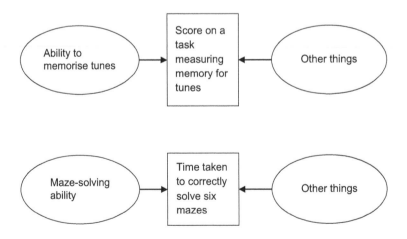

Figure 2.1 Model where performance on a task is influenced by the ability that each task is supposed to measure, plus other (unmeasured) things

in their ability to perform each task: this is why some people perform better than others. We are not at this stage trying to understand why some people *develop* different levels of abilities—the role of experience, education, genes and so on: that all comes later. But for now, we are just trying to establish how to conceptualise abilities.

In Figure 2.1, the arrow joining the ability to the task indicates that we believe that a person's level of some ability influences his or her performance on the associated task—rather than vice versa. Figure 2.1 also shows another oval attached to each task. This is there to show that we do not think that the *only* thing that affects a person's performance on the task is his or her level of ability to perform that task. Other things (e.g., tiredness, motivation, lucky guessing of answers to multiple-choice items) might also influence performance on each task. The second oval attached to each task represents all those other things that influence people's performance. So according to this very simple model, a person's performance on a task is determined by (a) the level of their ability, and (b) a host of other things, most of which we will probably not have measured.

The idea of abilities is not confined to humans. Some people are interested in the running ability of horses and greyhounds, the navigation ability of pigeons, and the ability of apes and other animals to solve puzzles in order to obtain food. The apparent ability of an octopus in Berlin zoo to predict the 2010 world cup football (soccer) results by crawling toward the flag of the country that would win their next game made headline news around the world. Thus although the physiology and lack of cognitive and language skills may limit the range of activities that a particular organism can undertake, the basic principles seem to apply across the board: abilities are simply measures of what animals can do. Indeed, we even describe the abilities of plants. Some types of rush are "better" than others at removing pollutants from pools of water; some trees are better than others for screening us from raw winter winds. I would not wish to labour this point, but you will appreciate that the concept of ability is a very broad one indeed. It seems that all one has to do is identify a task at which some people perform better than others, and argue that the reason for this is that some people have more ability than others to perform the task. What could be simpler?

However it does not take much thought to realise why this definition is flawed.

1.   The number of tasks is potentially very large.

The first problem is that the number of potential tasks is almost infinite. We could study ability to remember facts about the Norwegian economy. Or poems. Or the ability to memorise "nonsense words" such as 'thwork'. Or pairs of words such as 'contented emu'. Or tunes. Or events from one's own life, such as what you had for lunch last Thursday. We could measure recall on each of these tasks over the short term (recite text immediately after learning it, for example) or long term (minutes, hours, days, years later). And we can measure performance in several ways—for example, by asking people to recognise which of several alternatives is correct, or by asking them to reproduce (e.g., write or sing) the information.

It is clear from this trying to understand human abilities by producing great lists of tasks and measuring performance on each of them is likely to be doomed to failure just because of the sheer number of potential tasks available. The list of 'abilities' revealed by this sort of analysis will either be enormous (if one tries to measure a huge range of different abilities) or misleadingly arbitrary (if one measures performance on just a few tasks and is thus unaware of a huge range of other abilities).

You might perhaps think that it would be sensible to just combine scores on several tasks that you think measure the same thing. For example, you might want to work out a person's average score on the various memory tasks that we described earlier. This is dangerous, because you have no *evidence* at all that people's performance on one memory task is in any way related to their performance on other memory tasks—and it makes no sense at all to take the average if the tasks all measure quite different things. To see why, let us leave the psychology of abilities behind us for a minute, and consider a more general example. We could measure the amount of time a person typically takes to dress up and prepare for a night out, the time he or she spends watching television each week, and the time it takes him or her to push a button when a light comes on (reaction time). All of these can be measured in seconds, and you might think that it is sensible to average these three scores for each person[1] just because they all involve time.

The only problem is that this average score would be completely meaningless. An 'average' score could indicate that the person watches a lot of television, reacts quickly and takes an average amount time to preen himself or herself. Or that they take an inordinate amount of time to get ready, react quickly and watch little television. Any average score that is computed from three quite different psychological characteristics tells you nothing useful about how the person behaves, and so is of no use for anything. The same *could* be true of memory tasks—we cannot easily tell just by looking at the tasks whether they measure the same underlying ability, and so we cannot know whether it is appropriate to average performance across several of them.

It would therefore be dangerous to combine scores on all of the memory tasks described at the start of this section for example, just because they all seem to involve memory. This is because it could be the case that the cognitive processes that determine how well a person can memorise text over long periods of time are quite different from those involved in memorising tunes (for example). You will probably know from your study of cognitive psychology that there are several quite different types of memory (episodic, long term, visuo-spatial sketchpad, phonological loop), and so if different tasks measure different aspects of memory, a person's score that is averaged across several different tasks will be meaningless.

You can see that there is something of a Catch-22 situation here. The number of potential ability tasks is very large—almost infinite—and so it is not possible in practice to measure people's performance on all of them. The only practical solution is to consider only a sample of tasks. For example, we might decide, quite arbitrarily, just to look at one type of memory task. However the danger of focusing some tasks whilst ignoring others is that we might fail to measure some really important abilities, unless care is taken to ensure that all possible types of ability tasks are included.

Thus one major problem with the definition of abilities as being what people can do on various tasks is that there are just too many potential tasks that could be administered. And sampling just a few of these tasks, or averaging scores across tasks that appear to be similar, is hazardous.

2. The theory cannot be refuted.

One key thing about any scientific theory is that it should be falsifiable (at least in principle—in practice one might have to wait for large pieces of equipment such as Hadron colliders to be built). In other words it should be possible in principle to show that a particular theory fails to fit the facts if, indeed, it is flawed. This is a fairly conventional view of science laid out by Popper (1959) amongst others.

Newton's laws of motion are a classic example: one merely needs to measure how long various objects take to fall various distances when dropped to determine whether rate of acceleration is constant, whether the mass of the objects affects the speed with which they fall, and so on. If one were to find out that the rate of acceleration is not constant, or that objects having different masses fell at different rates, then the theory is clearly wrong and should be discarded or modified. This theory is clearly capable of being refuted.

Psychology is full of theories that are difficult or impossible to disprove and that are therefore unscientific. Freud's theory of the death instinct is an example of a theory that is untestable. This instinct supposedly propels us all toward death and destruction—but how could this theory be shown to be incorrect? Since all humans die for purely physiological reasons, there is surely no need to invoke the concept of a death instinct at all—and if one did want to invoke it, this 'instinct' should surely also be found in amoebae, trees and other forms of organisms that fit ill with the rest of Freud's theory! But the crucial point here is that it is hard to imagine what experiment one could perform to show that the death instinct does not drive us toward death. We all supposedly have this death instinct and we all die, but there is no obvious way in which the two can be shown to be linked. As there is no obvious way of measuring the instinct, it would not even be possible to determine whether people with high levels of the instinct tend to die early.

The theory of abilities outlined earlier in this chapter is that performance on any task reflects a person's level of ability on that specific task. How could this possibly be shown to be incorrect? How could one demonstrate that a person's performance on any task is not attributable to their narrowly defined "ability on the task"? If it is found that some people are better than others at memorising 200-word extracts of English poetry, how could we ever show that performance at a task measuring how well a person can memorise poetry is not due to their poetry memorising ability? This alone shows that the facile definition of abilities given at the start of this chapter must be discarded.

3. The theory does not demonstrate an understanding of the mechanisms involved.

By essentially saying that the reason why some people perform better than others on some task is because they have greater ability in that area, the door is closed to any attempt to develop lower-level models of behaviour. For example, one might wonder why it is that some people are better able to memorise chunks of text than are others. Is it related to the extent to which their parents talked or read to them? Perhaps the age at which they were introduced to reading is important? Or perhaps some genetic predisposition may be involved? Science operates by always trying to seek lower and lower-level explanations of phenomena. For example, acidity is useful to describe how chemicals behave, but simply naming the concept does not mean that one understands why certain substances behave in similar ways. For this one needs to think in terms of molecules, ions and so on.

The position seems to be the same for the psychology of abilities. Rather than saying that someone performs well at a particular task because they have a particular level of ability and making that the end of the story, it is necessary to delve further into what causes people to develop a particular level of that ability.

4.   The theory is not parsimonious.

Another key feature of good theories is that they are parsimonious. In science a few broad concepts (e.g., acidity) can be used for many things—for example, suggesting whether a particular substance might be used to rescue a too-sweet curry, to guide someone how to produce hydrogen by electrolysis, or to etch metal, all of which are uses for acids. Of course these broad concepts cannot explain everything perfectly: some acids might be fairly useless at etching metal whilst others would poison you or introduce unpleasant flavours as well as adjusting the flavour of your curry. But the odd exception does not mean that broad generalisations are valueless. Knowing that what is in a bottle of liquid is acidic (rather than a base, or a salt) gives you some guidance as to how it is likely to behave, and the strength of the acid (its pH) provides some guidance as to the potency of its influence.

But the model laid out in Figure 2.1 does not bring simplicity of structure to human abilities. There are as many abilities as there are tasks—and that number is near infinite.

A Model of Human Abilities

Perhaps there some reliable links between how people perform on different tasks. For example, is it the case that people who perform at a particular level on one type of memory task perform at a similar level on a seemingly rather different task? As an analogy, you might like to think about performance at sports. If someone excels at one sport (tennis, for example), does this mean that the person is also likely to perform above average at other sports, for example badminton, sprinting, or rowing? If there are clear links (e.g., if elite tennis players also to excel at other racquet sports, such as squash or badminton, but vary randomly in their ability at other sports) then rather viewing performance at each sport as being a separate ability, we can talk in terms of 'ability at racquet sports', 'ability at endurance sports' and so on.

This gets us away from the assumption that each task is associated with one unique ability, and the unwelcome conclusion that the number of human abilities is near-infinite, because the number of potential tasks than can be devised is near-infinite. Instead, we need to develop a model where there are far fewer abilities than there are tasks. We need to compile a list of human abilities (perhaps by experiment, perhaps by some exhaustive literature search) and determine how these influence performance on a range of tasks.

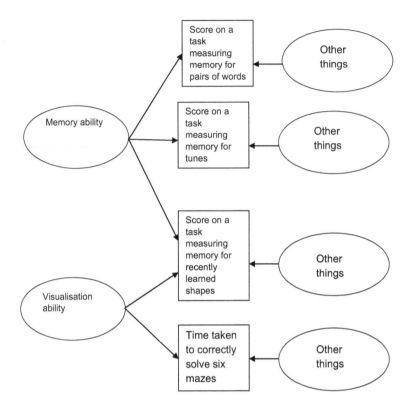

Figure 2.2 Model where each ability influences performance on several different tasks

This is shown diagrammatically in Figure 2.2. As before, squares represent tasks, ovals abilities, and lines indicate that a person's level of ability influences their performance on a task to some extent. Where there is no line linking an ability and a task, this indicates that a particular ability is irrelevant as far as performing that task is concerned: for example, a person's level of memory ability might be completely unrelated to their ability to solve a maze.

This new definition of ability is different from the previous one because it suggests the following:

(a) The number of mental abilities is smaller than the number of tasks that can potentially be devised.

(b) Each person has a characteristic level of each of these mental abilities, and this stays roughly constant over time and from situation to situation. These proposals can be tested empirically (i.e., through experimentation): they are not assumptions.

(c) Each mental ability influences performance on several different tasks. This too can be determined empirically.

The obvious question is how one can discover whether proposal (a) is in fact correct—and how one should go about discovering which abilities influence performance on which tasks. We argued earlier that it is wrong and dangerous to decide in advance to combine scores from several tasks that look similar (e.g., several different types of memory test). Thus, you may well feel some alarm that I am now proposing something very similar.

The key difference is that one should find a way to determine which abilities influence performance on which task(s) empirically. That is, rather than assuming that a group of memory tasks all measure one ability, one should perform experiments to test this and check whether reducing the number of abilities from a near-infinite to a more manageable set is statistically justifiable. Chapter 3 gives some guidance as to how this can be achieved in practice.

Examples of Tasks Measuring Mental Abilities

So far the discussion of tasks that may reflect abilities has been rather abstract, and so this chapter ends with some examples of the types of problems that have been used to measure individual differences in abilities.

I have so far avoided the word 'test' for two reasons. First of all, it sounds rather evaluative: if the word test is used, it implies that a person can either pass or fail it. Psychologists rarely, if ever, treat data like this. Any assessment normally measures the extent to which a person possesses a particular trait: the number of items that are correctly answered, or something similar. There are a few exceptions to this generalisation, where an arbitrary cutoff is applied: for example, the level of intelligence that an individual needs to show in order to be tried in court, or (in some American states) be executed. But the huge majority of psychological assessments measure and interpret the level of a person's performance. Second, psychological tests are carefully developed and are standardised by administering them to large, carefully constructed samples of the population—a process that can take years and cost huge amounts of money. So the main reason I have so far used the word 'task' is to allow us to talk about the sorts of assessment that you or I could design over the course of a day or two, and those carefully constructed "gold standard" assessments (tests) that are widely used in educational psychology, forensic psychology and clinical psychology to evaluate individuals. For example, these high-quality tests may be used to determine whether a child is dyslexic to the extent that special provisions should be made for that child at school, or whether a person shows signs of dementia.

Types of Tasks

The content of a task is sometimes guided by theory—for example, where a theory of creativity specifies that several different types of cognitive operations indicate that a person is creative. But more often, the choice of task seems to be fairly arbitrary. Sometimes, there is no theory to provide guidelines. For example, if a researcher tries to determine the number and nature of human cognitive abilities without much knowledge or expectation of what the results might be, his or her best strategy would be to develop a large number of tasks to measure as many different cognitive skills as possible by as wide a variety of methods as possible. But the exact nature of what goes into a test is seldom to clear cut.

Suppose that one is interested in measuring individual differences in mental rotation—a phenomenon that has been studied extensively by cognitive psychologists (starting with Shepard & Metzler, 1971). The idea is that a person is shown a picture of an object, then another picture that is either the same object or its mirror image, but on its, side, upside down or at some other angle. Given the opportunity, it would probably be best to administer such items by computer, showing the 'target' plus just one of the alternatives, and measuring how long it takes the person to mentally rotate the shape and decide whether or not it matches the target. This gives an accurate measure of time and allows us to calculate how long it would take a person to mentally rotate the shape through 180 degrees. But for group use, one would probably use a booklet with 100 or so sets of printed shapes rather as shown in Figure 2.3 and determine how many of these were correctly answered within 2 minutes.

(i)	(ii)	(iii)	(iv)	(v)

Figure 2.3 Mental rotation task. Which one of the five shapes could not be rotated to form the letter F?

This approach is much more crude. It is not possible to measure how long it takes a person to respond to each item, and so one cannot measure how long it takes a person to mentally rotate a shape through 180 degrees. Instead, one can only measure how many each person answers correctly within the allocated time. Some people may work carefully, checking each answer—which will appear to make them less able at performing the task. Others may be clumsy when it comes to marking the answer—a problem that can be exacerbated when the test uses a separate answer sheet. The best way of asking a participant to indicate their response to the type of item shown in Figure 2.3 would be to ask them to circle the one shape in each row that could not be rotated to give the figure shown at the top. If they were asked to mark a separate answer sheet (choosing one of the alternatives i . . . v) the test scores would be contaminated by the speed at which the person can find the correct place on the answer sheet to make their response. And given that one is searching for a rotated letter of the alphabet if the various alternatives had been labelled a . . . e rather than i . . . v this would probably have introduced another source of confusion, particularly if a letter such as B was ever used as the target.

Anyway, why use letters of the alphabet, rather than irregular shapes, pictures of asymmetrical objects (e.g., a teapot, a side-view of a cow), irregular, hard-to-name geometric shapes, or perhaps strings of letters? Would the same results be obtained whatever one used? When designing a task like this to measure some cognitive ability, the answers to these questions are rarely known because no one is likely to have developed a similar task before. So one has to rely heavily on common sense. It is necessary to identify as many possible sources of measurement error as possible, and designing the task so as to minimise their impact as far as possible, something that is more of an art than a science.

Even if one has a good knowledge of what one wants to measure ('mental rotation') the above examples show that there are many ways in which a task can be devised. The key aim must always be to try to eliminate random and systematic measurement errors. For example, the task shown in Figure 2.3 might perhaps be harder if the participants are not familiar with the English language. If pictures or random shapes had been used, this might perhaps be fairer. Though using random shapes might perhaps alter the cognitive demands of the task, as it would be harder to "subvocalise" and say to oneself "that's a letter F upside down" if, instead of a letter F, the person sees a random shape that resembles no recognisable object. Does this matter? No one knows, but the danger is that after one task is published in the literature, subsequent researchers will simply "lift" the same task (because it works), and so the issues raised above—such as whether the nameability of the shapes, or the effects of language skills on the ability to rotate letters—may never be explored. There is never any guarantee that a task, scale or test that is published in the literature (or sold commercially, for that matter) is the best one that could be devised to measure a particular trait.

It is usual (though not invariably the case: see the AH series of tests by Heim, Watts & Simmonds, 1970) for all of the items in one task or scale to be similar in content. One might measure how well a person can solve analogies, another could measure how well people can solve anagrams, and so on—rather than having a mixture of items in the same task. This allows us to determine whether apparently different tasks are related.

Another (fairly arbitrary) decision is how low-level the tasks should be. At one extreme, one could measure simple and choice reaction times, or ask people to push one of two buttons in response to problems such as

---

+

STAR IS NOT BELOW PLUS

*

Here participants are asked to decide whether each statement is true or false, which makes it possible to work out how long it takes for people to apply the "not" operation, for example. (Present a similar item with the star above the plus sign, and ask people to decide whether "star is below plus".) There was a flurry of interest in such "elementary cognitive tasks" in the 1980s (e.g., Kline, May & Cooper, 1986), but the problem is that these tasks (which tend to be based on paradigms developed by cognitive psychologists) are themselves fairly arbitrary. In addition, reaction-time-based measures can have quite a lot of measurement error associated with them. People sometimes lose attention and respond slowly. This can make the interpretation of data rather tricky.

Logical Reasoning Tasks

These problems involve pure logic—for example, working out whether a particular conclusion necessarily follows from a set of facts. For example:

Circles are always heavier than squares. No square is lighter than any triangle. Which of the following statements is true?

(a) Any square is lighter than any circle.   Y/N
(b) A square and a triangle could be the same weight.   Y/N
(c) Any circle must be heavier than any triangle.   Y/N

The context is not really supposed to matter, though most problems are phrased so that everyday experience cannot help some people solve the problem, as this would disadvantage people those who lacked specialist knowledge or experience. The example above could be rephrased as "golden retrievers are always heavier than spaniels. No spaniel is lighter than any Pekinese"—and phrasing the item like this may well make some of the statements easier to solve by making the problem more "visual"—if, and only if, the person answering the item knows anything about breeds of dogs. This type of problem will may be easier to solve if the participant is allowed to draw a diagram, and so the test instructions should make it clear that this is allowed.

Critical Thinking Tasks

These problems require some creativity for their solution—the ability to think laterally, and to come up with multiple ideas without getting stuck in a rut.

(a) Suppose that the earth acquired a second moon. What differences might we notice? (List as many as possible in 5 minutes.)
(b) Suppose that humans had evolved with their brains at the top of their body, where the head is—but with the eyes, nose, mouth and ears at waist height. What would be some advantages and disadvantages of that arrangement? (List as many as possible in 5 minutes.)

A second moon could well affect tides, there could be unpleasant consequences for Earth if they ever collided (meteor-like rocks), they would mean that the night sky is, on average, brighter than it is now (as the second moon would sometimes appear at the same time as the existing one), it might confuse animals that navigate by the moon, werewolves (if they exist) might well transform more often, there would be more eclipses of the sun, space exploration budgets would probably increase, . . . and so on. The more imaginative the ideas are the better: my suggestion about werewolves is somewhat tongue-in-cheek, but critical thinking problems frequently ask people to devise solutions that are as imaginative as possible, and so this would be acceptable. The test instructions should specify how bizarre the answers should become. You may like to attempt the second example for yourself.

Memory Tasks

Many tests have been devised to assess memory—for example, being given 2 or 3 minutes to learn 20 or so pairs of associated words ('pretty curtains', 'old wall', 'red shirt' etc.). Then there may be a period during which the person takes another task (so that the memory fades slightly) followed by pairs of words, only some of which had been shown previously. The wrong answers may be cunningly chosen to confuse participants; "pretty wall", "pretty shirt" etc. Participants might be asked to recall each pair of words, or (more commonly) be given the first word, and asked to choose the word that was linked with it from a list.

Tests of working memory are particularly fashionable at the moment. These involve the person holding something in mind whilst performing some rather different task. For example, you might be shown two or more letters together with a number, such as A D 2. The number 2 means that you should count forward two places in the alphabet—so A would become C, and D would become F. Thus the answer would be DF. This task requires you to remember the answer to the first part of the problem (C) whilst working on the second part, which is why it is thought to measure working memory. A negative number means that you should count backwards—so Z – 2 is "X". These problems sound quite simple, but if you try solving PLV – 5 without writing anything down, you can see that they can be quite challenging. Another genre of problems involves remembering the meaning of a story (for a comprehension test) and simultaneously rote learning the last word in each sentence.

Perceptual Speed Tasks

Participants are shown a list of symbols, each of which represents a number or letter of the alphabet—numbers in the example below. Participants are then asked to substitute the corresponding number for each symbol, and solve a simple addition problem using the numbers. (The letter version could involve spelling a word.)

$$\mathfrak{N}=1 \quad \mathbb{Q}=2 \quad \Upsilon=3$$
$$\maltese=4 \quad \text{\Leo}=5 \quad \maltese=6$$

Solve $\maltese + \text{\Leo} - \maltese =$

a) $\mathfrak{N}$

b) $\mathbb{Q}$

c) Υ

d) $\maltese$

Here the addition problem corresponds to $4 + 5 - 6$, the answer to which is 3: answer (c) is therefore correct, as that symbol represents the number 3.

Analogical Reasoning Tasks

One of the oldest types of reasoning problem involves tasks where the person is to deduce the rule that defines relationship between two "things" that could be anything from geometrical shapes to abstract concepts. To test whether they have correctly deduced this rule, most tasks then ask them to apply the rule to a third "thing". For example,

HOT	IS TO	COLD	AS	TALL	IS TO . . .
■	IS TO	■	AS	▲	IS TO . . .

Here the relationship between the words 'hot' and 'cold' is clearly that they are opposites, and so the correct answer to the first problem would be a word that means the opposite of 'tall'. In the second problem, the first shape becomes broader but not higher; applying this rule to the triangle produces a triangle that is about twice as wide as it is high, such as

Language Tasks

Many tasks have been developed to assess language ability—probably because of the importance of using language in education and commerce. Some involve measuring how well a person can understand or use language: comprehension, vocabulary, spelling, synonyms and so on. Others assess how well a person can manipulate letters within words—for example, solving anagrams. Sometimes test-constructors try to be a little more creative; the following example requires someone to work out from the context that one word might fit in both sentences,

> I sit on the river bank and watch people * * * past
> Disagreements can sometimes lead to a major * * *

That one is fairly straightforward: for a harder example, you might like to try

> The hunter stalked two * * * *
> A good joke usually * * * * make me laugh

where the word 'does' has two quite different pronunciations and meanings in the two sentences.

Measuring comprehension etc. does however raise several problems.

(a) It is necessary to ensure that everyone who is being assessed will have had broadly the same exposure to language, and there are obvious problems using such tests with those for whom the language being assessed is not their first language.

(b) It is not obvious that tasks that measure knowledge will necessarily correlate with other abilities. Language tasks require knowledge that is taught at school—vocabulary, spelling, rules of syntax and so on—and whilst it *might* be the case that people who have acquired this knowledge also tend to be good at reasoning, memory and other cognitive operations, one certainly cannot assume this in advance. We will look at the evidence for this in Chapter 3.

The Format of Ability Tasks

It should be obvious from the above examples that tasks differ considerably with regard to (a) what participants are shown, (b) what they are asked to do, and (c) how they are asked to respond.

Some tasks will involve participants being shown pictures, others may involve shapes, words, sounds, videos or even descriptions of hypothetical situations.

The participant will then need to perform some sort of cognitive operation(s) on this content—e.g., by working out which shape should come next in a series, which word was paired with 'weasel' in a list that was memorised, how to navigate to the centre of a maze, or deciding what action would be most appropriate if they suspect that a coworker has a drug problem.

Finally, each test will ask the participant to do something to indicate his or her response: this will usually involve ticking a box (or clicking a mouse) to indicate which of several alternative answers they feel is best, or writing/typing the correct answer to a problem. Though it could, in theory, involve virtually anything: assembling a jigsaw, singing, rearranging half a dozen pictures so that they tell a story, or countless other activities.

Open-Ended vs. Multiple Choice Questions

In an open-ended question, the person who is being assessed must write the correct answer—for example, he or she would write the word 'short' when answering the first analogy puzzle shown above. Multiple choice tests give several alternatives—for example (a) Lanky (b) Lukewarm (c) Short (d) High. Participants tick a box, circle or click on an alternative to indicate their answer. Such tests are popular because they are easy to score: a machine can do it, whereas a person will probably be needed to read handwriting. However some types of items do not lend themselves to multiple choice format. If the answer had been given to our language question above

("The hunter stalked two DOES"), just about anyone would be able answer the item correctly by working through each of the alternatives and seeing which one makes sense in both sentences.

Timed vs. Untimed Tasks

It is possible that some people might reason well but slowly, whilst others think faster. If our task has a tight time limit, the number of items answered correctly will be influenced by both a person's ability and their speed. For this reason, it is normal to impose fairly generous time limits for each task— long enough to allow almost everyone to attempt each item. However some form of time limit is essential, otherwise someone who is obsessional will sit there worrying at the last few items for hours. On the other hand, there are some tasks where solution time is measured—for example, in reaction-time tasks where the item is so easy that just about anyone could answer it correctly given sufficient time, as with the "star is above plus" example given earlier. There is a literature showing that there is a very substantial correlation between performance on tasks where people are allowed as long as they want to complete them, and performance on tasks where fairly lenient time limits are imposed. That is, although it is theoretically possible that some people could be smart and fast whilst others are smart but slow, the evidence seems to show that this is not the case: people who solve problems quickly also seem to be better at solving difficult problems (Vernon, 1961).

Computerised, Group and Individual Tests

Most tests are designed to be administered by computer or using pen and paper, though some require specialised equipment. Computerised tests allow for multiple choice or free response items, where words, numbers, etc. are entered using a keyboard. It is easy to control the amount of time for each section (or each item), and it is also possible to measure how quickly the test-taker responds to each item, though for technical reasons measuring very short reaction times is not straightforward. Computerised tests can administer items that include video or sound clips—something that is harder to do in other formats. It is also possible to use computers to perform 'adaptive testing'. Here the person's score on previous items is used to determine the difficulty of the item to be administered next: not every-one receives the same set of items. The scoring of adaptive tests is complex, and does not involve simply adding up the total score because some people have been given harder items than others. Two major problem with administering computerised tests remotely are the difficulty of ensuring that the person sitting at the computer is who they say they are, and the difficulty of checking that they have understood precisely what they are being asked to do in the test instructions.

Group tests normally involve a large number of participants taking the same pencil-and-paper (or computerised) test in the same place and at the same time. Participants are normally read the instructions, given the opportunity to ask any questions, and are told when to start and finish each section of the test.

Some tests are designed to be administered to individuals. These are normally tests where the accuracy of the assessment is paramount—perhaps because the test is to be used to make some clinical diagnosis (e.g., of dyslexia, or to determine whether a person is fit to stand trial). The one-to-one relationship between test administrator and participants might enhance motivation, make it easier to ensure that the person has understood what he or she is being asked to do, and allow test-designers to use items that would not be feasible with groups. For example, a participant might be given half a dozen jigsaw pieces and the time taken to correctly assemble them might be recorded. The main problem with these tests is the high cost of administration. Administration also involves quite a lot of technical skill—e.g., ensuring that the jigsaw pieces are always in the same initial position as indicated in the test manual, ensuring that questions are answered according to the guidelines in the test manual, and reading verbally administered items at a standard speed. Hence such tests can only be administered by specially trained individuals. As the tests frequently take over an hour to administer and score, the labour costs are appreciable.

Guessing

Suppose that a particular task comprises 20 multiple choice items, each having four possible alternatives. Someone with zero ability who guesses all the answers at random will answer approximately $20/4 = 5$ items correctly. Someone with greater ability who never guesses at all might solve four of the items correctly. So the person with zero ability who guesses would emerge with a higher score than the person with some ability who never guesses. To get round this problem, it is necessary to ensure that the instructions are very clear about whether participants should guess the answers to items when they are unsure. If guessing is not encouraged, wrong answers should perhaps be penalised—e.g., by deducting a mark for each wrong answer—and this should be mentioned in the test instructions.

Scoring Ability Tasks

Ability tasks are usually scored by awarding one point for each item that is answered correctly, although sometimes other methods are used—for example, awarding two points if a person solves an item within 30 seconds, and one point if they do so within a minute. The scores on the various items (all of which measure the same ability) are then added together to produce the "raw score". Computerised adaptive tests, in which participants are each given a different set of items whose difficulty is matched to their performance, are scored differently.

IQ and the Interpretation of Test Scores

Most researchers will simply analyse the raw scores that people obtain on each task—for example, by correlating them together, testing for gender differences etc. However, performance on cognitive tasks tend to improve during childhood, and so if participants vary in ages, this can lead to problems when interpreting test scores. A raw score that is excellent for a 9-year-old may be only average for a 12-year-old. There are several ways of converting raw scores into standardised scores to make them more interpretable. IQ is the best known. Here, scores on an ability test are rescaled by use of a table in the test manual. These tables vary from test to test, but might show that for a 9-year-old child, a score of 27 on the test corresponds to an IQ of 110. For a 12-year-old, a score of 27 might correspond to an IQ of 100.

The average IQ in any population of a particular age is 100 (by definition), and the standard deviation is (usually) 15. Thus someone with an IQ of 110 has an IQ that is two-thirds of a standard deviation above the mean. Consulting a table of the Standard Normal distribution shows that this puts them in the top 25% of the population. Likewise, only about 0.23% of the population has an IQ lower than 70, as you may care to verify. The key thing is that IQ scores correct for age-related changes in ability: each person is compared to peers of the same age. Because the tables that are used to convert raw scores on tests into IQs are extremely expensive to construct (they involve testing a cross-section of the population at various age ranges) only the most sophisticated commercial tests provide good tables to convert test scores to IQs. However they are invaluable for interpreting an individual's scores. Without them, we have no way of telling whether a person's score is good, average or below average. There are alternatives to IQ that you may sometimes hear mentioned—T-scores, stens and stanines all follow the same sort of principle, although with different means and standard deviations.

Overview

This chapter has just given a taste of the types of problems that psychologists have traditionally used to measure individual differences in human cognition. There are literally hundreds more, plus other tasks that have been designed to measure knowledge or attainment in school or at work: the number of memory tasks that could be developed is particularly large. The tasks can be developed either on the basis of some theoretical model—for example, to measure individual differences in each of the components of a model of human memory (e.g., Baddeley, 1986), in order to reflect some real-life need (for example, reflecting some of the cognitive skills that are thought to be important when flying an aeroplane or managing a company), or simply because someone somewhere has devised an interesting-looking task that seems to involve thought. It has also outlined how such tests may be administered and scored, and how the scores may be interpreted.

One popular misconception about tasks that measure ability is that they assess knowledge or learning—either the types of information that is taught in school, such as geographical or scientific knowledge, or general knowledge of some kind. You can see from the examples given above, and those in other sources (Eysenck, 1962 is still highly relevant) that this is not necessarily the case, if one assumes that all school leavers have basic language and numerical skills that allow them to understand the words in the problems. Solving the problems requires thought, be it metacognition (planning how to go about solving the problem), the actual solution process itself, and perhaps some error-checking at the end to ensure that the answer is sensible and has been recorded properly. Indeed, the tasks have been designed so as to minimise the effects of knowledge or familiarity, by using problems that are unfamiliar to everyone.

Note

1   Because the various scores differ in their mean and variance within the population, it is not a good idea to simply add the scores together as I imply here, as this will give more weight to the variable with the greatest variance. Just take this on trust if it is not obvious. It is better first to standardise a person's score on each measure so that each has the same variance—e.g., subtracting the mean score from a person's TV-watching time and dividing this by the standard deviation. The mean and standard deviation are found by testing a sample of people.

3

THE STRUCTURE OF
MENTAL ABILITIES

Even though we have narrowed the field of study considerably by excluding abilities with a strong physical, emotional or knowledge-based component, the number of tasks that rely on thought for their successful completion is still enormous. And we argued that it is extremely dangerous to make assumptions about which tasks reflect the same underlying ability just by looking at their content. For although tasks that assess spelling ability, creative writing, comprehending a passage of text, explaining the meaning of proverbs, solving anagrams or rapidly thinking of words that start with the letter 'b' and end with the letter 'n' all involve language, the cognitive processes involved seem to be very different. Thus it would be very dangerous to assume that they all measure some "verbal ability".

It follows from our discussion in Chapter 2 (see Figure 2.2) that since each ability is likely to affect performance on several tasks, someone with above-average levels of a particular ability will show above-average performance on several different tasks: someone will low levels of that ability will show low levels of performance on those same tasks. The only problem is that we have no way of telling in advance how many abilities there are, what they are, or which tasks will be influenced by which ability/abilities. Fortunately, there is a statistical method that allows us to determine this by collecting and analysing data.

This chapter outlines a technique that allows us to

(a) Find out how many different abilities influence performance on any collection of tasks.

(b) Determine which ability (or abilities) influence performance on each particular task.

The key thing to remember is that given the model of abilities that we developed in Chapter 2, you would expect each person to show a similar (e.g., high, low or intermediate) level of proficiency on every task that is influenced by the ability[1]. Think of the scores on each of the tasks as showing the rank-order of that individual relative to other people in the school, town, population or world. Indeed, there are three main possibilities.

First, at one extreme, it might be found that all abilities are independent. That is, there might be no relationship at all between how well a particular person can comprehend a passage of text, remember a face, solve anagrams, manipulate fractions, find their way through a maze, or find a creative solution to a problem. Scores on all of the various tasks might be 'uncorrelated'. This corresponds to the model that we proposed at the start of Chapter 2 and shown in Figure 2.1, where each task reflects a single, narrow ability. If this was the case, then if one wanted to appraise a person's strengths and weaknesses (as part of an employer's selection task, for example), it would be necessary to measure performance on a vast number of different tasks, as each task corresponds to a different mental ability.

Thus, if we were to plot four individuals' scores on eight different tasks (T1 to T8), the results would look rather as shown in Figure 3.1. (For convenience I have rescaled the tasks to have the same mean and standard deviation.)

You will notice that in this figure, there is little tendency for any person to perform consistently better or worse than other people: each person performs well at some tasks and poorly at others, and the rank-ordering varies considerably from task to task. Thus, to describe any one person's abilities, it is necessary to consider that person's performance on all eight tasks. There are as many different abilities as there are tasks: because they each measure something unique it makes no sense to average a person's scores across several tasks.

The second logical possibility is that there could be some areas of overlap between performance on the various tasks. Perhaps people who are below-average on Task 1 also perform below average on Tasks 2–4, and people who show above-average scores on Task 1 also show elevated scores on Tasks 2–4. Thus these four tasks form a group of related abilities that 'correlate positively' together. It might also be found that people who perform above average on one of Tasks 5–8 also tend to perform well at the rest of that group of tasks, so that these form another group of skills. But it might be found that performance on Tasks 1–4 is unrelated to performance on Tasks 5–8.

This is shown in Figure 3.2, where each person's level of performance (relative to the other three individuals) Tasks 1–4 is similar: Bob outperforms

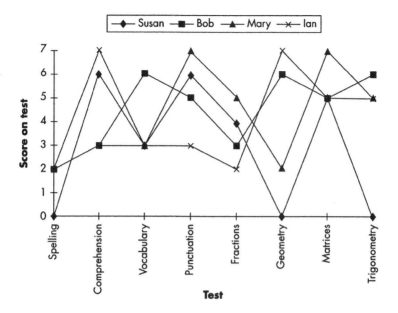

Figure 3.1 Scores of four individuals on four tasks of verbal skills and four tasks of numerical skills, showing no relation between any of the scores

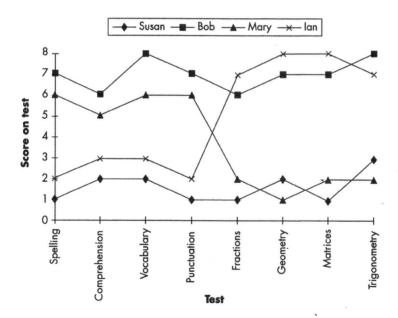

Figure 3.2 Scores of four individuals on four tasks of verbal skills and four tasks of numerical skills, showing that each individual performs to a similar level on all the verbal tasks and all the numerical tasks but that performance on the verbal task is unrelated to their numerical performance

Mary who outperforms Ian who outperforms Susan on each of these tasks. For Tasks 5–8, you can see that there is again some consistency in performance: Ian generally outperforms Bob whilst Susan and Mary both seem to have difficulties with these tasks. There is some consistency of behaviour within each set of tasks, but little or none *between* the two sets of tasks: someone who excels at Tasks 1–4 may or may not excel at Tasks 5–8.

If data show the sort of pattern shown in Figure 3.2, it is possible to infer that two separate abilities exist, one influencing performance on Tasks 1–4 and the other influencing performance on Tasks 5–8. We can describe a person's performance on the eight tasks fairly accurately by using just saying that he or she "is excellent at the first four and average at the second four tasks", for example. Whilst we could average together each person's scores on Tasks 1–4 to estimate the first ability, and estimate their scores on the second ability by averaging their scores on Tasks 5–8, it is important to appreciate that we could also estimate a person's level of each of these abilities by administering just two tasks—one selected from Tasks 1–4 and the other from Tasks 5–8. So we could probably estimate scores on the two abilities by just using two tasks—one selected from Tasks 1–4 and the second from Tasks 5–8[2].

The third possibility is shown in Figure 3.3. This is the simplest model of all. It suggests that someone who performs well on one task is also likely to

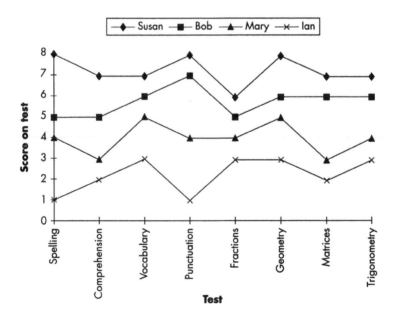

Figure 3.3 Scores of four individuals on four tasks of verbal skills and four tasks of numerical skills, showing that each individual performs to a similar level on all tasks

excel at all of the others; someone with an average score on one task is likely to show average performance on all the others, and so on. It implies a person's score any one task (or the average score computed from two or more tasks) would be adequate to describe each person's profile of scores, since each person performs at a similar level at all tasks. According to this model, we can either administer a few tasks and average them, or just pick one task at random to measure a person's level of general ability.

Factor Analysis

Examining graphs such as those in Figures 3.1–3.3 is not the most scientific method of examining the relationships between the children's scores to the various tasks. Instead, a statistical technique called 'factor analysis' is generally used. There are several good introductory texts (Child, 2006; Comrey & Lee, 1992; Cooper, 2010; Gorsuch, 1983) that cover the topic without going into too much technical detail, whilst the work of Tabachnick and Fidell (2007) is excellent for the slightly more advanced reader, and Eysenck's (1953) superb non-technical discussion of the logical basis of factor analysis remains as relevant now as it was half a century ago.

The technicalities of factor analysis need not concern us here: all you need to know is that a computer program reads in the scores of (100+) people on some selection of tasks and indicates:

- Whether there are any groups of tasks such that a person who scores above average on one task in the group also tends to score above average on the others. In Figure 3.2 there are two groups of variables, with just one group in Figure 3.3 and as many groups as there are tasks in Figure 3.1.
- Which variables belong to each group. For example, in Figure 3.2, the four verbal tasks comprise one group, whilst the numerical tasks form the other. In Figure 3.3, all the tasks belong to one group.

Groups of tasks are usually termed 'factors', and so we would say that two factors are needed to explain the data shown in Figure 3.2, and one factor explains Figure 3.3. The decision about which tasks belong to each group ('factor') is made on statistical grounds alone: it is not necessary to 'tell' the program that the first few variables are language problems and the remainder are mathematics items: the program can work out for itself which groups of variables measure the same things. It is quite possible for one factor to reflect performance on, say, six tasks, whilst another one reflects performance on just three others. Likewise, some tasks not to appear with any of the factors. For example, if we factor analysed people's responses to ten tasks we might find one factor of four tasks, another of three tasks, and another of two tasks—meaning that performance on one of the tasks is not influenced by any of the factors.

Factor analysis is a very useful technique because it allows one to find groups of items that seem to be measuring the same basic ability. If it is found that the four different memory tasks form a factor, this implies that someone who performs well at one type of memory problem is likely to perform well on all of them. Someone who performs poorly at one is likely to perform below average on all the rest, too. This is valuable for four reasons. First, it tells us that it is quite legitimate to construct a task based on a mixture of the four memory skills (the task will comprise a mixture of the four types of items)—for although the four tasks may look rather different in terms of what they ask people to do, the factor analysis shows that they are all influenced by the same underlying ability. The second point is practical: being able to develop tasks like this makes the applied psychologist's life much easier, since it means that instead of measuring performance at thousands of different tasks, the psychologist need assess only as many abilities as there are factors. Third, it is valuable in helping us understand the structure of ability. Are there any correlations between the memory ability factor and other factors? Finally, it leads to interesting research questions. What are the processes that cause a factor to emerge? Why should certain tasks form a factor, even though they may *appear* to measure quite different things? Do certain children excel at all aspects of memory because of the way they have been taught? Or because they carry out certain cognitive processes faster than others? Could it even be related to individual differences in the physiological structure or function of the brain? We shall return to these issues later.

Spearman's *g*

What actually happens when factor analysis is used to explore the relationships between several, seemingly rather different, ability tasks? One of the very first studies was performed by the British psychologist Charles Spearman (1904), who invented factor analysis for that very purpose. Other workers such as Alfred Binet (in France), Francis Galton (in Britain) and J. McKeen Cattell (in the United States) had previously studied rather simple tasks (e.g., time to perceive what a picture showed, or the time taken to push a button when a light came on) and used performance on these tasks to predict success in later life, with rather discouraging results. Spearman's data are interesting for two reasons. First, his work used somewhat more complex tasks than those chosen by Binet, Galton and Cattell—tasks that involved thinking. Second, he was not so much interested in predicting later achievements as in understanding the relationship between several (superficially very different) tasks.

Spearman developed some rather primitive tasks, including measures of the children's ability to follow complex instructions, visualisation, vocabulary, mathematical ability, ability to match colours accurately and ability to match the pitch of two musical tones. He administered these tasks to small samples of children (mainly from a village school in Hampshire), subjected the data to factor analysis and found that a single factor seemed to influence performance at all tasks. A child who scored well above average on one task also tended to perform well above average on all the rest. A child who performed at the average level on one of them was unlikely to either excel or perform much below average on any of the others. In other words, Spearman found that the model shown in Figure 3.3 fitted his data rather accurately. He called this factor *general intelligence* (or *general ability*), which is often abbreviated as *g*. Today many psychologists still believe that this 'g-factor' is one of the more useful ways of conceptualising human ability, and the search for the origins and correlates of g continues unabated (see for example Jensen, 1998).

One necessary implication of Spearman's finding is that when several ability tasks are correlated together, the correlations between them are invariably positive, a finding that is sometimes called *positive manifold*.

It is interesting to note that the tasks that measured knowledge (vocabulary etc.) emerged on the same g factor as those that required thought (e.g., ability to follow complex instructions). Thus for these children knowledge and ability to think logically are closely entwined.

Spearman's early work can certainly be criticised on many grounds. The tasks that he used may well have been influenced by certain aspects of the children's schooling, his method of factor analysis is now regarded as primitive and mistakes were made in some of his calculations (Fancher, 1985). In addition, his samples were both small (fewer than 40 children) and arguably unrepresentative of the broad population of British school children. Nevertheless, Spearman had stumbled on a very broad, powerful effect. We now know that it is impossible to find a half-decent ('reliable' and 'valid' being the technical terms) task that does not correlate positively with all other ability tasks. As Jensen (1997) observes:

> [g] is reflected by every cognitive task that permits responses that can be scored or measured according to an objective standard (e.g. number of correct responses, response time) . . . Since its discovery by Spearman in 1904, the g factor has become so firmly established as a major psychological construct in terms of psychometric and factor analytic criteria that further research along these lines is unlikely to disconfirm the construct validity of g or to add anything essentially new to our understanding of it.
>
> (Jensen, 1997, pp. 115 and 122)

Thurstone's Primary Mental Abilities

Although Jensen's comments reflect the modern consensus view, it was not always thus. In the 1920s and 1930s, Louis Thurstone, in the United States, examined the correlations between certain mental tasks in some detail, and reached conclusions that were diametrically opposed to Spearman's. Using a somewhat different method of factor analysis and a wider selection of tasks, Thurstone found several distinct ability factors rather than g. That is, he found that the model shown in Figure 3.2 fitted the data much better than Spearman's one-factor model (Figure 3.3). When he examined the correlations between 56 psychological tasks, Thurstone (1938) found not one factor but about a dozen of them, many of which seemed to make good psychological sense. For example, one factor consisted of those tasks that involved visualising geometrical figures: such as deciding whether or not the figure shown on the left of Figure 3.4 (lower part) could be rotated to look like the figure shown on the right.

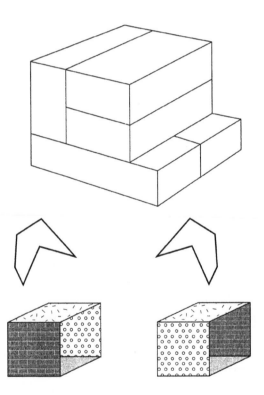

Figure 3.4 Typical items measuring spatial ability
Top: How many blocks (each of the same size and shape) are in the top figure?
Middle and bottom: Can the figure on the left be rotated to look like the figure on the right?

Thurstone's other primary mental abilities ('PMAs') are shown in Table 3.1, and examples of the actual task items used are reproduced in Chapter 2 of Thurstone (1938).

Thurstone believed that just as the three primary colours of light (red, green and blue) can be combined so as to reproduce any other colour of

Table 3.1 Some of Thurstone's (1938) primary mental abilities, with illustrative examples

Code	Name	Description	Examples
V	Verbal relations	Using words in context	Understanding proverbs, vocabulary, arranging words in order to form a sensible sentence, verbal analogies ("fish is to water as bird is to . . .")
P	Perceptual speed	Speed/accuracy in comparing items or shapes	Are the following two strings of symbols identical? 3%&@^f∂W 3%&@Af∂W
N	Numerical facility	Algebra and other forms of mathematical operation	Solve $y = x^2 - 3x + 3$. What is 40% of 60? Simplify $\dfrac{x^2 - 1}{x - 1}$
W	Word fluency	Tasks dealing with isolated words	Make as many words as you can from the letters A-B-D-E-R. Write down as many words as you can that start with 'A' and end with 'R'. Spelling.
M	Memory	Paired-associate learning and recognition	Pairs of two-digit numbers (e.g., 23 57), words and numbers ('egg 14'), or initials/surname (J.B. Foster) are learnt, and recalled on cue, e.g., 23 – ? –, – ? – 14, – ? – Foster.
I	Induction	Finding rules given exemplars	What is the next number in the series 0, 1, 3, 8, 15 . . . ? What do cows, tables and triathlons have in common? (legs)
R	Restriction	A strange mixture of multiple-choice tests	Is 3.1452 × 7.88814 (a) 24.8098 (b) 17.8848 (c) 21.9098 (d) 30.8848 A doge is (a) a magistrate (b) a ruse (c) a leaf (d) an idea
D	Deduction	Deductive logic	All tigers are dangerous. Tibbles is dangerous. Is Tibbles a tiger?
S	Spatial ability	Visualising shapes	See, for example, Figure 3.4.

the spectrum (e.g., yellow), it should be possible to predict a person's performance on any complex cognitive task (e.g., programming a computer, diagnosing electrical faults) through some combination of these PMAs (Thurstone, 1938).

Thurstone could find no evidence whatsoever for g. So how could Spearman and Thurstone, both employing similar research techniques (factor analysis) arrive at such different and seemingly irreconcilable conclusions? There are several reasons.

- Thurstone tested university students, rather than schoolchildren. This has two important consequences that were not appreciated at the time.
  - (a) If students are generally of above-average intelligence, the student group will (by definition) show less variation in g than does the general population. For purely statistical reasons, this will reduce the size of the correlations between the tasks, which will in turn affect the results of the factor analysis, and make it less easy to identify a g factor.
  - (b) Suppose that you take a sample of people from the population and divide this sample into two—the people of above-average intelligence in one group, and the people of below-average intelligence in the other. Then administer tasks measuring cognitive abilities, and factor analyse the results for each group separately. It is now known (Detterman & Daniel, 1989; Reynolds & Keith, 2007) that there will be a stronger g factor in the low-ability group, perhaps because people with high g specialize more and develop some of their abilities. So for this reason too, Thurstone's use of college students might be expected not to reveal as strong a g factor as he would have found in a more balanced sample of the population.
- Thurstone's tasks also had strict time limits, whereas Spearman's children were not hurried: it is possible that hurrying students may introduce some random error into the students' scores. I mention this as a logical possibility: however, research by P.E. Vernon (1961) suggests that this is unlikely to be a problem in practice.
- Thurstone administered a much larger sample of tasks than did Spearman (nearly 60, as opposed to about 7). The tasks were much better than Spearman's as they depended more on cognition and less on school learning. In addition, the increased size of Thurstone's sample (200+) can only improve the accuracy of his results. So perhaps Thurstone's research was just better than Spearman's.
- As I have observed elsewhere (Cooper, 1998, p. 99), a crucial difference between Spearman's and Thurstone's experiments lay in the types of

tasks that were used. Spearman added together scores on addition, subtraction, multiplication problems and so on to estimate the children's
overall mathematical ability. He included this *overall* measure of mathematical ability in his factor analyses. Thurstone, on the other hand,
treated addition, subtraction, multiplication etc. as separate tasks in his
factor analyses. Unsurprisingly, perhaps, his factor analysis revealed that
those who did well at addition and subtraction problems also excelled
at multiplication and division problems: these four tasks formed a factor. So the *factor* of numerical ability identified by Thurstone is almost
identical to the *task* of mathematical ability used by Spearman. The problem is not restricted to mathematical ability: Thurstone's collection of
tasks included some that appeared to be almost identical to other tasks
in the battery—for example, 'Reading 1' and 'Reading 2' that were
two almost-identical tasks of knowledge of proverbs. Since these tasks
are essentially identical, they are virtually *guaranteed* to correlate highly
together and form a factor.

How many primary mental abilities are there? This is, in fact, a very difficult question to address, since the choice of sub-tasks (and hence the nature
of the primary abilities that emerge) is largely arbitrary. Thurstone's (1938)
rationale for selecting that particular set of 56 tasks was to "include a fairly
wide variety of tasks covering verbal, numerical, and visual tasks in the hope
that some of the primary traits involved in current psychological tasks would
appear" (1938: 10). Quite why he concentrated on these three broad areas,
and why he chose some tasks rather than others was never made explicit.
This is problematical, since if none (or only one)[3] of the tasks in a battery
of tasks actually measure a particular primary ability, then no factor corresponding to that primary ability can emerge. Thus it is necessary to examine
performance on as many diverse tasks as possible. Later studies (e.g., Hakstian &
Cattell, 1976) *did extend* the list of tasks used, and discovered more primary
abilities as a consequence: the list of primaries now numbers at least 20, and
these take some 3 hours to assess. However, even this list is unlikely to be
complete, as there is always the possibility that some important mental abilities may have been overlooked.

It certainly *seems* as if there are some major gaps in the sorts of tasks that
have been considered. One might perhaps expect the main tasks used to
identify the main primary mental abilities to reflect current thinking in
cognitive psychology or developmental psychology: it seems reasonable to
ensure that a task battery includes those that experimental psychologists
use to assess memory for events, Piagetian 'conservation tasks', and so
on. However, this is manifestly not the case. Even the classic tasks used by

cognitive psychologists (e.g., Clark & Chase, 1972; Daneman & Carpenter, 1980; Halford, Baker, McCredden & Bain, 2005; Posner & Mitchell, 1967; Sternberg, 1969; Stroop, 1935) have generally been ignored in large-scale studies aimed at clarifying the main primary abilities, although Carroll (1983, 1993) and others have scrutinised the factors that emerge when small groups of these tasks are analysed, and have related them to primary mental abilities and other factors.

Practical considerations (such as the need for quick group testing) may have led to other omissions. For example, there have been few attempts to measure individuals' ability to sing a note in tune, learn a foreign language, track a moving object on a computer screen using a joystick, ignore information from one sensory modality when using another (e.g., ignoring words presented through headphones when learning words from a printed list) or measure the speed with which individuals can 'automatise' (that is, learn to perform automatically) novel tasks. There are often good practical reasons for these omissions, but it is likely that the number of potential primary abilities is very large indeed, and it is not obvious that we shall ever be able to identify them all. All we can hope to do when assessing abilities for the purpose of personnel selection, clinical diagnosis, the evaluation of educational intervention, or whatever, is to appraise what seem to us to be the factors that' emerge from those tasks that appear to be most relevant to everyday cognitive activities: reasoning, remembering and so on.

Individual difference psychologists may have a lesson to learn from occupational psychologists here. It might be worthwhile sampling the sorts of activities that people perform in their working and home lives and ensuring that any battery of tasks that claims to assess primary mental abilities actually measures all of these variables, in much the same way that occupational psychologists use 'job analysis' to identify the skills required for a particular post. Although the number and nature of the main primary ability factors depends crucially on the nature of the tasks included in the battery, and their 'level' (i.e., sub-tasks rather than tasks), Kline's (1991) book shows the primary factors identified by Ekstrom, French and Harman (1976) and Hakstian and Cattell (1976). Factors that are found in both batteries include perceptual speed (speed of comparing strings such as 1975623097 and 1975643097), numerical ability, spatial ability, verbal comprehension, inductive reasoning, deductive reasoning, memory span (recall of lists of digits), associative memory (memory for "sensible" phrases—e.g., 'happy sailor'), flexibility of closure (identifying simple shapes embedded in more complex ones), speed of closure (identifying words/pictures that have been partially obscured with correcting fluid), word fluency ("list as many words as you can that start with 's' and end in 'n'"), originality/flexibility of use of objects ("what useful object could you make from an empty tin, a stick and a tissue?") and fluency of ideas ("you have 2 minutes to think of as many words as possible that could describe your university/college").

To return to the conflict of views between Spearman and Thurstone, the finding that two researchers who both used factor analysis could come to such different conclusions about the structure of abilities made many psychologists wary of the technique. The debate was intense, as indicated by Thurstone's claim that "we have not found the general factor of Spearman, but our methods do not preclude it" (Thurstone, 1938). It suggested (to non-specialists) that factor analysis was a flawed procedure that was capable of "proving" anything—a notion that endures today. For example, Howe (1997) asserts that "it [factor analysis] does not identify any one unique correct solution", a claim that most would regard as being factually incorrect. But how can one resolve the problem that one researcher identifies a general factor of ability, whilst another finds at least 10? One solution to this conundrum is outlined in the next section.

Hierarchical Models of Ability

Several researchers (Cahan & Cohen, 1989; Carroll, 1993; Cattell, 1971; Gustafsson, 1981; Vernon, 1950) have shown that there is no necessary conflict between the views of Spearman and Thurstone and that both these models can be viewed as correct when considered as part of a hierarchical model of abilities. It all hinges on the realisation that the *factors* identified by Thurstone (numerical facility, verbal relations, spatial ability, etc.) might themselves be correlated. So it is entirely possible to apply factor analysis to the correlations between these factors.

In principle, it is a simple matter to follow the steps outlined below, which will reveal the structure of ability.

(a) Devise tasks to measure a very large number of rather "low-level" mental abilities: for example, tasks assessing ability to solve anagrams, knowledge of proverbs, ability to multiply two-digit numbers, ability to identify the aesthetically most pleasing picture from a series, ability to remember lists of numbers presented verbally. The key requirement here is that each task should comprise a number of similar items: there should be no attempt to mix items (e.g., vocabulary, spelling and comprehension items) within a task, since the assumption that these various skills are related is precisely the one that we wish to task. In practice, modern researchers may study the relationship between 50 or more such tasks.

(b) Administer these to large samples of volunteers.

(c) Work out the scores (number of items correctly answered) for each person on each task.

(d) Use a computer program to factor analyse these scores: that is, to determine

- how many factors (groups of tasks) are present.

- which tasks belong to which factor(s). The 'primary mental abilities' that emerge at this stage (verbal ability, etc.) are sometimes known as 'first-order factors', as they are found at this, first, step of the analysis.

(e) Repeat step (d) several more times, but instead of factoring scores on the tasks, we now factor the first-order factors (PMAs) to produce second-order factors (sometimes known as 'second-order abilities' or 'secondaries'. Then factor analyse the correlations between the second-order factors to obtain third-order factors, and so on—until either just one factor is found, or the correlations between factors are small. Thus, we first group the tasks to form first-order factors. Then we try grouping these factors to form second-order factors, and so on—until it is found that none of the factors can sensibly be grouped with any other factors, or until just one factor remains.

The answers to the question "how many ability factors are there?" thus depends entirely on the level of analysis that one wishes to use. To describe a person's abilities in most detail, one would want to measure all known primary factors, which would take many hours. The hierarchical model shows that it is possible to get a very good approximation to this figure by measuring second-order abilities (or primaries that are very closely correlated with the second-order abilities). Or one can get a very reasonable approximation by simply measuring general ability, g, which emerges as a third-order factor in most studies. Which level of the hierarchy is used depends on the purpose of testing: in particular whether the aim is to predict performance on just a few, highly specific tasks (such as those involved in clerical work, where tasks measuring a few primaries such as perceptual speed, verbal and numerical ability are the obvious choice) or to try to predict how a person will perform in a great many (unspecified) areas using a task measuring g. So both Spearman and Thurstone are correct in their conclusions: they are looking at different levels of the hierarchical model. Spearman looked at the topmost level, whilst Thurstone (because of his unfortunate choice of tasks, and his incorrect assumption that the primary mental abilities were uncorrelated) looked only at the bottom level of the pyramid.

In order to establish the structure of abilities, it is vitally important to ensure that the tasks that are selected are as diverse as possible. Consider what would happen if people were administered one task measuring inductive reasoning, and one each of tasks measuring logic, memory, perceptual speed and so on (say 10 tasks in total) together with 6 tasks measuring very similar abilities— for example, 6 tasks all of which involved quickly comparing pairs of things and deciding if they are the same. One task might involve strings of letters such as QLFBL and QGFBL. Another might involve familiar (and thus easy-to-name) shapes. Another might involve unfamiliar, irregular shapes, and so on. This creates problems because when all of these tasks are correlated together, the visualisation factor will appear much larger than it should; it might lead you to believe that visualisation is a more important ability than memory, for example. It is important that the tasks that are factor analysed form a random sample of all of the tasks that could have been devised, as recommended by Cattell (1971, p. 299) and Kline (2000, p. 141). Obviously if no tasks have been given that measure a particularly ability, that ability cannot emerge from a factor analysis. And if too many tasks have been administered to measure a particular ability, the factor that emerges will appear to be more powerful than it should be. This seems a very obvious point, but it is one that many psychologists overlook.

Horn and Cattell (1966), Hakstian and Cattell (1978), Undheim (1981) and Gustafsson (1981; Gustafsson, Collis & Messick, 2001) are amongst those who have used this approach to discover the structure of abilities, although some workers start from the level of primary abilities, rather than the lower-level   tasks. That is, they use scores on commercially published tasks measuring primary mental abilities, such as the Comprehensive Ability Battery (Hakstian & Cattell, 1976), the Kit of Cognitively Referenced Tasks (Ekstrom, French & Harman, 1976) or the Differential Aptitude Task (Bennett, Seashore & Wesman, 1978) rather than rediscovering the primary mental abilities as described in step (a) above.

The choice of which variables are entered into the analysis is therefore somewhat arbitrary and will often be based on those primary abilities that happen to be easily assessed by commercial tasks. This will itself influence that secondary abilities are found, and there is always the chance that including a few new tasks will produce additional primary and higher-order abilities.

An example may help. Suppose that we took a selection of tasks similar to those used by Thurstone, administered them to a large sample of people, calculated the correlations between every pair of tasks, and used factor analysis to identify the factors. We might represent the analysis graphically as shown in Figure 3.5. This shows the left-hand portion of a very wide diagram, where the squares to the bottom of this figure each represent some psychological tasks, such as those used by Thurstone. So T1 might represent a

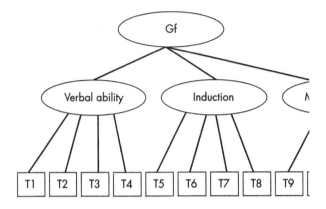

Figure 3.5 Part of a hierarchical model of ability, showing how primary mental abilities (verbal ability, inductive reasoning . . .) emerge from the factor analysis of sub-tasks, and how a second-order ability factor (fluid ability, Gf) emerges from a factor analysis of the primary mental abilities

task measuring understanding of proverbs (e.g., "a bird in the hand is worth two in the bush"), T2 a task of verbal analogies (a typical item being "cat is to kitten as dog is to …"), T3 vocabulary (e.g., "which word in the following list means the opposite of 'tiny'"), T4 a measure of comprehension (e.g., asking someone to read a piece of text and then asking questions to task the person's understanding of what has been read), T5 a task asking what certain groups of things have in common, that other objects do not (e.g., 'legs' in the case of tables and people, as opposed to snakes, fish and cars), T6 a task asking subjects to complete a difficult number series (e.g., 1, 4, 13, 40), T7 a task of verbal analogies (e.g., "petrol is to car as ? is to computer") and T8 might ask people to pick a shape that will best complete a pattern. T9 measures memory span (ability to recall lists of numbers read aloud).

You will remember that factor analysis is a statistical procedure that can show which (if any) of the tasks measure the same underlying ability as other tasks. Just as in the previous chapter, the ovals represent the factors ('primary mental abilities') and a line joining a task to a factor indicates that performance on that task is substantially influenced by the factor. So in the figure, we can see that Tl, T2, T3 and T4 are all influenced by one factor, whereas T5–T8 are influenced by a second factor. As it is clear from the nature of the problems in the tasks that T1–T5 all involve the use of language, we would probably call the first factor 'verbal ability' or something similar. Likewise it seems from their content that T5–T8 all involve inductive reasoning.

It might be found empirically that some factors (including the deductive reasoning and inductive reasoning PMAs) are correlated together and form a second-order factor denoted here as Gf, whilst other PMAs (such as 'digit span' or 'original uses') form other second-order factors. Likewise there is nothing to stop us exploring the relationships between the secondaries, perhaps finding one or more 'third-order' or 'tertiary' factors. Indeed, the process can continue either until all the factors are uncorrelated, or until just one factor remains.

Gustafsson (1981) studied the relationships between scores on some 20 tasks. These were found to form 10 primary mental ability factors, which were themselves found to be inter-correlated. This meant that it was legitimate to look for second-order factors, and Gustaffson found three main second-order factors (all of which had previously been identified by other workers using different selections of tasks: e.g., Hakstian & Cattell, 1978; Horn & Cattell, 1966). Fluid ability (Gf) was a factor that grouped together the primaries such as inductive and deductive reasoning, memory and ability to make logical inferences. Crystallised ability (Gc) bundled together primary abilities such as verbal ability, numerical ability and mechanical knowledge/ reasoning, primaries that involve both knowledge and abstract thought. Visualisation (Gv) encompassed those primaries that involved 'picturing' what figures would look like if they were moved. These three second-order factors were found to be correlated, and so it was appropriate to look for a third-order factor. This factor grouped together all three of the second-order factors. Thus Gustaffson's hierarchical model resembles that shown in Figure 3.5. As before, the ellipses represent factors and the squares represent tasks. (To keep the diagram to a manageable size, we have not shown all of the 20 tasks, or all 10 primary mental abilities.) Straight lines indicate which tasks (or factors) fall into groups, as shown in Figure 2.2.

Carroll (1993) used factor analysis to reexamine 461 sets of data, in order to determine which are the most reliably found primary factors. His 800-page discussion is well worth consulting, but in essence he suggests that the main primary abilities include the following:

- Three types of reasoning ability (inductive, deductive and that used in solving mathematical problems),
- Five memory factors (memory span and associative memory as discussed above, plus visual memory, memory for meaningful material, for example, 'happy sailor', and free recall memory), together with one "speed-of-learning" factor,
- Between five and eight visual perception factors, including perceptual speed, spatial ability, speed of closure, flexibility of closure (all described above) and visualisation,

- Twelve auditory factors, including ability to hear faint sounds, to localise sounds in space, understand distorted speech and remember tunes,
- Nine factors tapping the speed with which ideas can be generated or expressed, including ideational fluency (e.g., "how many words can you think of which could be used to describe a new red car?" with a time limit of 2 minutes) and word fluency (e.g., "how many words can you think of which start with S and end with N" with a time limit of 2 minutes),
- A great many factors associated with language use,
- Several factors associated with school achievement/knowledge and social skills,
- Speed of speaking and speed of writing.

When tasks measuring some of these primary abilities are administered to large groups of people, and the correlations between these tasks are factor analysed, the main second-order factors that emerge include those identified by Gustafsson (1981) and described above, namely fluid intelligence (Gf), crystallised intelligence (Gc) and visualisation (Gv). Carroll's analyses also include second-order factors of memory ability (Gm), cognitive speed (Gs) and retrieval (Gr) identified by Cattell (1971), the latter having large loadings from tasks such as 'word fluency' or 'originality' requiring information to be retrieved quickly from long-term memory. Carroll's list also includes a factor of auditory perception, plus a rather strange factor that is a mixture of Gc and Gf. When the correlations between these second-order factors are analysed, a factor of general intelligence (g) is found at the third level.

It should now be clear how this "three-stratum model" (Carroll, 1993) reconciles the work of Spearman and Thurstone. The model shows that it is perfectly reasonable to describe the correlations between the tasks either in terms of rather a lot of primary mental abilities (the first-order factors), or in terms of a few second-order factors, or in terms of general ability (the third-order factor). It is a matter of convenience which level of analysis one chooses.

A concrete example may make this clearer. Suppose that, instead of asking people to carry out cognitive tasks, you asked them to rate (on a 7-point scale) how much they enjoyed certain films. The list of films would be a long one, and should cover the whole spectrum, just as a great many varied tasks are administered when researching the structure of abilities. It would be easy to factor analyse people's responses to the various films using a standard statistics package. Remember that factor analysis will try to identify variables that individuals like to a similar extent, and so one would probably find that *Gunfight at the OK Corral* and *The Magnificent Seven* formed one factor (which we might call 'Westerns'), *Reservoir Dogs* and *Pulp Fiction* formed second ('Urban Reality' films), *Alien* and one of the *Star Trek* films, a third (Science Fiction) factor, *When Harry Met Sally* and *Pretty Woman*, a fourth ('Romantic') factor, *Police Academy* and *The Full Monty*, a fifth ('Comedy') factor and *A Nightmare on Elm Street* and *Friday the 13th* a sixth ('Horror') primary factor. We could then factor the correlations between these six primary factors and might well find three secondary factors. I would guess that the first of these factors would comprise the Science Fiction and Horror factors, and so might be labelled 'fantasy films', the second secondary factor might include 'Romantic' and 'Comedy' films (perhaps called 'relaxing films') and the final factor might show that the Westerns and Urban Reality films also went together ('violent films'). And finally, we might factor the correlations between these three second-order factors and obtain a single, general, factor.

Consider now how you might explain why a particular person likes any particular film—*Alien*, for example. At the narrowest level of generalisation (first-order factor) you could 'explain' it by pointing out that people tend to like science fiction films to a certain, characteristic extent, and this is why the individual enjoys *Alien*. Or we could move up a level, and note that the factor analysis reveals that some people enjoy fantasy films (of which science fiction films form one type) whilst others do not, and this is why *Alien* appeals. Hence the person may enjoy *Alien* because it is a fantasy film. Or we could explain it by resorting to the third-order factor, which reveals that some people like *all sorts* of films (of which fantasy films are one example) whilst others are not keen on any sort of film: our viewers might enjoy *Alien* just because they enjoy *all* films. But all three explanations are correct, and useful in trying to explain why an individual may enjoy the film. Which level of explanation we use ('because the person likes films', 'because they like fantasy films' or 'because they like science fiction films') is entirely up to us. Suppose that we wanted to predict how the *Alien* fan would enjoy *Friday 13th*. We might find it useful to make the prediction on the basis of their liking for 'fantasy films', as both science fiction and horror films fall into that category. If we wanted to predict whether they would enjoy *The Full Monty*, it would be sensible to consider their liking for films *in general*, since only this will filter down to these two particular films.

It is exactly the same when analysing the structure of abilities. One can 'explain' a person's performance on a particular psychological task either in terms of a primary mental ability (as did Thurstone), in terms of a second-order ability factor (e.g., Gf, Gc, Gv, Gr or Gm) or in terms of their general ability, g (as suggested by Spearman). Most research has, however, focused on g. There seem to be several reasons for this. First, it is the simplest possible model, and in science, it is normal to start off by exploring simple models, only making them more complex if they do not adequately fit the data. But it has been found that g is a more useful predictor of real-world behaviour than are primary or second-order abilities (see Chapter 7) and it is surprisingly strongly linked to various biological and psychological variables, as described in Chapters 5 and 6. So the simplest model may turn out to be the best.

One g or Several Different gs?

The hierarchical model discussed above works out the structure of abilities by giving participants a large number of tasks, each designed to measure some ability, and analysing the results using factor analysis. In an ideal world, we would have sampled the tasks carefully—ensuring that we analysed a sample of all the tasks that could possibly have been devised. However, (a) it is not obvious how one would go about doing this, (b) there is a legacy of old data built on rather ad-hoc selections of tasks and it would seem a shame to throw this away, and (c) the matter can be resolved empirically.

Wendy Johnson (Johnson, Te Nijenhuis & Bouchard, 2008) reported an analysis of 500 Dutch seamen each of whom had been given five different sets of ability tests in the 1960s. These tests varied considerably in content. For example, one was a traditional measure of fluid intelligence. Another test was widely used for personnel selection and had scales measuring how well participants could put pegs in holes, assemble small objects, identify tools and so on. Three other ability tests with scales measuring between 7 and 13 different abilities were also given. The key point is that there was a lot of variety in what each test assessed. Some had some scales measuring language skills: others had none measuring language. Some had scales measuring memory: others had no memory component. Some focussed on assembling objects: others completely ignored such abilities.

Johnson et al. (2008) factor analysed the scales from each test independently, using a hierarchical model as described earlier in this chapter. This produced five measures of g, one from each of the tests. And these measures of g were virtually identical: most of the correlations were above 0.9. This shows clearly that it simply does not matter what the content of the test is (in terms of the scales that were administered). The g calculated from a test involving one group of cognitive tasks is almost identical to the g from a test whose content looks quite different.

The importance of this cannot be stressed too strongly. It goes back to an idea put forward by Spearman called the "principle of indifference of indicator". Spearman believed that general ability, g, is essentially raw reasoning ability that can be applied to just about any task. It influences performance on each and every task that required thought. If this is the case, then it does not really matter which tasks one administers in order to measure g. This is in stark contrast to some others such as Guilford (1967) who wrote (without a shred of empirical evidence) that "[g] is not an invariant variable but changes almost with every battery of test that is analysed". Johnson's work shows that Guilford was quite, quite wrong.

Other empirical studies come to much the same conclusion as Johnson et al. (2008). For example, what happens if you give a large sample of people 45 cognitive tasks to perform and then randomly put (say) 8 of these into "test A" and another 12 or so into "test B". Then factor analyse the correlations between the tasks, find the g factor from test A and correlate it with the g factor from Test B. This has been done using hundreds of different tests, rather than the two we have assumed here (Floyd, Shands, Rafael, Bergeron & McGrew, 2009). These authors conclude that "g remains quite invariant across many different collections of tests . . . and across batteries of varying sizes".

What happens if we take Johnson's approach a little further and look at the g factor from a cognitive ability battery (similar to the ones that Johnson used) and another g factor from a battery of tests designed to measure school attainment. The first test uses several scales to measure thinking, not knowledge: the second set measures knowledge, and not much thinking. Is the g from the school-based tests essentially the same as the g that comes out of the tests that require thinking, not knowledge? It turns out that the correlation between the two gs is 0.83 (Kaufman, Reynolds, Liu, Kaufman & McGrew, 2012). The g derived from school-based tests is very similar indeed to the g derived from tests that require thinking rather than knowledge. It seems that there is a very strong link between general ability and overall academic achievement. So whilst I was very careful in previous chapters to caution that performance at tests of language, arithmetic and other school-based subjects might be influenced by language competency, quality of schooling etc., it seems that this was over-cautious. There is a very strong tendency for children who show high levels of general ability to perform well at school. However it is not obvious from these analyses whether school makes you smart, or whether being naturally smart makes you perform well in school—issues that we will consider in Chapters 4 and 7.

An Alternative Hierarchical Model of Abilities

More recently, Johnson and Bouchard (2005a) have suggested a rather different hierarchical model. They administered four ability tests to a sample of adults. The first was Cattell's Comprehensive Ability Battery, measuring

14 primary mental abilities. The Hawaii Battery comprised 15 tests measuring mainly spatial, language and memory skills, though with one knowledge-based scale. Eleven subtests of the Weschler Adult Intelligence Scale were also given: they measure various verbal and non-verbal abilities. The final test was Raven's Matrices, which is a non-verbal test of general ability. Thus they gave a sample of tests that mainly measure primary mental abilities, though with more far more spatial tasks than is usual: 11 of the 42 tasks measured some form of spatial ability (e.g., mental rotation, imagining what a 3-dimensional object would look like from another perspective, or solving jigsaws). By contrast, there were only 5 memory tasks in the test battery.

Various confirmatory factor analyses were performed although the logic for this was always not made explicit—for example, in their interpretation of the "fluid/crystallised" model, 4 tests loaded a second-order "verbal facility" factor and 12 tests the "crystallised ability" factor—and both of these were thought to load on a third-order "school" factor. This does not seem to feature in the models put forward by Cattell or by Carroll that they were supposedly replicating. More seriously, although the selection of tests included several "creativity" tests that would be expected to load on the Gr factor (fluency: speed of producing ideas) the model did not include this factor. These tests seem to have been lumped in with the rest of the "verbal" tests when the authors tested Cattell's model. The rationale for this is unclear, particularly as a "fluency" factor was included in one of the other models that they tested. And the decision to use six second-order factors was made on the basis of a rule which is known to be seriously flawed (Cooper, 2010, Ch. 17). Given all this, the over-representation of perceptual tasks in the test-battery and the somewhat odd way in which tasks were assumed to be assigned to second-order factors, it is hard to know what to make of the authors' conclusion that there are three main third-order factors: verbal, perceptual and image-rotation, all of which load onto a fourth-order factor of general ability as shown in Figure 3.6. They found that this model fitted the data somewhat better than the more conventional three-stratum model where g emerges at the third level, not the fourth.

Putting it simply, if one includes a lot of tasks of one kind in the test battery (spatial tasks), it is hardly surprising that they seem to form an important factor, given that the "importance" of a factor is directly related to the number of tasks that load appreciably on the factor. To understand the structure of abilities, it is necessary to analyse a random or representative sample of all the tasks that could possibly have been devised to measure cognitive skills. That said, the model found by Johnson and Bouchard (2005a) has been replicated in other sets of data, although there are definite oddities. For example,

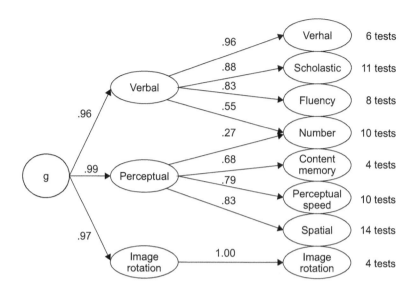

Figure 3.6 Verbal, Perceptual and Image Rotation model of abilities proposed by Johnson and Bouchard (2005a)

Thurstone's multiplication task belonged to the "speed of rotation" factor in Johnson and Bouchard's (2005b) replication study, which seems extremely strange. So too did Thurstone's "identical numbers" task—which required people to check whether numbers in a list were the same as the one at the top of the column, without a hint of mental rotation being required. Given these problems and the over-representation of perceptual tasks in their test battery, it is not clear that this model necessarily represents as much of an advance as its proponents suggest.

Summary

This chapter has introduced the method of factor analysis—a valuable tool that can identify which (if any!) of several task scores tend to vary together from person to person. Although Spearman and Thurstone both used factor analysis to explore the structure of abilities, they came to very different conclusions (one factor of general ability, g, versus a dozen primary mental abilities). We suggest some reasons for this confusion and note how both these "explanations" for the structure of abilities can be correct when viewed within the context of a hierarchical model that includes second- and third-order factors. The best-established primary and second-order ability factors are described. There is some debate about the number and nature of the second-order factors, but good agreement that a single factor of general ability, g, is found at the top of the hierarchy.

The most important finding is that g is essentially the same, no matter what tests are used to measure it. This supports Spearman's idea that g represents raw thinking ability, which affects our performance at everything we do that requires thought. Even tests based on school performance (rather than the decontextualised thinking problems of ability tests) measure g quite well.

Notes

1   This assumes that the tasks have been devised so that each task measures only one cognitive ability: for example, a task that sets out to measure spatial ability should not make many demands in terms of vocabulary, memory, mathematical knowledge or any other ability. This should be the case when using simple tasks of the type shown in Chapter 2. It would not apply if more complex tasks were used—e.g., performance at computer games.
2   Or one task that is a mixture of the four verbal tasks and another that is a mixture of the four numerical tasks.
3   A factor is, by definition, a *group* of tasks that measure the same psychological construct. Thus one task cannot constitute a factor.

4

ALTERNATIVE VIEWS OF THE STRUCTURE OF ABILITIES

Whilst chapter 3 focused on attempts to use factor analysis to understand the number of distinct abilities and the interrelations between them, not all theorists have followed this route. For there are some phenomena (such as 'streetwise' intelligence) that the models of ability described in Chapter 3 were not designed to explain, and this chapter explores some ways of understanding the nature of intelligence that are not based on factor analysis. We first briefly consider three arguments that suggest that the approach of the previous chapter is misguided; they suggest that our definitions of ability are arbitrary, that how people *perceive* their intelligence is what matters, and that our approach is flawed because it cannot explain the behaviour of some clinical groups. We then build on this to consider in some detail the theories of Gardner, Sternberg and Howe all of whom developed theories of abilities that are not based on the factor-analysis models of Chapter 3.

The Social Construction of Abilities

One approach that must be considered at the start is that human cognitive abilities are purely social constructions. This viewpoint suggests that the definition of what is intelligent will vary from culture to culture, rather as the meaning of terms such as 'beauty' vary over time (pale skin was valued a century ago but less so now; blonde hair is far more highly regarded in Hong Kong than in the West). The larger female figure idolised by Baroque artists such as Rubens is the exact opposite of today's size zero to which many aspire today. This implies that there is no such thing as a person's objective level of beauty: it is not something that can be objectively measured using some sort of test or machine, and so beauty cannot be used to explain why people behave in a particular way.

Is intelligence like this? If so, it follows that psychologists would be quite wrong to use the term to explain how people behave. For example, one could never argue that "a child performs well at school because he or she is intelligent". This is because a term such as intelligence might perhaps not refer to a real property of the child's psychological makeup. It could instead be an arbitrary term, the meaning of which could change from culture to culture or over time.

Gardner (1993) amongst others argues that this is the case. Some cultures may view memorising holy books as representing the pinnacle of human achievement, and so a person's intelligence will be measured against this criterion; other cultures may value scientific progress, catching fish or making money. According to this view, intelligence is culturally determined. The skills that are regarded as intelligent for one culture may be viewed as irrelevant by members of another culture. This issue is important because it could mean that our conception of intelligence is arbitrary and/or culturally biased, and that other ways of viewing abilities are at least as valid as the evidence-based approach that we considered in Chapter 3.

I have a major problem with social constructivism. We earlier defined mental abilities as performance on tasks that rely on thinking for their successful solution, and suggested in Chapter 3 that this should involve measuring performance on as many such tasks as possible. Thus the memory skills required for recalling passages from holy books, or the perceptual skills required for spearing fish and so on should have been included on that list of abilities. The factor-analytic approach should therefore have been based on all the mental skills that define intelligence in *any* culture, and so the results that are obtained by it should have general relevance rather than being culturally bound. And indeed, the literature shows that the basic structure of abilities described in Chapter 3 is fairly similar across cultures (e.g., Demetriou et al., 2005; Hakstian & Vandenberg, 1979) although levels of performance do vary somewhat—for example, levels of spatial ability are higher in Japan than in the West (Lynn & Hampson, 1986).

As was made clear in Chapter 3, our understanding of the nature of human abilities is not based on merely performing a survey and asking people what qualities they *believe* to be important aspects of human thinking. The answers that emerge from a survey such as this would indeed probably vary over time and from culture to culture, and so may well be social constructions. But they also need not have any basis in reality. Spiritualism was very popular 100 years ago, and so if such a survey had been run then, the ability to contact dead people would have been seen as an important mental ability by some people. But it does not follow that it ever was a genuine ability at all!

We have seen from Chapter 3 that the evidence for a *g* and other ability traits comes from a careful analysis of the evidence of how people actually behave when solving various types of problems: not what the general population *believes* to be important. Thus a reference to "newer, more democratic conceptions of intelligence" (Oakes, Wells, Jones & Datnow, 1997) shows an alarming level of misunderstanding that seems quite widespread in sociology. It suggests that intelligence is a social construct, the meaning of which can be changed quite arbitrarily depending on political attitudes, personal preference and so on. It is simply incorrect to regard human cognitive abilities as revealed by factor analysis as being social constructions because they are based on attempts to sample all possible thinking skills, rather than arbitrary opinion, and because the evidence shows that pretty much the same hierarchical structure is found in different cultures (Hakstian & Vandenberg, 1979). Whilst no one would seriously talk about "democratic conceptions of height" when addressing the issue that some people are taller than others, sociologists sometimes seem to show ignorance of the fact that modern theories of human ability are firmly founded on a century's worth of hard data: the models of intelligence described in Chapter 3 are simply the most appropriate ways to describe the correlations between the various abilities. Being based on hard fact, these theories are far from being arbitrary or socially determined. Instead, they reflect parsimonious models for describing how people actually think.

Self-Ratings of Ability

There is a considerable literature on self-ratings of ability (e.g., Beloff, 1992). For example, a group of people could be told what general intelligence means (abstract thinking, etc.) and then be asked to rate themselves as to how intelligent they are. Sex differences are found (males tend to rate themselves as more intelligent than females), and there are national differences too. But I can never understand why anyone finds this interesting—particularly as much of the early research never even bothered to address the fundamental question of whether males rate themselves as being more intelligent than females because they actually *are*[1] more intelligent.

Such studies do not seem to say anything useful about a person's actual level of cognitive ability, which is the focus of this book. There are some formidable methodological issues with this work too. To start with, it is necessary to explain to non-specialists who have probably never heard or thought much about intelligence what the psychologists actually mean by intelligence: this is by no mean feat in itself, given that popular opinion confuses intelligence with general knowledge and educational attainment! Most studies ask people to rate their level of intelligence using something like a 5- or 7-point scale, where the middle point means average. But how can anyone sensibly do this? People are being asked to rate themselves relative to the rest of the population (which includes people with learning and developmental difficulties, people of very different ages, and so on). How can the university students on whom most of this work has been conducted have a feel for how intelligent the population as a whole is, when it is likely that most of their friends are also in college, and they may not have socialised with people of below-average intelligence for several years? This probably explains why the correlations between self-rated intelligence and actual intelligence are consistently less than 0.3 (Ackerman & Wolman, 2007).

Thus although it has been found that men typically think that they are more intelligent than women (Hogan, 1978), that these differences may be linked to sex differences in personality (Stieger et al., 2010) and that these biased estimates are found in widely different cultures (e.g., Von Stumm, Chamorro-Premuzic & Furnham, 2009) and using different abilities (e.g., Ackerman & Wolman, 2007), I cannot share social psychologists' excitement about these results. They do not seem to have a close link to people's actual powers of thought and reasoning.

Social psychologists may be interested in exploring the processes that may lead some groups to develop lower opinions of their own abilities, and might be keen to see whether and how a low belief in one's own abilities (low self-efficacy) might relate to other things, such as educational performance. There is evidence that this level of belief in one's own abilities—self-efficacy—is an important predictor of how well a child performs in school (e.g., Pajares & Miller, 1994). Unfortunately, the social psychologists who carry out this research do not usually bother to ask themselves whether a person's self-belief in mathematics competency (or whatever) is itself linked to how well the child can solve mathematical problems. It seems likely that a child who finds mathematical problems easy to solve will therefore develop high levels of self-efficacy in this area, whereas a child who struggles will (quite rightly) appreciate that they are probably not wonderful at mathematics. So just because self-efficacy correlates with academic performance, it does not necessarily follow that self-efficacy is the *cause* of good or poor performance. It could well be that a child's level of ability influences both their feelings of self-efficacy and their academic performance.

The evidence shows that this is indeed the case (Pajares & Kranzler, 1995) with g affecting both mathematics performance and feelings of self-efficacy, and self-efficacy then also influencing mathematics performance. In the case of self-ratings of performance at biology, ability has a much larger effect than self-efficacy (Lawson, Banks & Logvin, 2007). However there are surprisingly few such studies in the literature. Most naively assume that self-efficacy is the key predictor, and do not bother to ask whether abilities might perhaps influence levels of self-efficacy. My view is that it is far simpler to measure abilities and determine how these influence performance, and only then explore the relationships between abilities, self-efficacy and performance. To study the links between self-efficacy and performance without considering abilities seems to me to be very odd, given the substantial causal links between cognitive abilities and educational success that we discuss in Chapter 7.

Unusual Abilities

The factor-analytic models discussed previously sought to describe how well "normal" individuals perform. There is a literature summarised by Howe (1989) and Conners (1992) indicating that individuals with severe learning difficulties may nevertheless be capable of exceptional cognitive performance in some highly specific areas. For example, Howe cites case histories of individuals whose scores on tests of general ability placed them in the lowest few percent of the population, but who could nevertheless perform prodigious feats of memory (e.g., memorising chunks of a telephone directory), playing recognising and identifying music, and performing complex calculations with dates (e.g., being able to work out on which day of the week January 3, 1893 fell).

He argues that such findings pose major problems for conventional theories of human abilities. Some others have argued that this sort of evidence suggests that there is no place for g in any theory of intelligence/cognition. Instead, it might be more appropriate to view human cognitive performance as representing the activity of several specialised cognitive modules (Ceci, 1996) somewhat as proposed by Fodor (1983). For example, one module may perform face recognition, another may allow us to learn language, and a third may allow us to perform multiplication.

It is evident that these modules are highly specific. The face-recognition module can only deal with faces (not music, numbers or language), for example: they are the "engines" that carry out various computational tasks. Logically there have to be modules rather like this; for example, as humans spontaneously learn language (without having to be taught it), there has to be some module somewhere that allows this remarkable feat to be accomplished. But saying that there is a module does not mean that we understand how it works!

Interestingly, Fodor never suggested that thought involved the operation of only these very narrow, domain-specific modules. He also argued that there is a need for a general-purpose problem-solving system that was highly unlikely to be modular, given that it allows information to be combined from several different modalities (for example, it would have to determine how a problem should be represented in order to solve it: it needs to determine which modules should be involved and in which order), and it can operate on any type of data (language, diagrams, sounds . . .). This could well be where individual differences in cognitive abilities arise, rather than at the detailed domain-specific modules that actually process the information, a point also made by Anderson (1998). So the existence of individuals with unusual patterns of abilities probably does not toll a death-knell for g.

To draw another analogy, it is difficult to see whether studying the most common "abnormal" behaviours seen by clinical psychologists (schizophrenia, depression etc.) would provide many insights into "normal" personality functioning. Well-established "normal" personality traits such as Extraversion, Conscientiousness or Openness to Experience would not seem to emerge from such an analysis. Clinical syndromes may be qualitatively different from normal personality functioning, rather than representing extreme levels of the most common "normal" personality traits. So finding that individuals who show very low levels of g when they are assessed using conventional ability tests can sometimes perform prodigious (and highly unusual) performance in one or two very specialised areas does not mean that the factor-analytic results discussed in the previous chapter are flawed. It just seems to imply that some highly specific (possibly "hard-wired") cognitive mechanisms have been spared.

Sternberg's Triarchic Theory of Ability

Robert Sternberg's (1985) triarchic theory is so named because it seeks to explain how three different types of intelligence operate. Sternberg felt that the sorts of problems that psychologists typically asked people to solve did not reflect a person's full range of abilities. Specifically, by being abstract and decontextualised, they did not allow people to bring existing knowledge and skills to bear. A literature suggests that children who have problems solving a maths problem when it is administered abstractly (e.g., $10 - 3 \times 2.44$) find it easier to solve when it is tied to some context that matters to them, such as checking the change that one gets after buying three loaves of bread

(Carragher, Carragher & Schliemann, 1985). Nor (he argues) do existing tests allow one to measure how well a person creatively adapts to new problems—for example, how he or she conceptualises the problem and how quickly he or she automatises commonly used skills.

Three Types of Cognitive Components

Sternberg is a cognitive psychologist, and his theory is distinctive because he tries to analyse the cognitive operations that a person must perform in order to solve various sorts of problems—both the types of problems found in intelligence tests, and real-world problems that might require some "common sense" or background knowledge for their speedy solution, or that require "thinking outside the box". He calls these cognitive operations 'components' and has drawn up a complex and highly speculative theory that specifies what these might look like.

Each component is assumed to have three characteristics:

- Duration (how long it takes to perform),
- Difficulty (the chances that the component will produce the wrong answer),
- Probability of execution when solving a particular problem.

For example, the component that compares the colours of two objects is likely to be quick to execute; might give the wrong answer on 10% of occasions (particularly if one is colour-blind or the lighting is poor) and is likely to be executed very often when solving a jigsaw puzzle. The cognitive process that identifies that a couple of bars of music were probably penned by Mozart is likely to be slower, is more likely to give the wrong answer, and will never be used when solving a jigsaw puzzle. Individuals are almost bound to consider how to solve the jigsaw puzzle most efficiently (a 'metacomponent')—but even if they muse for hours, they may overlook an obvious strategy.

A 'component' is defined by Sternberg (1985) as "an elementary information process that operates upon internal representations of objects"—a thought process, in other words. And whilst some of these components are very broad (e.g., thinking about how to structure that essay, and what you should and should not include), others may involve rather precise descriptions of cognitive behaviour (e.g., deciding whether two words or shapes are identical, rather like Fodor's modules).

Some components describe high-level planning of how to solve a problem (metacomponents). Some are involved in acquiring the knowledge/information that are necessary to solve a particular type of problem (*knowledge acquisition components*), whereas others describe the low-level cognitive operations (e.g., encoding strategies) that actually get the problem solved (*performance components*). Thus, there are three types of components: metacomponents, knowledge acquisition components and performance components.

Metacomponents

Metacomponents are involved in planning how to solve problems. Consider solving a jigsaw puzzle. One might first decide on a sequence of strategies to use, such as

(a) Sorting the pieces that have a straight edge into several piles, according to their colour.
(b) Consulting the picture on the box to decide which coloured pieces of border go where.
(c) Assembling chunks of same-coloured border by searching for those that have appropriately shaped contours and testing whether they fit.
(d) Joining these sections of border together.
(e) Repeating steps (a)–(d) for similarly coloured/textured areas within the main body of the puzzle until it is ultimately solved.

Sternberg suggests that metacomponents are used to

• *decide precisely what the problem is that needs to be solved.* This is obvious in the case of the jigsaw, but may not be immediately clear to an arbitrator who is involved in a longstanding, complex and emotional dispute between an employer and a union, or to students who are keen to find a boyfriend or girlfriend but do not know what, precisely, they are doing wrong. (Is it political views? Shyness? Body odour?) Metacomponents may also affect performance on quite simple tasks, when the experimenter probably intends that they should not. In my student days, I once took part in an experiment on Piagetian conservation of volume, was shown a lump of modelling clay and was asked whether it would always displace the same amount of water when dropped into a tank. I said that it would not, arguing to myself that a dense clay ball could be crafted to have a hollow, air-filled pocket in the centre and would still sink, and so the volume of water displaced by the clay could perhaps be larger than expected. Because I approached the task as one of extreme logical reasoning, I failed to show conservation of volume.

- *select appropriate performance components* in order to solve the problem. There are usually several ways of solving each problem; should one approach the jigsaw by simply trying to randomly fit pieces together? Is it best to find the corner pieces first?
- *decide how to represent information*. For example, consider whether a diagram might help when solving an abstract reasoning task, such as an anagram.
- *decide how to combine lower-level components*. For example, consider whether to sort for colour, texture and a straight edge simultaneously, or in three stages, and how to decide that a particular chunk of the puzzle seems to be wrong.
- *decide how much time to allocate to each component*. Should each component be performed slowly but accurately, or is it better to aim for quick and possibly faulty analyses?
- *monitor the success* of the solution. That is, check how one's solution is progressing according to the initial plan.
- *incorporate feedback*. Be alert for improved ways to solve the problem that are noticed by chance.

Taken together, the metacomponents describe how a particular problem is to be conceptualised, and which methods (procedures, strategies) may allow its successful solution. They are likely to be particularly important for complex real-world problems.

Knowledge Acquisition Components

Sternberg argues that we almost always acquire new knowledge by relating novel information to what we already know. For example, in the previous section, I tried to help you understand metacomponents by helping you relate them to issues (jigsaws, finding a partner) with which you are probably familiar. This existing knowledge can be general knowledge or knowledge about strategies for acquiring and knowledge (how to browse the contents page of a book, or strategies such as mnemonics to help readers to memorise information). Sternberg argues that increasing one's vocabulary is an important aspect of knowledge acquisition, and this is highly dependent on being able to deduce the meaning of a word from its context. On reading "the Himalayan klob melted in my colourless drink", you will probably suspect that 'klob' is another word for ice, because it is hard to think of anything else that melts and would be associated with a drink. You know from experience that the temperature of drinks is normally somewhere between the freezing point and boiling point of water, so klob is unlikely to refer to metal melting in your drink, and you also know that other substances such as candle wax that could melt in a hot drink would not taste pleasant.

Selective encoding is the process whereby a person decides what might be relevant and what can safely be ignored when ascertaining the meaning of a word: it probably does not matter that the drink is colourless, whereas the fact that klob melts in a drink probably is important.

Selective combination involves examining all the important aspects of the sentence ("melting", "is found in a drink") that have been selectively encoded, and coming up with hypotheses about what klob probably is. Is Himalayan klob a special sort of ice—for example, octagonal crystals? Or is it just another name for ice from the freezer? Selective combination involves scouring the encoded information for answers.

Selective comparison then relates klob to other concepts with which you are familiar. If you find information elsewhere in the text to make you realise that Himalayan klob is indeed a form of frozen water with eight sides, then the word will enter your vocabulary by linking it to ordinary ice: "Himalayan klob is basically the same as ordinary ice but comes in eight-sided crystals".

The principles apply to higher-level problems, too. When researching an essay, you will flick through books, journals and abstracts until you find something that looks relevant. Then when you read several papers you do not try to remember everything—you will focus on various results that seem relevant to what you have read elsewhere (perhaps one researcher finds a highly significant correlation between two variables, whilst the other finds nothing and so you decide to explore why this might be). These are all examples of selective encoding. Then you will scrutinise how the two papers differ in their methodology, and relate what you have read to your knowledge of experimental design and statistics, eventually coming up with a hypothesis about why the studies differ (selective combination). For example, you may realise that the second study used a very small sample. Then having discounted the second study as being flawed, you will want to link your new-found knowledge to other, related concepts with which you are familiar (*selective comparison*) and come to some conclusion about what the literature implies for theory and practice in the area.

Performance Components

These are the basic building blocks of problem solving and include many of the cognitive operations (e.g., encoding and retrieving material from memory, mental rotation) that are required in order to perform a task. If one was to draw up a flowchart showing the sequence of operations that a person performs in order to solve some puzzle, the boxes in the flowchart would be the performance components. Sternberg identifies three types of performance components. These include various *encoding components* (noticing what stimuli look like), *comparison components* (deciding whether two stimuli follow some rule, e.g., are the same colour or shape) and *response components* (deciding to do something, e.g., deciding to push one button rather than another).

Sternberg's first experimental studies into performance components began with an approach known as componential analysis (Sternberg, 1977). This was a brave attempt to understand the cognitive processes that took place as people solved individual items in ability tests. For example, suppose that a person is shown two words on a computer screen and asked to push one button if they mean the same thing, or another button if they differ in meaning. What mental operations must a person perform in order to make this decision? One simple model might suppose that a person will have to

(a) read the first word,
(b) retrieve its meaning from some internal dictionary (the time taken to do so being known to depend on features of the word such as its frequency or length) and store this meaning in working memory,
(c and d) do the same for the other word,
(e) evaluate whether the two words are "sufficiently" similar,
(f) decide on the appropriate response (e.g., by pressing one of two buttons),
(g) physically make the response.

Thus an individual's reaction time to this item is a simple sum of the durations of all of these cognitive processes. It is possible that each of the first six stages listed above (sometimes called *elementary cognitive operations* or ECOs) takes a fixed amount of time for a particular individual. For example, it may take me 0.05 seconds to retrieve words of a particular length and frequency, whilst another individual may be able to perform this operation in 0.03 seconds. Using some ingenious methodologies, Sternberg was able to estimate the durations of several such ECOs. (Note that Sternberg used a rather different task from that shown above—one that did not require the use of language.)

To see why this work is important, suppose that we have estimated the duration of one person's ECOs from one task, and know the nature and sequence in which some of these operations are performed in *another* task. We should be able to "plug in" the durations of the ECOs and predict quite accurately how long it will take the individual to perform the second task. Unfortunately, however, there is so much measurement error associated with the estimated duration of the ECOs (and/or in deciding which model is the most appropriate) that this is not possible in practice (May, Kline & Cooper, 1987).

It turns out that even for simple tasks, the number of potential cognitive models becomes very large. This is because some operations may perhaps be performed in parallel, rather than sequentially. This makes it much harder to work out which model is the "best", and to estimate the durations of the ECOs. However, the basic idea from this research is that *cognitive components* may affect performance on ability-test items. Performance components are heavily implicated in the types of tasks that require clear, logical thought—they are at the core of Sternberg's Analytic Intelligence.

Evaluation of Cognitive Components

The idea of components is problematical for two reasons. First, as Kline (1991) discusses in some detail, many of them are 'non-contingent' concepts. That is, they are concepts whose existence is necessarily implied by the problem, rather than proper theoretical constructs whose presence or degree of influence can be determined empirically in order to test the model. For example, it is clearly impossible to solve any problem without 'encoding' it (making some representation of it). So there must, by definition, be an encoding performance component. Likewise when solving a problem, there *has* to be some sort of 'response component' (even if it only involves saying 'aha!' to oneself). Surely problem solving is by *definition* using metacomponents to decide how to represent the problem, devise strategies for solving it, and so on. And how is it possible to learn anything *without* using selective encoding/combination/comparison? It is not at all obvious that this part of the theory is scientific as it cannot obviously be falsified. How could you conduct an experiment where the null hypothesis is that there is no such thing as selective combination (for example)?

Second, the broad definitions of 'components' given above mean that it is impossible to specify the level at which behaviour should be analysed. Take one of the very simplest 'performance components'—deciding to push a button when a light comes on. One could simply measure the duration/ probability of execution/success of execution of this button-pressing component (using some form of chronometric experiment to estimate the duration of encoding and comparison components, and subtracting these from the total reaction time). Or one can go down to a lower level of analysis, look at what is happening in the neurones and regard this activity as a (more complex) set of response components. Having mastered that, we could even try to conceptualise what goes on at a biochemical level. Or take the encoding component. Is this really a single process, or is it possible (necessary, even) to explain encoding in terms of other lower-level sub-processes? As each component may possibly spawn many simpler sub-processes (for "no claim is made that any of the components are elementary at all levels of analysis" [Sternberg, 1985, p. 98]), the types of models used to describe even simple behaviours can rapidly become very, very complex and impossible to test.

The unlimited complexity of the componential sub-theory means that it is difficult to test in practice. One reviewer is even more ascerbic:

> things like 'recognition of just what the nature of the problem is' and 'understanding of internal and external feedback concerning the quality of task performance' are not separate elements in any genuine mental process; they are more like chapter headings in books on how to think.
>
> (Neisser, 1983)

Just defining several different tasks as examples of a particular type of component seems to this author to be rather unhelpful. Why is it useful to specify that—for example—listening to a passage of music and reading a word are both encoding processes, given that they probably use quite different parts of the brain? However as any task will require the use of high-level planning strategies (metacomponents), this might well explain why so many different tasks all load on one factor (g). General ability may reflect individual differences in the efficiency of people's metacomponents: a view which is somewhat at odds with theories considered in Chapter 5 that suggest that g is related to speed/efficiency of neuronal information transmission.

Whilst Sternberg seems to have categorised the processes which people might use to solve problems, it is not obvious whether or how we can ever measure the components' duration, and so on, for an individual, and so it is uncertain as to whether the notion is useful. But according to Sternberg, these components lead to three different types of cognitive ability—the triarchic theory of intelligence.

Three Types of Intelligence

Sternberg argues that as well as the analytic, problem-solving intelligence problems considered in Chapters 2 and 3, psychologists ought to consider real-world problems in which background knowledge or common sense can be brought to bear ("If it takes 5 minutes to boil one egg, how long does it take to boil two"—answer: 5 minutes) or where new information needs to be acquired, used or automatised (so that cognitive operations can be performed with little or no conscious thought).

Analytical Intelligence

This seeks to explain how we conceptualise problems, plan how to solve them, select strategies or shortcuts, monitor the success of our efforts (and perhaps modify the approach being used) and perform the basic mental operations necessary to reach a solution. This form of intelligence corresponds closely to Spearman's *g*, as measured by the "traditional" ability tasks considered in Chapters 2 and 3. Inductive reasoning (working out which number or shape should come next in a series) and deductive reasoning (working out whether a conclusion necessarily follows from a set of statements) are typical tasks, though there are many more possibilities.

We have seen from the examples given above that performance components are likely to be heavily utilised in such tasks, where the emphasis is normally on fast, accurate and logical reasoning.

Practical Intelligence

Practical intelligence corresponds closely to what most people recognise as common sense. It reflects a person's ability to use tacit knowledge to make sensible decisions when solving real-world problems. We are probably all familiar with the difference between what we are taught is necessary to do a job, and the knowledge of shortcuts, rules of thumb and so on that make it all much easier—and that you only really learn through experience. This is essentially what Sternberg means by practical intelligence, and strong claims have been made for its importance. For example, Sternberg (2000) claims that "practical intelligence is a construct that is distinct from general intelligence and that . . . [it] is at least as good a predictor of future success as is the academic form of intelligence that is commonly assessed by tests of so-called general intelligence [*g*]".

Tacit knowledge is knowledge that is picked up through experience or observation rather than being explicitly learned: "tacit knowledge includes things like knowing what to say to whom, knowing when to say it, and knowing how to say it for maximum effect" (Sternberg, 2000, p xi). Sternberg also claims that practical intelligence determines how individuals adapt their environments, adapt to their environments, and select their environments in an "intelligent" manner. If one is unhappy with the university course that one has chosen, the options include adapting to it (trying to develop an interest or reminding oneself that one has to study the subject for only another 18 months), modifying it (by making constructive sugges-tions for change) or selecting a different environment (by changing course or institution).

Rather than being tied to abstract contexts, practical intelligence examines real-world problems that tend to be poorly defined, and may well involve implicit knowledge, "cunning" and so on. They may also have several pos-sible solutions. For example, a person might be given a problem to which he or she can relate in their everyday life, such as how to get the best possible mark in a statistics test, if he or she has not been to many classes, or how to manipulate voters into electing them. A real-life example involved studying how a teenager learns the ropes to function effectively as a gang member (Venkatesh, 2008). Here practical intelligence seems to have huge life-or-death consequences: if a gang member misreads the mood of the gang or his position within it, he could easily die.

Inventories have also been developed to measure individuals' levels of practical intelligence (Cianciolo et al., 2009). This sounds odd. How can one assess practical intelligence, given that different people will be adapting to different environments? However these authors claim that it is possible to identify common environments, such as adapting to college or university life, which are shared by large groups of individuals.

The theory sounds intuitively sensible, but it is fraught with problems. For how else can one interact with one's environment other than by adapting oneself, modifying the environment or changing the environment? Once again, these seem to be necessary ('non-contingent') concepts, implying that the theory cannot be falsified, and so may not be scientific.

This definition of intelligence also means that a great number of other fac-tors, psychological, social and experiential, will together determine what is the most "intelligent" option for an individual. For students who is unhappy with their chosen course of study, these will include:

- The nature of subjects studied prior to university, university regulations and academic practices that may constrain the possibilities that are open to an individual,
- Motivation,
- Personality (e.g., self-confidence),
- The structure of an individual's social networks,
- Social construction processes,
- Expectations about the consequences of changing course, and so on.

The list is potentially very long indeed. This means that the evaluation of whether or not a person has made an "intelligent" response to environmental demands has to be made using different criteria for each individual: changing the subjects studied at university or college may be eminently sensible for one person, but not for another. So assessing whether a particular behaviour is intelligent in a particular environmental context is a remarkably complex procedure.

It is difficult to test whether the theory of practical intelligence is correct as it is very hard to understand the precise context in which another individual operates. Motivation, values, background, personality etc. will all constrain the options that are available to the individual, and influence the perceived merits of various courses of action. So, it is not at all obvious how one can ever evaluate how "intelligent" an individual's behaviour really is in a particular situation, since the situation is unlikely ever to be completely understood by someone else.

Creative Intelligence

This considers how people approach novel tasks and also build on past knowledge and experiences when solving problems. The novelty of a task can either require people to think of alternative uses for objects—for example, insight problems where you might need to appreciate that a pen can be used to push an object (rather than be used for writing)—or combine various known facts to come to a novel conclusion (as with Watson and Crick's discovery of the structure of DNA). These could be examples of selective encoding and selective combination components.

Sternberg also claims that creative intelligence is linked to development of automaticity. This is where complex sequences of cognitive operations can, after practice, be performed swiftly, smoothly, accurately and almost without thought. Driving, moving a character around the screen when playing a computer game or multiplying single-digit numbers are obvious examples of tasks that initially required a lot of thought and attention but that, after considerable practice, require little or no conscious thought. When one is first exposed to a particular type of unfamiliar problem, it is high in novelty. After solving several similar problems, most people will start to automatise parts of the process, which frees up more resources to deal with the novel and unique challenges of each problem.

Most tests will involve a mixture of highly automatised skills and novel skills, and Sternberg (1985) suggests that tests and test-items measuring the second-order factor of fluid ability (Gf) typically measure individual differences in solving novel problems (e.g., analogies, identifying the next number in a series), whilst those that tap crystallised ability (Gc) determine how well automatised certain operations have become (e.g., reading comprehension).

An Evaluation of Sternberg's Theories of Intelligence

Were Sternberg's claims correct, then the whole focus of this book would need to shift to cover these theories in detail. My reason for not doing so is that there is little or no hard evidence supporting Sternberg's theories. The theories are complex, highly abstract, and (as we have argued) likely to be untestable in practice. So rather than analyse them theoretically, it might be easier to test a few of his key propositions empirically.

The key reason for the development of triarchic theory was the belief that the focus of conventional ability tests was too analytical and that important aspects of cognition were therefore ignored. Introducing two completely different aspects of ability (Practical and Creative Intelligences) should redress the balance. However both Brody (2003) and Koke and Vernon (2003) note that that contrary to Sternberg's theory, Practical and Creative Intelligences correlate substantially with conventional tests of general intelligence. If anything, Creative Intelligence correlates better with g (0.78) than does Analytical Intelligence. Second, adding Practical and Creative intelligence to Analytical intelligence makes hardly any difference to the value of R-squared when these three intelligences are used to predict school performance. So Practical and Creative intelligence add little or nothing useful and are certainly not that much different from g.

Sternberg's own test (Sternberg, Ferrari, Clinkenbeard & Grigorenko, 1996) was used to measure his abilities, and given all the complexity of triarchic theory and the theory of cognitive components, one might expect the items to look rather special. Two sample items for Creative Intelligence are the following:

> *Example 1:* There are three underlined words. The first two underlined words go together in a certain way. Choose the word that goes with the third underlined word in the same way that the first two go together.
>
> Each question has a "pretend" statement. You must suppose that this statement is true. . . . Think of the statement, and then decide which word goes with the third underlined word in the same way that the first two underlined words go together.
>
> Money falls off trees.
>
> Snow is to shovel as dollar is to
>
> A. bill B. rake* C. bank D. Green

Example 2: Students are required to describe how they would reform their school system to produce an ideal one.

Practical Intelligence was assessed by items such as

John's family moved to Iowa from Arizona during his junior year in high school. He enrolled as a new student in the local high school 2 months ago but still has not made friends and feels bored and lonely. One of his favorite activities is writing stories. What is likely to be the most effective solution to this problem?

A.   Volunteer to work on the school newspaper staff.*
B.   Spend more time at home writing columns for the school newsletter.
C.   Try to convince his parents to move back to Arizona.
D.   Invite a friend from Arizona to visit during Christmas break.

(Howard, McGee, Shin & Shia, 2001)

Gottfredson (2003) has also made a careful scrutiny of the evidence for the distinctiveness and importance of Sternberg's notion of Practical Intelligence and has found it wanting. She concludes that Sternberg backs up his claims "mostly with the appearance, not the reality, of hard evidence", and her careful analysis concludes that

There is a solid, century–long evidentiary base upon which researchers are busily building. Simply positing a new and independent intelligence to explain much of what remains unexplained (and much of what has *already* been explained), while simultaneously ignoring the ever-growing evidentiary base, does not promise to advance knowledge. The concept of tacit knowledge does, I suspect, point to a form of experience and knowledge that lends itself to the development of what might be called wisdom— a gradual understanding of the probabilities and possibilities in human behavior (and in individual persons) that we generally develop only by experiencing or observing them first-hand over the course of our lives. This is not a new form of intelligence, however, but perhaps only the motivated and sensitive application of whatever level of *g* we individually possess. Sternberg et al. could better advance scientific knowledge on this issue by probing more deeply and analytically into the role of tacit knowledge in our lives rather than continuing to spin gauzy illusions of a wholly new intelligence that defies the laws of evidence.

(Gottfredson, 2003)

In addition, McDaniel and Whetzel (2005) make the point that Sternberg's practical intelligence has been extensively studied by occupational/ organisational psychologists through 'situational judgement tests'. The literature on these tests suggests that there is little or no evidence for a single factor of practical intelligence as proposed by Sternberg. The evidence instead shows that general intelligence influences performance on tasks based on implicit knowledge, contrary to Sterberg's claims. Whilst this all seems fairly damning, the problem is that practical intelligence, heavily promoted by Sternberg in books rather than peer-reviewed journal articles, refuses to die. But the theory probably does not merit any more detailed attention here.

Howard Gardner's Theory of Multiple Intelligences

The psychometric model of abilities outlined in Chapter 3 is what cognitive psychologists would call a bottom-up or data-driven model. Factor analysis is used to determine how many abilities are necessary to explain people's performance on a wide but fairly arbitrary selection of mental tests. And so, there are plenty of phenomena that this model was not designed to explain—for example, the abilities of "unusual groups", such as geniuses, brain-damaged individuals or children with severe learning difficulties. Nor does it seek to explain how and why abilities develop over time, nor indeed the processes that *cause* individual differences in these abilities to emerge in the first place (for although some such models are examined in Chapters 5 and 6, these do not spring from the data-driven model of factor analysis).

Gardner, on the other hand, has set out some criteria that he regards as essential for a theory of ability *within a particular culture*: he has been influenced by social constructivism. Unusually, Gardner also regards intelligence behaviourally: intelligence is what a person can *do*. His work ignores one of the main findings of factor-analytic research—*g*. Instead, he claims (without a shred of empirical evidence) "that there exists a multitude of intelligences, quite independent of each other" (Gardner, 1993). If Gardner is correct, and all of his intelligences are indeed uncorrelated, then he is exactly correct: there could be no such thing as *g*.

Gardner believes that the only reason why there are correlations between the various primary and secondary abilities (such as discussed in Chapter 3) is because all these tests rely on the use of language or logic. A child who is good at language/logic will perform well at all of them; a child who has difficulties with language/logic will perform poorly at all of them. According to Gardner, if we were to control for ('partial out' is the statistical term) the effects of language and logic from ability tests, the intelligence factors would really be uncorrelated. This view is slightly surprising given that some primary and secondary abilities—e.g., memory for strings of digits, pairs of random letters, pitch perception, spatial ability, visualisation—do not seem to rely extensively on either language or logic. And if Gardner's explanation were correct, how could there possibly more than one or two second-order factors (corresponding to language ability and/or logical ability)?

Gardner rejects factor analysis as a tool for determining the structure of abilities on the basis of some rather specious arguments put forward in Steven Jay Gould's book, *The Mismeasure of Man* (Gould, 1981).[2] Instead, Gardner suggests that an intelligence should be identified by identifying:

(a) abilities that all disappear (or are all retained) following damage to some area(s) of the brain;
(b) abilities that are found together is prodigies or those with severe learning difficulties ('idiots savant');
(c) a genetically programmed set of cognitive operations that operate on particular stimuli (e.g. those involved in pitch-perception, or imitation);
(d) clear development of the system as the child ages;
(e) tasks that interfere with each other (in dual-task experiments) or that transfer together to new situations—and so, that are likely to share a common neural mechanism;
(f) intercorrelations between psychometric tests measuring these cognitive operations; and
(g) the development of systems of symbols to represent concepts—e.g., language, mathematics, music.

Thus, rather than focusing on a single type of evidence, Gardner draws on physiological psychology, several aspects of cognitive psychology, developmental psychology and clinical psychology in order to find groups of abilities that seemed to come and go together. These, he believes, constitute different forms of intelligence. Gardner then searched the psychological and medical literature to try to find intelligences that conformed to these criteria. In total he identified seven classes of intelligence that met most or all of them. These were linguistic intelligence, musical intelligence, logical-mathematical intelligence, spatial intelligence, bodily-kinaesthetic intelligence, and two forms of personal intelligence (integrity of self-concept and quality of interactions with others). They are described in some detail in *Frames of Mind* (Gardner, 1993) along with some fascinating suggestions about how certain historical figures (ranging from Freud to Gandhi) exemplarise particular abilities. More recently naturalistic intelligence (being in touch with nature) and existential intelligence (spirituality) have also been proposed.

I do not propose to discuss these "intelligences" further here—not because they are uninteresting, but because the first four of them seem to correspond very closely to some of the main ability traits identified by factor analysts, and discussed in Chapter 3. Intrapersonal and interpersonal intelligence certainly seem to resemble emotional intelligence, discussed later in this chapter. And bodily-kinaesthetic intelligence, which is concerned with coordination and grace of movements, is arguably not a *mental* ability. Thus, whilst Gardner's work is useful in that it adopts a completely different approach to the mapping of human abilities, much of it merely reinforces what the factor-theorists had already suggested.

One problem with Gardner's approach is that it is not obvious that the list of intelligences can ever be complete. There may be others that have not been identified. Sexual performance is one variable that has a clear developmental trend, can be affected by damage to certain areas of the brain or by drugs (e.g., alcohol), is very highly regarded within some cultures, has its own set of symbols, and so on. So why is there no factor of sexual intelligence?

Gardner's theories have become extremely popular, particularly with teachers and educators, as they paint a much more egalitarian picture than the hierarchical model outlined in Chapter 3. For if there *are* a number of completely separate intelligences, and a child underachieves in one area (e.g., linguistic or logical-mathematical intelligence), then the teacher could and should look around for areas of strength that can be developed. If the various intelligences are uncorrelated, a child would have to be very unlucky to be seriously below average in all of them! However, the positive correlations between the ability factors that are implied by the hierarchical model suggests that if children are below average in one area, they are rather unlikely to excel in others. There will be some variation in performance, but it is improbable that a child who is one or two standard deviations below the mean on verbal or mathematical ability will be one or two standard deviations above the mean on anything else. We might all wish that it was otherwise, but this is what the data clearly show, as discussed in Chapter 3.

Like Guilford's (1967) theory of the structure of intellect, which also postulated a theoretical model of ability (rather than examining the actual correlations between tests and between factors), Gardner presents no evidence for his crucial claim that the various intelligences are independent. Without this, his theory seems to be entirely compatible with the hierarchical models considered in Chapter 3.

It comes as a shock to discover how educators actually assess Gardner's intelligences. How should we try to measure musical intelligence, for example?

It is probably best not to assess musical knowledge (e.g., "Beethoven's third symphony is sometimes known as the _____") or a person's performing ability, as different people will have acquired knowledge in different areas reflecting their interests (rather than ability), and so a test asking questions about classical music would not be fair to someone whose passion was jazz or rock music. Second, some privileged children may have been taught an instrument, whilst those from poorer backgrounds with equal talent may not have had their skills developed. Thus measuring someone's level of achievement may not be a fair way of assessing future potential (musical intelligence).

You might perhaps think that the best way to assess musical intelligence would be to give a person some unfamilar tasks to measure his or her performance—perhaps playing a tune or a rhythm once and asking the person to remember it, asking him or her to identify which of two notes is higher in pitch, compose a tune, or identify a musical interval. There are plenty of tests that assess musical talent in this sort of way (e.g., Gordon, 1989). But that is not the way that Gardner's followers assess musical intelligence. Instead, the child will be asked questions such as "did you ever take part in a choir, band or orchestra", "can you easily remember a tune that you have heard once" and so on[3]. Tests such as these provide no hard evidence that the child actually has the level of expertise that they claim; they certainly look as if they measure motivation as much as ability. I can certainly think of some choir members who persevered despite having a very low level of musical ability, and likewise, it is possible that some talented solo performers—piano players, perhaps—will never have taken part in the group activities mentioned, and so might have their ability underestimated. In addition, it is very tempting for a person to distort their score by lying should they want to do so. There are several scales like this (e.g., Armstrong, 1994; Shearer, 2007), some of which are widely used despite a lack of peer-reviewed evidence that they measure what they claim to assess. The scales used to measure other intelligences are no better: mathematical intelligence is assessed by asking children how much they enjoyed mathematics, and kinaesthetic intelligence by asking how quickly they can pick up new dance steps etc. What about the child who is good at mathematics but hates it? What about the child who wants to present himself or herself as a genius? What about the shy child who is too self-conscious to dance (but who might excel at it)? This naive approach to assessment may alarm psychologists, but teachers and educators seem to be blind to these problems.

There have been few decent attempts to test Gardner's claim that the various "intelligences" are independent of each other (i.e., uncorrelated). Visser, Ashton and Vernon (2006) gave two technically adequate tests of each of

Gardner's eight intelligences plus a test of general intelligence to a sample of 200 students. Their analysis looked at the correlation between each test and general ability: they found that contrary to Gardner's claims, these were substantial for all of the cognitive tests (though not for tests measuring non-cognitive skills, such as Bodily-Kinesthetic Intelligence). So Gardner's claim that his intelligences are independent is simply incorrect. These researchers also found that the correlations between pairs of tests that (according to Gardner) should measure the same intelligence were generally weak, or came about because both of the tests were influenced by g. These results indicate that Gardner's theory is seriously flawed. The data provided far better support for the hierarchical model of abilities discussed in Chapter 3.

Emotional Intelligence

The term 'emotional intelligence' became popular following the publication of a popular book by Daniel Goleman (1995) that argued that understanding emotions was an important skill in the workplace, and in many other aspects of life. Why is it that some individuals are "good with people", whilst others are abrasive? Why are some people sensitive to their own and others' emotional states and emotional needs, whilst others seem unaware of this and may show unpredictable emotional outbursts? The answer (if you believe Goleman) is emotional intelligence.

It turns out that emotional intelligence has two quite distinct meanings in psychology. Recognising emotions in oneself and other people, and deciding how to use them, is a cognitive skill, because it is clearly possible to evaluate performance; an astute therapist will be able to recognise that a client is experiencing low, depressed mood, and will be able to convey this understanding to the client. You can see how (in principle) one could ask therapists to identify which emotion a person was experiencing, and compare this with the client's answer: the client could also rate how well he or she felt the therapist understood his or her feelings. So this form of emotional sensitivity is clearly an ability, as argued by Mayer, Caruso and Salovey (1999). Of course, this sort of emotional intelligence—known as ability emotional intelligence—is not confined to the consulting room: some people may be better able than others to monitor their own emotional state (e.g., recognising their shock and fear after some stupid driver almost kills them) and also modify their emotions (e.g., overcoming nerves during a job interview or public speaking).

The other meaning of emotional intelligence (called trait emotional intelligence) describes how a person usually performs across all sorts of different settings. People who agree with statements such as "I like to hug those who are emotionally close to me", "I often use my intuition in planning for the future" and "I believe I can do almost anything I set out to do" are thought to be high on trait emotional intelligence. These statements look as if they measure personality traits rather than cognitive abilities, because they describe how a person usually behaves. And this is what the literature shows. Questionnaires measuring trait emotional intelligence tend to correlate with personality traits (Petrides, Pita & Kokkinaki, 2007), whilst a test of ability emotional intelligence (which measures how well a person can identify emotion from a photograph of a face and similar tasks) also correlates with g (Schulte, Ree & Carretta, 2004). Given the focus of this book, I will only consider ability emotional intelligence here.

As far as I am aware, only one test exists for measuring ability emotional intelligence. The Mayer-Salovey-Caruso Emotional Intelligence Test (MSCEIT; Mayer, Salovey & Caruso, 2002) supposedly measures how well people can identify emotions (in photographs, and in art), whether individuals are aware how emotions may combine and interact, whether they can anticipate what the likely emotional impact of events will be, and whether they can manipulate their own emotions (e.g., controlling anger or depression). These four scores of the MSCEIT (perceiving, understanding, using and managing emotions) are generally combined to give an overall emotional intelligence score, although most researchers find that there are problems with the 'using emotions' scales that makes including this score inadvisable. This literature is summarised by Maul (2012).

The "correct answers" to each item in the MSCEIT were determined by asking people to identify the best answer to each question: the majority view was assumed to be the correct answer. One version of the test uses the views of experts as defining the correct answers: another version is based on the opinions of the general population. (There is a lively debate as to whether the small group of 21 experts really were experts—all we know is that they attended a conference on emotions in 2000.) The problem is that even the experts might not always agree on what the answers to each item should be, and as far as I can see, the extent to which they agree with the answers to each item are not shown in the test manual. So, we cannot tell how much consensus there is that the "correct" answer to each item is, in fact, correct. Nor is there any guarantee that just because everyone *believes* an answer to be correct, it actually *is* correct. However statistical analysis of the test scores should be able to identify any items that had been wrongly scored, as they would not load on the factors that they were supposed to measure.

Some researchers find that the MSCEIT correlates appreciably with a measure of g (Webb et al., 2013) using a measure of g such as the

Wechsler scales that measure a mixture of fluid and crystallised ability. Other researchers have found that the overall emotional intelligence score (and especially the "understanding emotions" scale) correlates substantially with Gc, crystallised intelligence, but that its correlation with fluid intelligence (Gf), and hence g was close to zero in two separate studies (Farrelly & Austin, 2007). This work is important, as it also found that scores on the MSCEIT were unrelated to Inspection Time. Inspection Time is thought to reflect biological speed of information processing that is the mechanism underlying g: it is discussed in some detail in Chapter 6. Almost all conventional ability tests are correlated with inspection time in much the same sort of way that they correlate with g (even tests such as memory and creativity correlate significantly), and so this work suggests that whatever the MSCEIT is measuring, it is rather different from the cognitive abilities measured by conventional ability tests. To make matters worse, one study also find that scores on the MSCEIT seem to be more influenced by social desirability ($r = 0.35$) than g (Rode et al., 2008). This is a major problem, as it suggests that people with high scores on the MSCEIT are not particularly good at identifying emotions, working with emotions etc., but just tend to give the most socially desirable answer to each item. This work needs to be replicated.

All in all, the status of the MSCEIT is uncertain at present. It certainly has some problems; its small correlation with fluid ability and inspection time make it hard to argue that ability emotional intelligence is just another second-order ability, like Gm (memory) or Gv (visualisation). Yet scores on the MSCEIT correlate with crystallised intelligence, Gc. Perhaps this suggests that emotional intelligence should be regarded as a component of crystallised ability (rather like mathematics performance) rather than a broad second-order ability factor in its own right. Or perhaps, it is only people who have excellent levels of verbal ability (a component of Gc) who can understand the language used in the MSCEIT, as suggested by Wilhelm (2005). Then there is the problem that the MSCEIT scores seem to be sensitive to socially desirable responding—something that certainly should not be the case if it measures a genuine ability. Despite some marketing hype that claimed (completely without evidence) that emotional intelligence matters more than IQ when predicting real-world performance (Goleman, 1995), there is little evidence to suggest that scores on the MSCEIT are able to predict real-world criteria such as life satisfaction or academic performance (Rode et al., 2008) over and above traditional measures of intelligence and personality. Ability emotional intelligence is probably best described as work in progress.

Summary

This chapter first examined three views of abilities that are incompatible with the factor-analytic literature discussed in Chapter 3. The first of these views abilities as arbitrary terms—"social constructions"—the nature of which will vary from culture to culture and from generation to generation. If this is so, then the factors identified in Chapter 3 are no more sensible that any list of abilities that you and your friends could construct off the top of your heads over a glass of wine. The second view argues that abilities are best conceptualised as specific modules: Howe (1988b) considers that the cognitive performance of some individuals with profound learning difficulties supports this view. He suggests that the hierarchical model of intelligence (with g at the apex) is inappropriate for this reason. And finally, we considered the value of studying self-assessments of cognitive abilities, as some social psychologists seem to view this as an important aspect of ability research. Finally, we consider three rather different alternatives to the factor-analytical models described in Chapter 3. Sternberg's theory suggests that abilities should be seen within a certain experiential and cultural context, although to do so is far from easy in practice, as this requires a detailed understanding of each individual's motivation, personality, values etc. Sternberg's componential sub-theory might be useful, in that the higher-order planning components (metacomponents) may perhaps explain g. A person's ability to select appropriate strategies for problem solving might explain why some individuals are more able than others at solving all kinds of cognitive problems, which is what g implies. Against that, some aspects of Sternberg's theory are non-testable in principle.

Gardner's theory provides a surprising amount of support for the psychometric model of ability outlined previously, despite considering rather different criteria. Four of his intelligences seem similar to factors in the psychometric model, two resemble emotional intelligence, bodily-kinaesthetic intelligence may not be a mental ability, whilst it seems likely that naturalistic and existential intelligences may be linked to crystallised ability, Gc, though as far as I am aware no one has tested this. Gardner's claim that his various 'intelligences' are independent of each other runs counter to the psychometric model, and the empirical evidence shows clearly that Gardner's claim is incorrect.

Finally, we looked at ability emotional intelligence. Although there is scant evidence to support claims that it can matter more than g in everyday life, being in tune with one's own and other people's emotional state does seem to be a genuine mental ability. However scores on the only available test of ability emotional intelligence seem to correlate better with tests of crystallised intelligence (i.e., knowledge) than they do with reasoning ability, and so it is not yet clear where precisely ability emotional intelligence fits into the hierarchical model of abilities outlined in Chapter 3. Is it a component of crystallised ability, Gc? Or is it a second-order factor in its own right? I do not think we know for sure at present.

Notes

1   Sex differences in general ability are not particularly large, and they do not account for the observed differences in self-rated ability between men and women. However my point is that these issues should have been checked at the outset.

2   This is widely regarded as a seriously misleading and partial book that is frequently factually incorrect, and is "crafted in such a way as to prejudice the general public and even some scientists against almost any research concerning human cognitive abilities" (Carroll, 1995): the rest of this review from one of the most widely respected figures in individual differences research contains even stronger phrases, and I would urge anyone who has read Gould's book to also consult this review.

3   For copyright reasons, I cannot reproduce the exact items used, but the examples shown are similar to and certainly no worse than the originals.

5

SOCIAL AND BIOLOGICAL
ORIGINS OF ABILITIES

One problem with the analyses described in Chapter 3 is that they attempt to define what the main human abilities are (through analyses of data that reveal the number and nature of primary mental abilities, second-order abilities and so on) they do not they do not explain how or why certain children develop certain levels of abilities. It is all very well producing evidence that people who perform above average on one type of task also tend to perform above average at other particular tasks, but why *do* some people perform better than others in the first place? What is it that makes people differ in their levels of *g* and other abilities?

Process models try to explain this. They explore the reasons why people develop a particular level of some ability by trying to understand their origins. So such studies involve experimentation rather than simply measuring and correlating scores on ability tasks. Some models that are developed to explain why some people show higher scores than others may be biological: for example genetic makeup or environmental factors might influence the size or operation of various brain structures in an individual or the speed/ accuracy with which information can be transferred along or between nerve cells. The explanations may be cognitive: the amount of information that can be held in a memory buffer for a particular amount of time might perhaps influence a person's level of some cognitive ability. Perhaps social deprivation affects mental abilities either directly (e.g., through lack of parental encouragement or environmental stimulation) or indirectly (perhaps as a consequence of a less balanced diet, or because socially deprived children might be likely to attend poorer-quality schools, leading to a lack of knowledge or language skills. Maybe social deprivation results in low self-esteem or low motivation toward cognitive tasks that might result in poor performance. Developmental factors may also matter as it is possible that children whose brains mature quickly may have an advantage that persists through life, or childhood illnesses might perhaps have an effect on later cognitive development.

It is necessary to make sure that the processes used to explain individual differences in cognitive abilities are truly more simple than the cognitive abilities that they are supposed to explain. For example, it would make little sense to "explain" why some people are better able than others to mentally rotate letters of the alphabet by measuring how well they can mentally rotate random shapes, because the two tasks are virtually identical. Likewise would seem to be crazy to "explain" individual differences in general ability, g, by giving tests some of which are themselves well-known measures of g such as memory span or ability to recall digits backwards. This has however been done in the context of working memory research (e.g., Alloway, 2010). It is necessary to develop some sort of theoretical model—a flowchart—of the *simpler* more basic processes that might be involved in the solution of a particular type of task, and to test how well this model fits the data. Statistical methods such as structural equation modeling are well suited for this.

One obvious question is how basic such explanations ultimately need to be. For example, is it enough to "explain" individual differences in intelligence using cognitive models such as working memory capacity, or do we need to drill down further and try to explain why it is that (for example) some people may have a greater working memory capacity than others, or may be able to encode information more quickly than other individuals. Such explanations are likely to be biological: for example, a purely developmental account of the impact of childhood illnesses on brain structure and function are probably not appropriate, since the illnesses have effects on the individual's physiological makeup. Similarly, although discovering that low birth weight is linked to low levels of general ability in adulthood is interesting, this then leads to the question of what causes babies to differ in birth weight. Once that is known, it is necessary to establish whether birth weight is itself a cause of low cognitive performance, or whether some lower-level variable (e.g., maternal alcohol consumption) influences both birth weight and the child's cognitive performance, and so whether this (rather than birth weight) is the true causal influence.

It is clear from this that establishing the basic structure of abilities, as described in the previous chapters, is the easy part of research into human cognitive abilities. Once the structure of abilities is established, the really interesting research involves trying to understand why people grow up to have different levels of abilities. This is where most modern research effort is focused.

But where should one start? Rather than exploring models more or less at random, is it possible to find out what broad areas influence abilities? Fortunately there is a technique that allows us to do just this. It can show the extent to which three different influences on children impact upon intelligence and other abilities. The three spheres of influence are as follows:

(a) The family environment. This includes everything that the parents provide for the children in the family—the assumption being that all children will experience them all to a similar extent. If the family environment influences abilities, it is necessary to find out precisely which of these influences are important. Does encouraging children to perform well at school impact upon their intelligence? Does providing plenty of books, mind-stretching puzzles, and so on matter? Can reading aloud to children cause them to become smarter (or at least better at reading than they might otherwise have been)? If parents frequently argue, can this affect the children's cognitive development—and if so, how? Assuming that all children from a family attend the same school, does quality of schooling influence mental abilities? These are just some of the avenues that could be explored if the childhood family environment turns out to have a major influence on intelligence.

(b) Environmental influences, outside the family. Not all environmental influences are the same for all of the children within a family. Children will probably have different friends, different relationships with teachers, and different hobbies. All of these could, potentially, influence their mental abilities. Likewise their birth orders will be different. Some children will catch childhood diseases that may influence their brain development, whilst their siblings stay well. If the "non-shared" environment is found to influence cognitive abilities, these are some of the models that could be explored. (Non-shared means that the environmental influences are different for each child in the family.)

(c) Finally, it is possible that the children's genetic makeup might influence their levels of mental ability. If this is the case, it makes sense to look for biological explanations of abilities, because the only thing that a gene can do is cause a piece of protein to develop somewhere in the body. If genes influence intelligence, they must do so by leading individuals to develop nervous systems and brains that are subtly different in their structure and/or function. For example, it might be found that some areas of the brain are larger in some children, and this might be reflected in their level of one or more mental abilities. Or some children may develop nervous systems that processes information unusually quickly or that forms efficient neural networks to perform computations.

The effects of genes and environmental influences on human cognitive abilities is one of the best-researched issues in the whole of psychology, and Plomin and Asbury (2005) or Bouchard and McGue (2003) offer clear and non-technical summaries of the research methods in this area that are well worth consulting. This work is important because it tells us whether we should look at family dynamics, parental behavior and so on, whether we should focus on things that the children experience outside the family, or whether we should forget about social explanations completely and focus on biological models. Thus, one important outcome of the nature–nurture debate (as this is sometimes known) is to suggest whether we should look at biological factors or developmental/social influences when trying to understand why some people are more intelligent than others.

A Little Biology

Chromosomes are long (5 cm) strands of a protein called DNA that are tightly packed into the cell nucleus. Each of these strands of DNA comprises a long sequence of chemical bases. Stretches of DNA represent genes that (in various ways) control the synthesis of amino acids and proteins. Twenty-three pairs of chromosomes are found in the nucleus of almost every cell in our bodies.

Most of our DNA is identical: it is this that makes sure that we have the correct number of heads in the correct place, and so on. However about 1% of human DNA shows variations from person to person. It is possible that variations in these parts of our DNA may be linked to differences in our mental abilities. In other words, some people may be predisposed to perform in a particular way (e.g., be able to show great creativity, spatial ability etc.) if they are exposed to an environment in which the relevant genes can express themselves.

Many of the pioneers of this approach took a right-wing stance, suggesting that society would be improved if highly intelligent people were encouraged to have plenty of children, whilst less intelligent people should be actively discouraged (or prevented) from doing so. For as they believed that general ability was largely inherited, this course of action should increase the overall intelligence of the nation. This became known as the Eugenics movement;

the Eugenics Society still exists today, and there is still some controversial debate on the subject, with Richard Lynn (1996, 2001) spelling out the merits of a eugenic policy.

Despite this politically suspect past, the issue of the heritability of abilities is a perfectly legitimate scientific question because it can show whether it is sensible to explore biological or social models of intelligence: if biological makeup has no influence on abilities whilst the family environment is all-important, then the methods outlined in this chapter would reveal this clearly.

Unfortunately, many authors who should know better choose to ignore the possibility that behaviour might be, to some extent, influenced by genetic makeup. Suppose that that the amount of time that the mothers and children spend reading together is measured, and is found to predict the child's later language ability. It would seem obvious to many psychologists that the mother's behaviour influences the child's ability. This simple environmental model is shown in Figure 5.1a: arrows indicate causal relations. So this suggests that parental reading behaviour causes children to develop good reading skills.

However this inference could be completely incorrect. It might be the case that only those mothers with high levels of language ability choose to read to their children. Language ability has a very substantial genetic component: 0.65 (Plomin et al., 2013). Thus the more linguistically able mothers will also have passed on some of their language-facilitating genes to their child. So the mother's reading behaviour could be driven by her genetic makeup, as might the child's later language skills. Reading with a child might have no direct influence on its later language skills, and if this is the case, it is unlikely that an expensive education programme, encouraging mothers to read with their children, would have any effect. This purely genetic model is shown in Figure 5.1b.

This model too is unrealistic, since it denies the possibility that the way in which parents behave toward their children can have any influence on their performance. Thus the model shown in Figure 5.1c is the most appropriate. This suggests that both the parents' genes and the behaviour of the parents (or adoptive parents) may influence the child's language ability. The size of each influence can be determined empirically.

'Genetically informed' research designs (for example, family/twin/adoption studies) can be used to determine the relative importance of the environmental and genetic effects, and a number of studies (summarised in Thompson, 1993) suggest that genetic influences on the abilities of even young children are far too substantial to be ignored. Genetically naïve designs such as that shown in Figure 5.1a will confuse individual differences

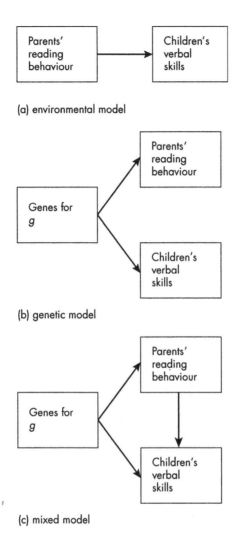

Figure 5.1 Three models to explain why a child may develop verbal skills (a) environmental model (b) genetic model (c) mixed model

due to shared genes with those that result from the environment. They will overestimate the importance of the environment if an ability has any genetic component whatsoever. However, many psychologists are unaware of the literature discussed in this chapter (or were influenced by Kamin's post-hoc criticisms of some of the early studies), and so such studies are quite common in the literature.

The same basic argument applies to almost any area in which two related individuals interact (do children really become violent because they witness domestic violence, for example?): ignoring any possibility of genetic influences on behaviour is sloppy science, but all too often researchers tend to assume (completely without evidence) that behaviour is socially determined, and ignore the possibility that our biological makeup can have any influence on how we behave.

This is not the place to get deep into this literature, but even good journals seem to publish papers that may make dubious claims about the likely efficacy of intervention programmes because they ignore the fact that parents and children tend to be related. For example, one meta-analysis concludes that "the available data on book reading support intergenerational literacy programs intended to stimulate parent-preschooler reading in order to better prepare young children for beginning reading" (Bus, Vanijzendoorn & Pellegrini, 1995) even though behaviour-genetic analyses show that the family environment (which will include parental reading behaviour) has minimal influence on childhood literacy whilst the genetic influence is substantial (Wadsworth et al., 2002).

Although they have the word genetic in their title, the methods outlined below do not fall into this trap. They do not presuppose that abilities have a biological basis, but seek to test this empirically. This is, after all, the way science operates: it would be poor science to search for purely social/environmental influences on abilities because those are the influences that appeal to one's political agenda!

There are several ways of determining the extent to which genetic makeup or social factors can influence any behaviour or ability.

Selective Breeding Studies

The first method involves experimentation, and it can only be applied in animal research for obvious reasons. The logic of this procedure is simple. If genes affect some ability (for example, how quickly a rat can find its way through a maze in order to reach a food pellet), it is possible to take a sample of rats (all of the same strain) and measure their performance on this task. Two groups of rats may then be identified: one group that performs well above average on the task ("maze-bright" rats) and another group that performs below average ("maze-dull" rats).

If genetic makeup affects performance on the task (and if all the rats have experienced a similar environment since birth), it is probable that the maze-bright rats have some of the genetic variants that enhance performance, whilst the maze-dull rats have the variants that hamper performance. In order to increase the concentration of genetic variants that affect performance, the maze-bright rats are then interbred, and their offspring are tested. Once again, the very best maze-runners are identified and interbred: this procedure is repeated for several generations. The same happens to the maze-dull group. They too are interbred, and the worst performing offspring are themselves interbred for several generations.

This procedure will produce two distinct strains of rats if, and only if, genetic makeup influences performance on the task. One strain will perform well, because they will all have variants of the genes that enhance maze-running. The rats that have been selected and interbred because they are hopeless at this task will have acquired variants of the genes that impair maze-running after a few generations. If genes do *not* affect performance at maze-running, this attempt at selective breeding will not work, and there will be no difference in the maze-running performance of the two groups of rats. The rats cannot have inherited any predisposition to behave in a particular way.

Tryon's (1940) work showed clearly that it is possible to breed selectively two strains of rat (maze-bright and maze-dull). This was the first scientific study proving that a behaviour may be influenced by selective breeding. Thus, it seems reasonable to ask whether individual differences in any other types of ability, such as general intelligence, spatial ability or any of the other abilities discussed in Chapter 3, might perhaps be influenced by genetic makeup as well as environments in humans. It is also possible that our genetic makeup may influence personality, attitudes etc., but a discussion of this is beyond the scope of the present book.

Tryon's work is important because it shows that behaviours based on thought can be influenced by genetic makeup, in just the same way that physical features of organisms such as size or eye colour. It therefore raises the possibility that the genetic makeup of humans may predispose them to show individual differences in cognitive ability. Needless to say, all this is predicated on the availability of suitable environmental stimulation. In the same way that a bean that has the potential to produce a vast crop of pods will fail to do so if it is planted in poor soil and deprived of water light or heat, genes that affect human cognition are only likely to have a noticeable influence if people are all given a "good enough" environment: for example, with adequate nutrition, exposure to language, education and so on. The interaction between genetic makeup and environmental factors is crucially important.

Molecular Genetics

There is another method that is sometimes used to discover which genes influence various traits, and unlike the previous example, it can be used with humans. It is called molecular genetics, and involves analysing DNA to find out which genetic variations are related to which behaviours. There are many different ways of achieving this end; I shall just mention one possibility. Suppose that DNA is collected from a group of prodigies—those with exceptional levels of g, for example. It can be presumed that these individuals will only have developed exceptional g if they have both a genetic predisposition and have been fortunate enough to experience a supportive environment that allows the genes to express themselves. So if the DNA from members of this group is compared with the DNA of a control group of people from similar backgrounds but who show only average levels of g, any consistent differences in their genetic makeup may point directly to individual genes that predispose individuals to showing high levels of g. Unlike the method of behaviour genetics described below, this approach can identify precisely which genes on which chromosomes are involved.

This approach has two main difficulties. First, the number of sites is so vast that it is very difficult to know which ones to compare between the two groups, so finding the genetic variations that are relevant is rather like looking for a needle in a haystack. The second problem is that if many genes influence a particular trait, the effect of each (examined individually) may be very small, particularly if genes also interact. So the prodigies may differ from the rest of us because each of a large number of genes has a small influence on their g, rather than half a dozen genes having a massive effect. This will make it very hard to detect which genetic variations influence a behaviour. Think of performing say 50,000 t-tests to test differences between the two groups on 50,000 gene variants. It should be obvious that if all of the tests are independent, about 50,000 x 0.05 = 2,500 of these t-tests will be significant at the 0.05 level, even if there is in reality no effect of genetic makeup on g. (That is what "alpha = 0.05" implies.) Suppose that you find that 2,550 of the t-tests are significant: slightly more than you would expect by chance. This suggests that it is possible that about 50 of the 50,000 genetic variations may be linked to g—but which ones? Trying to work out which of the "significant" differences are genuine, and which represent Type-I errors ('false positives') is not trivial, and findings have to be carefully replicated in different samples to make sure that they are genuine. Only if the same variants are also linked to g in a second sample can we be confident that the relationship exists.

Although this sort of study is time-consuming and expensive to perform, it does provide a very precise picture of precisely which genetic variations are linked to abilities, which is why workers such as Robert Plomin (e.g., Plomin et al., 1995; Plomin & Petrill, 1997) actively pursue this line of research. An excellent summary of the issues is offered by Plomin, Kennedy and Craig (2006).

Unfortunately, the literature in this area tends to be highly technical, which makes it hard for mere psychologists like ourselves to grasp. Posthuma and de Geus (2006) offer a reasonably non-technical outline of the molecular genetics of intelligence. They observe that although several genetic variants have been linked to g, these usually fail to replicate. Only one genetic variant appears to have been linked to g in two samples, and this variant only explains a small (under 1%) fraction of the variability of g. Deary, Johnson and Houlihan (2009) offer a rather more detailed summary of the field, which is if anything rather more pessimistic. Variations in just one gene do not seem to lead to be closely linked to intelligence. This could well be because many genes each have a small influence on g, rather than a few genes having a substantial effect.

A paper by Davies et al. (2011) shows that this is indeed the case. Their work is important because it examines the influence of over half a million genetic variants using a sample of over 3,500 people, and attempted to predict people's levels of intelligence purely on the basis of an analysis of their DNA. This genome-wide study shows that 40% to 50% of the variation in intelligence between adults is directly linked to variations in genetic makeup (Single Nucleotide Polymorphisms) that are established through analysis of DNA. The estimate of 40% to 50% is based on simple additive effects: the authors discuss why this analysis will somewhat understimate the "true" heritability of general ability. Non-additive effects (dominance, epistatis etc.) will also increase this figure. This analysis shows clearly that a great number of genes each have a small influence on general ability, and taken together, this influence is substantial.

Behaviour Genetics: The Theory

The third method for exploring the links between genetic makeup and intelligence is known as behaviour genetics, or sometimes behavioural genetics. It does not set out to show which precise areas of DNA influence a particular behaviour or ability, but to determine the extent to which our overall genetic makeup and by various aspects of our environment influence some behaviour or ability. It is particularly useful as it can also demonstrate whether the home environment is a potent influence on levels of intelligence: for example, whether the extent to which some families stress academic success, provide learning opportunities and so on is related to intelligence.

When an egg is fertilised, the offspring receives half its chromosomes (and so half its genetic makeup) from the mother, and half from the father. If we assume that the parents are unrelated to each other (that is, share a chance number of the genes that vary from person to person), it follows that siblings share about half the genetic material that varies in people. A parent and their child also share 50%, whereas a child and their grandparent or uncle/aunt share 25% of this material.

Fraternal ('dizygotic' or non-identical) twins result when two sperm fertilise two eggs: they too share half the genes that vary, and so on average are no more similar (genetically) than any other siblings. It sometimes happens that the fertilised egg splits in two or more clumps of cells during the early stages of growth. These clumps of cells may each develop into an individual, and these people are genetically identical (we ignore any mutations in the womb), hence known as identical twins.

Genes can influence behaviour in several different ways. In the simplest case, each of a number of genetic variations can have a small influence on some characteristic of the organism. For example, it might be that several genes determine height: the more of these genes that are present in an individual, the taller that person is likely to be (given a suitable environment: adequate nutrition, etc.). The more of these genes one has, the taller one is likely to be, and so this is known as the 'additive model'. Or genes can interact. It may be that a certain characteristic will emerge only if a person has one or more genes present at the same position in a pair of chromosomes. If the person has neither of them, then the characteristic will not be seen. Sometimes characteristics emerge only if certain genes are present at a number of different positions on the chromosome. Although the majority of the research to be discussed below assumes a simple additive model, behaviour geneticists are actively researching more complex models too.

The environment, too, may well influence behavior, as discussed above. Two types of environmental influences have traditionally been studied. The first, the common environment (also known as the shared environment), describes all those features of the environment that are shared by all the brothers and sisters in a family. For example, parental income, parental attitudes to education, the parents' behaviour and style of child rearing, the number of books in the house and the type of food provided is likely to be broadly similar for all the children in one family, assuming that levels of income are stable and that the parents stay together. Sharing a common environment will tend to make members of the same family behave in similar ways.

Each child also experiences a unique environment. Individual children will develop their own friends, may each be influenced by a different teacher at school, read different books, may develop different hobbies and skills, and miss different chunks of schooling (or suffer damage to different parts of the nervous system) because of childhood illnesses. The unique environment describes any environmental influences that will tend to make members of a family *different* from each other.

The basic aim of all the behaviour-genetic studies considered below is to determine the extent to which individual differences in cognitive abilities are influenced by individual differences in genetic makeup, and individual differences in the common environment and the unique environment. For example, we may wish to discover the relative importance of the common environment, the unique environment and genetic makeup on children's levels of spatial ability. However, before going on to discuss some research designs and findings, it is important to appreciate what this approach implies.

Cautions for Interpreting Empirical Findings

(a) Estimates of the relative importance of genes, the common environment and the unique environment will depend on who is tested. If these are unrepresentative of the population (e.g., by excluding homeless, substance abusing and institutionalised individuals), then it will be unwise to extrapolate estimates of the relative importance of the common and unique environments and genetic influences to the general population.

(b) Heritability estimates are based on the range of environments that are usually found in a society, and so should not be applied cross-culturally. For example, if the range of environments experienced by children in some cultures varies far more than in our society (some children going hungry, suffering disease and living in squalor whilst others experience an extremely affluent lifestyle), this will affect the relative importance of environmental and genetic influences.

(c) Even if an ability is 100% genetically determined, it can still be changed by environmental intervention: it may well be possible to boost (or lower) children's levels of general ability, through environmental manipulations, because a child's genetic potential can only be expressed given a suitable environment. Unless all children are brought up in environments that allow them to develop fully their full range of abilities, some will fail to show their full potential because of environmental constraints.

(d) The relative importance of the common and unique environments and genetic makeup are features of the *sample*, not of the *individual*: it would be meaningless to claim that about half of a particular child's intelligence is determined by the environment and about half by the parents' genetic makeup, for example.

(e) Whilst early studies ignored the age of participants, it is now thought vital to conduct developmental studies to investigate the development of abilities over the lifespan, as the influence of the family is known to be greater at some ages than others, whilst certain genes may influence behaviour only at certain ages. What of experience? Even if some individuals start life with some genetically endowed advantage, are these benefits outweighed by environmental factors (such as quality of education, work experience) by the time one reaches adulthood? Or do early genetic advantages continue through life?

(f) Although twins and adoptees are used to discover the extent to which genes and the common and shared environment influence behaviour, the findings from these studies apply to everyone in the population— not just to twins and adoptees.

Age

It may well be important to consider the age of children who take part in these studies. Perhaps the influence of the family environment is important in childhood, but becomes less important in later life. Or perhaps a sound, supportive and stimulating family background early in life sets children up for life? Maybe genetic factors may matter early in life, but as children grow up their experiences and interests might take over and swamp any initial genetic advantage they may have had. Or perhaps, any genetic advantage that some children have in childhood will persist into old age. The important point is that it is sensible to ensure that participants in these studies are of similar ages, so that if the relative importance of family, genetic and extra-familial influences change over the lifespan, this does not confuse the picture.

Quantitative Behaviour Genetics: The Methods

The previous section sought to provide a conceptual of understanding of how studying twins, adoptees etc. can indicate whether or not the genes, the common environment and/or the shared environment influence abilities. For example, we showed that the influence of the shared environment can be determined by looking at the similarity between adopted children and other children in the family. However, we have not yet tried to quantify these influences, and I would hope that readers will by now be asking themselves, "but how can we know that the influence of genes is four times as important as the common environment" or suchlike.

There are many ways of discovering the extent to which the common (family) environment, the unique environment and genetic background influence a trait. For convenience I will assume that the trait in question is general intelligence (g) but the same principles can, of course, be used for absolutely any trait or behavior.

All of the studies involve studying how similar pairs of people are. For example, we might identify a few hundred families with two or more children of a particular age, and give two children from each family the same test of g. We can then correlate their scores together (using a special form of the correlation coefficient): this will show us how similar siblings tend to be. We can then do something similar, only using families where one of the children has been adopted, and so is not related to the other children in the family.

In the first case, children share their family environment and also share some genes (because they have the same parents). In the second case, children share only their family environment (because the adoptee and the other child in each family are not related to each other). So if genes have zero influence on g, the two correlations should be identical; it will not matter that the pairs in the first sample are genetically more similar than the pairs in the second sample. On the other hand, if genes do influence g, one would expect the children who are related to each other and who also share the family environment to be more similar than children who just share the family environment. As we will see below, it is a simple matter to quantify the extent to which genetic makeup, the family environment and the unique environment influence g, and so these studies give useful guidelines as to whether we should look at the family environment, influences outside the family, or biological mechanisms when we try to understand why some children grow up to be more intelligent than others.

There are a near-infinite number of other experimental designs available, too. For example, one could look at pairs of identical twins and pairs of same-sex non-identical twins who are brought up normally by their parents. The pairs of identical twins are genetically identical. Does this result in their being more similar in terms of g? Or one could look at correlations between the intelligence of parents of children who was given up for adoption and the adopted children (we would have to ensure that the parents had not been in contact with the children). Any similarity could only come about because of genetic similarity, as the parents will not have influenced either the family environment or the unique environment that the adopted-away children experienced. There are countless other possibilities, too.

The aim of quantitative genetic studies is to determine (for a given population, experiencing a particular variety of environments) the relative importance of shared genes, the shared environment, and the unique environment for determining some behaviour or trait such as g. In the following sections, I shall derive some very simple formulae for estimating the relative importance of genetic and environmental influences. I do so to demonstrate how simple correlations between pairs of twins and other family members can be used to draw powerful inferences about the relative importance of genetic and environmental influences on ability. Should you be expected to reproduce these equations, it will be easier to derive them as needed, rather than relying on memory.

Adoption Studies

The logic of these studies is straightforward. When psychologists study adopted children they look at children who are brought up by people to whom they are not biologically related. Children who are brought up by a relative (e.g., grandparent) would not be included. The key thing is that the child who is adopted has no biological link to anyone else in the adoptive family. So the only thing that can make adopted children similar to another child in the adoptive family is the family environment, which both children share. On the other hand, when a child is brought up with its biological brothers and sisters, the child shares both the family environment and some genes with their brothers and sisters.

If genes influence intelligence, you would expect the correlation between the test scores of children and their brothers & sisters to be higher than the correlation between adopted children and other children in the adoptive family—because the biological parents and their children share both genes and the family environment, whilst the adopted children and the other children in the family share only the family environment.

Good studies (from a statistical point of view) will involve samples of hundreds of adopted children. The adopted children will have been adopted at a very early age and will have had no contact with their biological parents. And the adopted children will have similar backgrounds to children who have been brought up by their parents—for example, it will be necessary to ensure that the adoptees were not given up for adoption because of health issues, that their mothers behaved similarly during pregnancy (rates of drinking, smoking), and so on.

Denoting the genetic contribution as A, the common (shared) environment as C and the unique environment as E, we first assume that

Total variation in scores on a trait $= A + C + E = 1.$ Equation 5.1

That is, that the common environment, the unique environment and genes together explain all the variation in an ability. The figures A, C and E thus represent the relative importance of these three influences.

Consider a child that is not adopted, but that is brought up alongside one of its biological siblings. Since they share half their variable genes and the common environment, we may write

$$r_{bc} = \frac{A}{2} + C \qquad\qquad \text{Equation 5.2}$$

where r_{bc} denotes the correlation between the general ability of biological siblings. Note that E does not appear in this equation—or in any of those that follow—as the children do not (by definition) share their unique environments.

For an adopted child, we express the correlation between another child in the family and the adopted child, r_{ac}, as

$$r_{ac} = 0 + C \qquad\qquad \text{Equation 5.3}$$

as the adopted child shares a common environment (but no variable genes or unique environment) with the other child.

Subtracting Equation 5.3 from Equation 5.2 gives

$$r_{bc} - r_{ac} = \frac{A}{2}$$

and thus

$$A = 2(r_{bc} - r_{ac}). \qquad\qquad \text{Equation 5.4}$$

Thus, if we know the correlation between the test scores of an adopted child and another child in the adoptive family, and the correlation between the test scores of pairs of siblings who are brought up together, these figures can be inserted into Equation 5.4 to estimate the proportion of variance in general ability that is genetically transmitted.

We have not mentioned a figure for r_{bc}. Bouchard and McGue (1981) report a result (averaged across a number of studies) of 0.42, whilst $r_{ac} = 0.13$. So how heritable is general ability? From Equation 5.4, we can see that it is (0.42 − 0.13) × 2, or 0.58. That is, variations in genetic makeup explains rather more than half of the variation in general ability within this sample.

It is also possible to estimate the relative importance of the shared and the non-shared environments—indeed, Equation 5.3 shows this directly. So here the common environment explains 13% of the variation of general ability, as you should check for yourself. The remaining 100 − 58 − 13 = 29% of the variation is due to individual differences in the children's unique environments (see Equation 5.1).

The models applied here (which stem from the work of Jinks & Fulker, 1970) are very simple, and fail to take into account any non-additive genetic effects: interactions between different genes (epistasis) and the presence of dominant/recessive genes. 'Narrow heritability' is the term used to refer to the additive effects only; 'broad heritability' encompasses both additive and non-additive factors. Thus broad heritability is always at least as large as narrow heritability.

The studies considered above also cannot allow for the possibility that adopted children may not be treated *exactly* the same as other members of the family. More complex models have been derived to take account of these difficulties; P.E. Vernon (1979) describes some of the older models, and Stevenson (1997) and Pedersen and Lichtenstein (1997) discuss some new approaches, based on a statistical method known as path analysis. Some of the more recent literature can become rather technical.

Twins Reared Together and Apart

Much research in genetics has focused on twins, as pairs of identical twins reared in the same family share the same genetic makeup and shared environment, whilst non-identical (fraternal) twins reared together form a useful control groups: they too shared the same environment from conception onward, as well as having all the environmental similarities caused by being the same age. Most studies consider only fraternal twins who are the same gender, to provide a still better match. Major twin studies that have produced a large number of publications include those based on the Swedish Adoption/Twin Study of Aging (e.g., Finkel, Reynolds, McArdle & Pedersen, 2005), the Louisville Longitudinal Twin Study (Wilson, 1983) the Western Reserve Twin Project (Thompson, 1993), the MacArthur Longitudinal Twin Study (Plomin et al., 1990) and the Twin Infant Project (DiLalla et al., 1990). There are also many older studies, summarised by Bouchard and McGue (1981).

Identical twins reared together share all their genes and their common environment. Using the convention where r_{mz} indicates the correlation[1] between pairs of monozygotic (identical) twins and r_{dz} the correlation between dizygotic (fraternal) twins, we may write:

$$r_{mz} = A + C \qquad\qquad \text{Equation 5.5}$$

whilst non-identical twins share just half their genes and their common environment, so

$$r_{dz} = \frac{A}{2} + C. \qquad \qquad \text{Equation 5.6}$$

Subtracting Equation 5.6 from Equation 5.5 gives

$$r_{mz} - r_{dz} = \frac{A}{2} + C - A - C = \frac{A}{2}$$

and multiplying both sides by 2 gives

$$2(r_{mz} - r_{dz}) = A. \qquad \qquad \text{Equation 5.7}$$

So to estimate the heritability of a trait from twins reared together, one simply subtracts the correlation between the test scores of pairs of non-identical twins from the correlation between the test scores of pairs of identical twins, and doubles the result. To estimate the importance of the shared environment, C, both sides of Equation 5.6 may be doubled, and then Equation 5.5 subtracted from it, giving

$$2r_{dz} - r_{mz} = A + 2C - A - C = C \qquad \qquad \text{Equation 5.8}$$

whilst the importance of the unique environment can be estimated (using Equation 5.1, Equation 5.5 and Equation 5.7) as

$$\begin{aligned} E &= 1 - C - A \\ &= 1 - (2r_{dz} - r_{mz}) - 2(r_{mz} - r_{dz}) \\ &= 1 - 2r_{dz} + r_{mz} - 2r_{mz} + 2r_{dz} \\ &= 1 - r_{mz}. \qquad \qquad \text{Equation 5.9} \end{aligned}$$

Thus, it is possible to estimate the relative importance of the genes, common environment and unique environment for determining the general ability of a member of a certain society simply through inserting the correlations between pairs of identical (monozygotic) and fraternal (dizygotic) twins who have been reared together into Equations 5.7, 5.8 and 5.9.

Very occasionally, identical twins are separated shortly after birth and brought up by different families, never having contact with each other. These separated identical twins share all their genetic makeup, but do not share a common environment (or unique environment). So the correlation between the scores of pairs of identical twins who were reared apart is a direct measure of the influence of genetics.

Gene-Environment Interactions: The Theory

The principles outlined above are a little simplistic. We have assumed that the parents treat all of their children similarly (instead of reacting to individual differences in children's personality and abilities) or more generally that there is no interaction between genetic makeup and the family environment. We have assumed that the parents tend to choose each other at random, whereas in fact couples who meet at university or at work may have rather similar levels of intelligence; we also assume that there are no sex differences in intelligence. And we have chosen to focus 'narrow heritability' that assumes that there are no interactions between genes; it is possible to estimate the broad heritability of intelligence that allows for interactions between the two copies of each gene (one inherited from each parent) and interactions between different genes. Broad heritability is, for reasons that should be obvious, at least as large as narrow heritability.

The problem is that in order to assess gene-environment interactions, it is necessary to be able to quantify environments. It is usual to do this by measuring parental socio-economic status (SES)—a measure based on the parents' income, education and occupation. Whilst it might sound desirable to look at narrower measures, such as attitudes to education, parental education and family income separately, this would not be easy to achieve in practice because we will see in Chapter 7 that all these variables tend to be quite substantially correlated. This means that it is difficult or impossible to untangle their individual effects—a problem known as multicollinearity. The usual assumption is that high SES parents are more likely to be able to develop their children's talents either through the common family environment (greater availability of books, private education, encouragement to do well at school) or as part of the unique environment (reacting to children's abilities and interests such as providing music lessons if a child seems interested in music). Putting it simply, being raised in a wealthy family might result in children being exposed to environments in which any genetic potential for cognitive abilities is likely to be realized. Although most children reared in more modest circumstances will have access to state schools, libraries, and so on, it is possible that some of them will not. For example some children may have to leave school early to earn a wage, and so will not benefit from academic stimulation offered by university or college. Disruptive classes, unchallenging curricula, poor teaching or lack of parental support and assistance may prevent them from developing their cognitive skills to their maximum.

It therefore seems possible that genetic influences might be larger in children raised in affluent surroundings. For them, their genetic makeup, rather than their educational and social environment, is likely to be the factor that limits their intellectual development. On the other hand, some children who are raised in socially deprived families may not receive the environmental stimulation to allow them to realize any talents they have. For them, the social environment is will often limit their intellectual development, and so variations in social environment will have a larger influence than will genetic effects.

Quantitative Behaviour Genetics: The Results

The literature here is vast, and has been summarised in a great many thoughtful reviews and empirical reports (e.g., Bouchard, 1995; Bouchard & McGue, 1981; Neisser et al., 1996; Pedersen & Lichtenstein, 1997; Plomin & McClearn, 1993; Scarr & Carter-Saltzman, 1982; Thompson, 1993). It is also remarkably consistent: different types of studies all reach broadly similar conclusions about the extent to which genetic makeup, the family environment and the unique environment influence general ability at a particular age. In this section, I have stressed the types of methodologies used, and given one or two examples of some typical results. Other results will be found in the sources listed above. Most of the studies have focused on measures of general ability, g, rather than primary or secondary abilities.

Bouchard and McGue (1981) summarised 111 older family studies of general ability and worked out average correlations for identical and non-identical twins reared together and apart, amongst others. Thompson (1993) reviews some more recent work. Bouchard and McGue reported that levels of general ability of pairs of non-identical twins reared in the same family correlated 0.60 (based on 5,546 pairs), whilst for identical twins brought up together the correlation was 0.86 (4,672 pairs). This implies (as you should verify, using Equations 5.7–5.9) that general ability has a narrow heritability of approximately 52%, with the shared environment and the unique environment accounting for 34% and 14% of the variation respectively. However, these studies averaged across several age ranges, which is undesirable given what is now known about how heritability changes with age. Thompson (1993) estimates heritability to be 50% in 6- to 12-year-olds, with the shared and unique environments accounting for 42% and 8% of the variation—figures that agree well with the earlier studies.

Studies involving separated twins are even easier to understand. Two identical twins who are separated shortly after birth and reared in different environments will share only their genes. So for separated twins, $A = r_{mz}$. For separated dizygotic twins, $A = 2r_{dz}$. Bouchard, Lykken, McGue, Segal and Tellegen (1990) report values of r_{mz} ranging from 0.69 to 0.78 between pairs of identical twins who were reared apart and then given three tests of general ability. This implies that genes account for up to three-quarters of the variation in general ability. However, very few identical twins *are* separated at birth, and so the numbers are small (fewer than 50 in the above study). Furthermore, those twins who do manage (or choose) to find their identical twin and volunteer for testing may not be a representative sample of the population. Thus I would caution against making too much of the separated identical twin data—although curiously this is the only sort of behaviour-genetic study discussed and criticised by Howe (1997).

Adoption studies are much easier to work with. If it is found that adopted children tend to have levels of *g* that are similar to other members of the adoptive family, then this provides good evidence that the common environment is important for the development of *g*. Several large-scale studies (Bouchard, 1993, gives references) have been instigated to keep track of adoptees, such as the Texas Adoption Study, the Colorado Adoption Study, the Minnesota Adoption Study, and the Swedish Adoption/Twin Study of Ageing.

In order to test the importance of the common environment, it is necessary to trace several hundred adopted children, measure their level of ability, measure the level of ability of *other* children in the same families, and use a statistic called the 'semipartial correlation' to decide whether the variation *within* families is smaller than the variation *between* families, as one would expect if the family environment is all-important for determining levels of the ability.

The evidence shows that in early childhood, adopted children do tend to have similar levels of general ability to other members of the adoptive family. However, they become less (rather than more) similar to other children in the family as they grow up. Loehlin, Horn, and Willerman (1989) analysed data from the Texas Adoption Study comparing the general ability of adopted children and other children within the same family—both fellow-adoptees and biological offspring of the adoptive parents. The childhood correlations of 0.11 and 0.20 (which indicate the influence of the common environment) fell to −0.09 and 0.05 ten years later, when the children were aged between 13 and 24. This suggests that the influence of the family environment becomes negligible as the children grow into adulthood. Where the adoptive parents have two children of their own, the correlation between their levels of general ability (which are influenced by both the family environment *and* their genetic similarity) is 0.27 in childhood and 0.24 ten years later. This suggests that genes may influence *g* to. Plomin and Daniels (1987) report much the same thing, from a different sample of twins.

Several studies have tested twins repeatedly over their lifespan in order to determine whether general ability becomes 'swamped' by the effects of life experiences as one gets older, or whether any early genetic advantage endures. The usual finding is that the heritability of general ability increases steadily, peaking at a value of about 0.7–0.8 at age 40 (Pedersen & Lichtenstein, 1997), and then declining, perhaps because of variability in the onset of senile decay. Somewhat confusingly, the heritability of g seems to vary as a function of year of birth (as well as age): groups of Norwegian twins who were born in different years were tested at the same chronological age by Sundet, Tambs, Magnus and Berg (1988), and the heritabilities were found to cycle up and down. No one really understands why this should be the case.

Haworth et al. (2010) have performed a massive analysis based on a sample of over 11,000 pairs of twins showing a linear increase in the importance of genetic factors as children age from 9 to 17: the heritability of g is 0.41 at age 9, and 0.66 at age 17, whereas the influence of the family environment drops to a mere 0.18 at age 17.

Thus, it seems that children develop similar levels of general ability in adulthood only if they are biologically related. Merely being brought up in the same family does not make two unrelated children develop remotely similar levels of g. This study suggests that both the common environment and genetic makeup affects general ability in childhood, but the influence of the common environment declines in adulthood whilst genetic influences endure.

These findings are both consistent and surprising. One might have expected that the effects of any genetic advantages may have been swamped by the different experiences (inside and outside the family) that affect children's development. It "seems obvious" that attending good schools rather than chaotic schools, or being fortunate enough to have parents who provide a stimulating environment rather than providing no encouragement or support at home, will have a massive influence on a child's cognitive development. However these data show clearly that this "obvious" presumption is completely incorrect. The reason that some children grow up to be more intelligent than others is overwhelmingly due to the genes that they inherit from their parents, rather than what the parents actually do to them.

This is not to say that the environment does not matter at all. Heritability figures refer to children in *general* in the sorts of environments that are *typically* found in Western society. Severely deprived or abusive environments may, and probably do, have a severe influence on individual children's intellectual development. If an individual child is cruelly deprived, then their intellectual development may well suffer. That said, studies have been carried out which suggest that the cognitive scores of children who suffer quite severe deprivation in early life bounce back later (van Ijzendoorn, Juffer & Poelhuis, 2005) following adoption and become "remarkably normal" in terms of cognitive development.

What of the link between the adopted children's levels of general ability, and the levels of general ability of their biological and adoptive parents? Children's levels of general ability were related to that of both their adoptive mothers (r = 0.13) and their biological mothers (r = 0.23) in a sample of over 200 adopted children (Loehlin et al., 1989). Ten years later, the intelligence of these adults/adolescents was still correlated with the intelligence of their biological mothers (0.26). However, the correlation with their adopted mothers' general ability fell to 0.05. This too suggests that the influence of the common environment on general ability is negligible by adulthood.

Gene–Environment Interactions: The Results

Several studies have examined whether the heritability of intelligence varies according to the SES of the family in which the children are reared. We argued earlier that if high-SES children enjoy environments that allow them to reach whatever genetic potential they may each show, the effects of genetics will be larger than for low SES families where some potentially highly able children will be held back because their environments cannot allow the cognitive skills to develop. Two key questions are whether such effects are, indeed found— and whether or not this gene x SES effect persists into adulthood.

Turkheimer, Haley, Waldron, D'Onofrio and Gottesman (2003) found clear evidence that the SES of the family in which children are brought up influences the heritability of g in a study that included a large proportion of very low SES families in the United States. In well-to-do families, the heritability of g in 7-year-old twins was about 0.6. However in the most socially deprived families, the heritability was close to zero, and variations in the shared environment were the most potent influence on intelligence. Children born into extremely low SES families may not be able to develop any intellectual potential that they may have (although there are other possible explanations, too). However although some authors have managed to find a similar effect in different samples (Bates, Lewis & Weiss, 2013; Turkheimer, Harden, D'Onofrio & Gottesman, 2009), there have been many problems replicating this work. For example, there is absolutely no sign of such an interaction in adolescents in Hawaii (Nagoshi & Johnson, 2005), British 4-year-olds (Asbury, Wachs & Plomin, 2005) or adults in Holland (van der Sluis, Willemsen, de Geus, Boomsma & Posthuma, 2008). The key issue seems to be that some of the United States families in Turkheimer et al. (2003) were very socially disadvantaged; other studies may not have included families with such extreme deprivation.

This work comes as a timely reminder that genetic potential may count for nothing if a child is brought up in abject poverty. The heritability estimates discussed earlier in the chapter are based on samples that probably exclude families with extremely low SES: for example, adoption agencies are unlikely to place a child with an extremely socially deprived family. It also suggests that enhancing the environments of the most socially deprived children may have profound effects on their cognitive development.

Multivariate Genetic Studies: The Theory

The evidence demonstrating the huge importance of genetic factors and the rather trivial influence of the family environment on adult intelligence are discussed in some detail above because some psychologists still appear to be ignorant of the mass of data that show that human intelligence is best regarded as a biologically determined (rather than socially determined) phenomenon. Having established this some years ago (hence the rather elderly references above), researchers have now moved on to study the molecular genetics of intelligence. However the methods of behavioural genetics can be extended to address another interesting issue: whether the genes that are relevant for one ability also influence quite different abilities.

For example, it might be found that verbal ability and numerical ability are correlated together in a sample of people. It might also be found (from twin studies, adoption studies etc.) that both verbal ability and numerical ability have a reasonably substantial genetic component. So the logical next question is whether the same genes that influence one of the abilities (verbal ability, say) also affect the other ability. It might be the case that one set of genes influence verbal ability, a second set of genes affect numerical ability, and the correlation between verbal and numerical ability arises just because of environmental influences. For example, it seems plausible that attending a good school will make a child perform well on both these tasks. Or some parents might encourage their children to perform well at school, providing computers, a quiet place to work and perhaps tutoring, and ensuring that homework is completed. Others might leave their children to do as little work as they choose. Such environmental factors are likely to affect the performance of all children in the family on all abilities. Thus it quite possible that children from the same family might perform better/worse on both tasks than children from other families purely because of the amount of support and the quality of education that they have received. Although one set of genes might influence verbal performance and another set of genes might influence numerical performance, the reason why the verbal and numerical tests correlate could well be entirely due to the family environment. The genes that influence verbal ability might have no influence on numerical ability, and vice versa.

At the other extreme it might be the case that that many or all of the genes that influence verbal ability might also influence numerical ability. So it could be that the correlation between verbal and numerical abilities arises because the same genes influence both abilities. This second possibility is exciting, because if true it hints that general intelligence, g, may have a direct genetic origin. In other words, there may possibly be some "generalist genes" that influence performance on many or all ability traits, and that cause them to be intercorrelated.

Multivariate behaviour genetics is a method that allows us to find out whether the genes that affect one ability are the same as the genes that influence other abilities. It is incredibly useful for understanding the nature of g—and far simpler than its name suggests.

All it involves is recruiting large samples of monozygotic and dizygotic twins. Each participant is given the same two tests measuring the traits whose genetic overlap is being investigated. In the above example, each of the twins would be given a verbal ability test and a test of numerical ability. Then one correlates together the verbal and numerical ability scores for the sample monozygotic twins, and also for the sample of dizygotic twins.

Clearly if the correlation between the verbal and numerical scores is genetically mediated (i.e., some genes affect performance on both tests), the correlations between the pairs of monozygotic twins' scores on the two tests will be higher than for the dizygotic twins. This is because members of each pair of monozygotic twins are genetically identical, whilst dizygotic pairs are not. So if genetic makeup is responsible for the correlation between the two tests, then you would expect the monozygotic twins to be more similar. If genes are not the reason why scores on the tests correlate, then the correlation between the two test scores for the dizygotic twin pairs should be about the same as for the monozygotic twin pairs. This would indicate that the reason that the tests correlate is environmental—for example, because members of each twin pair (be they monozygotic or dizygotic) received similar levels of encouragement/support at home, attended the same school that may have developed (or held back) their academic performance, and so on.

Multivariate Genetic Analysis: The Results

So what do the data show?

There is good evidence that, in children at any rate, the correlations between quite different abilities are mediated by the same sets of genes (Davis, Haworth & Plomin, 2009). This occurs in high-ability individuals

(Haworth, Dale & Plomin, 2009) as well as those with problems in one or more area (Haworth, Kovas, et al., 2009; Plomin and Kovas, 2005). The importance of this finding can hardly be overstated. It implies that these genes perform precisely the function that general intelligence performs— causing seemingly disparate abilities to be correlated. Of course, large-scale studies involving many abilities have not yet been performed as this is still a very new and developing field; to my knowledge at the time of writing, no one has tested whether the main primary or second-order ability factors such as spatial ability, memory, or creativity correlate with other abilities because of these generalist genes. This is probably because of the important practical importance of understanding why some children have difficulties with mathematics and/or language. However these generalist genes clearly closely resemble the way that the g factor, identified by factor analysis, operates. They cause a number of human cognitive abilities that look as if they involve quite different cognitive processes to be correlated together.

g and reaction time correlate, as shown in Chapter 6. Does this come about because both g and reaction time are influenced by the same genes, and hence involve the same brain mechanisms? A multivariate genetic analysis by Baker, Vernon and Ho (1991) shows clearly that this is the case. They showed that the correlation between speed of information processing and intelligence arises because the same set of genes influence performance at both types of task. The effect of environmental factors was miniscule.

There is also a literature on the genetic/environmental basis of elementary cognitive tasks (e.g., Petrill, Luo, Thompson & Detterman, 1996), and physiological variables considered in Chapter 6, such as nerve conduction velocity and event-related potentials (e.g., Katsanis & Iacono, 1991, Rijsdijk, Boomsma & Vernon, 1995a).

Methodological Objections

Not everyone agrees with the interpretation of the data from behavior genetic studies. Kamin (1974), Rose, Lewontin and Kamin (1984), Richardson and Norgate (2005) and Howe (1997) are amongst those who raise a number of criticisms of this work. They highlight important concerns about some aspects of the studies that may weaken their findings. For example,

(a) At what age were children adopted into other families? If late in childhood, it may be the influence of the shared environment during some crucial early period (rather than shared genes) that makes the adoptees similar in later life.

(b) Adoptive families tend to be vetted by social service agencies, and so few children are likely to be adopted into extremely poor or abusive homes. The range of adoptive environments will be reduced, and this will lead to the importance of the common environment being underestimated.

(c) Selective placement may be a problem: children from working-class mothers may be adopted into working-class homes, whilst those from middle-class mothers may end up in middle-class homes. Hence the correlations between the biological mothers' and the adopted children's level of general ability may reflect similarities of social class (shared environment) and not genetic similarity.

(d) Do "separated" twins truly never see each other, or might they live close to each other, meet at family gatherings (if adopted by a family member) and even attend the same schools? If so, it could be this contact (rather than genes) that makes them similar.

(e) Might identical twins who are raised together have similar levels of ability because they are often mistaken for each other, and basically treated much more similarly by teachers and parents than are non-identical twins?

(f) Perhaps children put up for adoption do not form a representative sample of the population. They may well have been abused, and the very process of adoption may be traumatic for the child.

(g) The psychologists administering the tests may "encourage" twin-pairs to perform well, so manufacturing support for a genetic explanation.

Bouchard (1993) and Brody and Crowley (1995) discuss some of the points made briefly below, and provide data to demonstrate their validity.

(a) Some children in the older studies *were* adopted quite late in life, so the similarity to the biological mother might be explained by their sharing an environment for several years, rather than sharing genes. However, several modern studies are based on babies adopted during the first year of life; babies adopted earlier than 6 months show the same results as babies adopted a little later (Bouchard, 1993) and, in any case, adoption studies and family studies yield similar findings. Also, if crucial early-lifetime experiences (rather than genes) explain why children who are adopted into different families show similar levels of ability, why should adopted children become less similar to their adoptive families over time? And why is the relationship with the biological parent so strong?

(b) If restriction of range of the shared (adoptive) environment was a real problem, then there could not be an appreciable correlation between the scores of adoptees and other family members during childhood.

(c) Selective placement cannot be the full explanation, for why should the correlation between the biological parents' and adoptees' general ability remain constant over time, whilst the correlations between the adopted children and their adoptive parents and other members of the adoptive family decrease? If only one mechanism (shared environment) is at work, all three sets of correlations should change in similar ways. In any case, more recent studies (e.g., Bouchard et al., 1990) now statistically control for the effects of selective placement, which is assessed by correlating the adoptive and biological parents' IQ and social class indices, physical facilities, educational achievement, etc. It has been found that although the parents' and the adoptive environments generally are correlated, neither of these is a good predictor of the children's level of general ability (Bouchard et al., 1990).

(d) Some supposedly "separated" twins were in contact with each other in the early studies. However, later work (e.g., Bouchard et al., 1990) took care to ensure that twins really were reared independently, and came to exactly the same conclusions as the earlier studies.

(e) Monozygotic twins are unlikely to become alike because they are treated more similarly by their families than are dizygotic twins. Baker and Daniels (1990) found no relationship between the ways in which monozygotic twins were treated when young and their later similarity, and little variation in the ways in which parents treated monozygotic and dizygotic twins.

(f) It is quite possible that adoptive children do not form a representative sample of the population, are more likely to have been abused, and may suffer distress at the adoption process. But why should this cause them to have similar levels of general ability to their biological mother? Or virtually no similarity to other same-aged children adopted into the family at the same time?

(g) Twins are nowadays tested by different investigators who are unaware of the other twin's score. Anyway, encouraging all twin-pairs to perform well will not improve the correlation: to do so it would be better to encourage just the monozygotic twin pairs to perform well.

All of the above objections suggest that the importance of genetic factors may have been overestimated. Yet there are also some important problems with the design of some of the experiments that may lead them to underestimate the role of genes. For example:

(a) Test scores all have some measurement error associated with them. The effect of this will be to underestimate the true correlations between individuals. It can be shown (applying the formula on p. 220 of Nunnally, 1978 to equation 5.7) that this will lead to the underestimation of genetic effects.

(b) We do not select partners at random, but may choose others who share our interests—and level of general mental ability. It has been found that pairs of partners have a correlation of 0.33 to 0.45 between their levels of g (Brody, 1992). If there is a genetic component to general ability, this is likely to mean that the parents are likely to share some of the 'variable' genes that influence general ability. Thus, fraternal twins will be more genetically similar than if their parents were selected at random, and this will lead to the underestimation of the role of genetic factors and the overestimation of the influence of the common environment on abilities.

Early behaviour-genetic studies were sometimes flawed for the reasons given above. However, methodologies have improved, and modern behaviour-genetic studies are much better designed, are based on large samples of individuals, ensure that adoptees are separated early and are genuinely reared apart, and take account of the problems raised by selective placement. They also provide remarkably consistent results. There is, of course, plenty more work to be done. Efforts are under way to actually measure the "shared environment", to find out precisely which parts of it seem to influence children's cognitive ability. But this is harder than it seems, as Chipuer, Plomin, Pedersen, McClearn and Nesselroade (1993) found that people's *perceptions* of the family environment have a substantial genetic component! So asking people questions about their home environment will not provide an objective measure of the quality of that environment.

Even more curiously, the scores on one inventory measuring family surroundings *as rated by an external observer* show a genetic component. This sounds most odd. How can scores that an independent observer makes about the family environment be linked to the genetic makeup of the child? Saudino and Plomin (1997) suggest that this reflects an interaction between genes and environment; the parents who have genetic makeup that causes them to show high levels of intelligence may, for example, also tend to produce home environments that facilitate the development of intellectual skills. They may encourage their children to take up intellectually demanding activities, provide good nutrition, and will probably earn more money than the norm (see Chapter 7). But the key suggestion is that this comfortable middle-class environment comes about not by accident but in part because of the parents' genetic endowment. Some of these genes will be passed on to the children.

This may be why the family environment seems to be linked to the genetic makeup of the child.

It has also been found that the child's unique environment is under genetic control, for similar reasons. A child with many genetic variations that give them the potential for high g is likely to do things that allow them to develop their intellectual talents—perhaps playing chess, joining a library, choosing other smart children as friends and so on. Rather being a passive victim of their environment, children may actively tailor it to suit their genetic propensities (Plomin, Defries & Loehlin, 1977; Scarr & McCartney, 1983). Plomin and Daniels (2011) provide an excellent discussion of these issues, with an accessible summary of modern trends in behavioural genetics in Plomin and Asbury (2005).

The nature–nurture debate remains one of the most hotly debated and politically charged issues in psychology, with several other important issues surfacing periodically in the press and scientific journals. These include the following:

- The belief that because abilities have a substantial genetic component abilities cannot be changed. This ignores the finding that about 30%–50% (depending on the age) of the variation in g is due to environmental influences.
- A concern that because genes are the most potent predictor of abilities within several cultural groups, differences in mean levels of g between cultural or racial groups is also due to genetic effects: some races may be genetically "inferior" to others. There is not strong evidence from transracial adoption studies where twins from one race are adopted by families from another race suggesting that racial differences in g are genetically mediated (Brody, 2007).
- Concerns about the activities of the eugenics movement. Such groups argue that high levels of g within a society make it successful within a capitalist worldwide economy, g has a genetic component, and as there is a negative correlation between g and the number of children one has (Herrnstein & Murray, 1994), this will cause a gradual decline in levels of g within the society unless measures are taken to restrict breeding amongst low-IQ groups—a chilling prospect.
- A more general suspicion that attributing g to the genes facilitates a right-wing agenda, rather than one that deals sympathetically with educational and environmental improvements for the disadvantaged. However, if genes had no effect on g then no child raised in an awful environment would have any chance whatsoever of excelling intellectually: the genetic basis of g will reduce the impact of poor or abusive environments.

- Confusion about whether the heritability statistics discussed above refer to individuals or groups. It is wrong to conclude that because the shared environment has but a modest effect on levels of g, the family environment will not influence any children. It will influence some. It will not influence others. The 'modest' figure is an *average* within the population.
- The assumption that because the common environment has a small influence on g, extremely good (or unspeakably awful) family environments will have little effect on children's abilities. The heritability estimates given above are average figures, based on the sorts of environments that children typically experience in countries such as the United States, Sweden and the United Kingdom. Expose children to an environment quite unlike that experienced by others, and it is impossible to say what will happen.

Overview

As Mackintosh (1995) observed, recent evidence about the heritability of general ability "has made an already pretty well established conclusion well-nigh irrefutable . . . no prudent person would now accept that the heritability of IQ was zero. That question is settled". Snyderman and Rothman's (1987) survey of psychology academics also revealed that most academics now accept that general ability has a genetic component, and the American Psychological Association's *Task Force on Intelligence* reached much the same conclusion (Neisser et al., 1996). All that remains is to identify the individual genes and their patterns of interaction.

Several different types of evidence lead us to this conclusion. The results of family studies of twins, studies of separated siblings and twins (and their biological and adoptive parents) and other family studies not discussed above have shown a very consistent picture. Genetic makeup has the most potent influence on levels of general ability in Western society (accounting for 50 to 60% of the variation; rather less in childhood, and rather more in adulthood) along with the common environment (which is important in childhood only) and the unique environment that each individual carves out for himself or herself. In order to understand why some people are more intelligent than others, it makes no sense to look at what goes on in the "normal" family, as we know that this has a vanishingly small influence on adult intelligence.

Multivariate genetic analyses show that the same genes that influence one mental ability—verbal ability, for example—also seem to influence other quite different mental abilities. A group of genes influences performance on just about all tasks that require thought, and so reflect exactly what the factor analytic studies say about the role of g. This is exciting, because it suggests that what we are measuring with simple tests of general ability reflect individual differences in our biological makeup. We now have evidence that g is a real property of organisms, linked to the biological makeup of the brain and/or nervous system. It cannot be a mere social construction.

The finding that the family environment has little or no direct influence on children's intelligence is both surprising and important. It is important because it indicates that trying to devise strategies to boost the intelligence of children by improving the family environment will be unlikely to have a major effect across the board (although it might have an influence for the most socially deprived children). And it shows that whenever psychologists identify some parental behavior that is associated with an ability (e.g., discovering that children whose parents read to them develop better language skills than those whose parents did not), they should be very cautious indeed about assuming that there is a causal link. Both the parent and the child might be fulfilling their genetic potential by reading: the child may have read voraciously whatever the parent did. Adoption studies, etc. are needed in such cases.

Perhaps the most important finding is the strong and consistent support for a biological model of human cognitive abilities that emerges from this literature. It shows that in order to understand the origins of human intelligence, we need to look at brain structure and function, rather than family dynamics. And so this is the content of our next chapter.

Note

1   When correlating the scores of pairs of twins, a statistic known as the "intra-class correlation" rather than the more usual Pearson correlation is used. This is because in each pair of twins it is arbitrary which twin is in Group A and which is in group B when the scores are being correlated.

6

ABILITY PROCESSES

Whilst chapters 2–4 spelt out in some detail what is known about the structure of individual differences, they said nothing about how or why they emerge. In order to have a proper scientific understanding of cognitive abilities, it is crucial to understand what causes people to differ in g and other abilities. Merely establishing the structure of abilities is not enough, in the same way that just being able to identify the symptoms of various diseases does not mean that we understand them enough to develop cures. A proper scientific understanding of any topic requires that we should be able to establish the basic structure (lists of diseases, lists of cognitive abilities), understand their interrelationships (discovering classes of diseases, such as infections or cancers; establishing the hierarchical structure of abilities), and finally developing models (to explain what causes some people to develop various diseases, or to develop a particular level of some cognitive ability). Models are usually developed piecemeal, by identifying weaknesses in the previous models and successively refining them. But even a partial understanding of how bacteria cause infections or how nervous system activity can affect intelligence can be of considerable practical use.

Chapter 5 shows that a sensible place to start looking for the roots of intelligence is in the biology of the nervous system, since general ability has a substantial genetic component. So it should be possible to find correlations between g and physiological measures. Individual differences in brain functioning might show up in the structure of the nervous system. For example, g may be related to the thickness of various areas of the cortex. Or g could be reflected in individual differences in the ways in which individuals' nervous systems operate. For example, the amount of glucose an individual's metabolises whilst solving some problem might reflect how adequate their neural networks are for performing the necessary computations. However, it is hard to determine precisely what is going on at the neural level in the cortex; for example, it is difficult or impossible to identify which neural networks an individual has evolved. So, it is also useful to look at the correlation between *g* and some psychological variables (e.g., reaction time) that might reflect individual differences in physiological makeup or functioning.

However, it is also clear from Chapter 5 that a purely biological model cannot be the sole explanation of individual differences in *g*. It seems to explain only 50% to 70% of the observed variation in scores. So the search should also consider other factors, such as cognitive processes, social processes, educational processes, and so on. The problem with studying these variables (rather than biological ones) is that it is difficult to distinguish between cause and effect. Does high *g* cause a child to read books, or does reading plenty of books boost *g*? It is very difficult ever to be certain. For this reason, many researchers prefer instead to test some rather simple biological models. This chapter mainly focuses on biological models, but it also considers some cognitive approaches. Because the family environment has zero relationship to adult intelligence (see Chapter 5), there is no sensible reason to try to examine how parental behaviour may influence intelligence in "normal" children in Western culture—for the evidence shows that it does not. Empirical studies also show that acute social deprivation after the age of 6 months seems to have rather little impact on later levels of intelligence (Croft et al., 2007).

The Speed of Processing Hypothesis

Many researchers in this area have concentrated on trying to explain general ability, or *g*—that is, developing an understanding of why scores on all ability tests (of very different kinds, some involving language and others not) are positively correlated together. One possible explanation for this is that some individuals are simply able to process information more quickly than others. General ability might reflect a basic property of the nervous system that affects *all* cognitive operations that make up an individual performance. Jensen (1993a) considers this sort of argument in some depth, and his book *Clocking the Mind* (Jensen, 2006) provides an excellent resource for this area of research. In it, he summarises 25 years of research linking various aspects of speed to general intelligence and develops some theories to explain why this relationship might come about.

Two slightly different theories relating g to cognitive performance have emerged, but they are in most instances interchangeable, and so will be considered together. Several writers (Eysenck, 1967; Galton, 1883; Jensen & Munroe, 1974) have suggested that either the speed with which information is transmitted within or between neurones, or the *efficiency* of neural transmission, may be the key to g. Efficiency simply refers to how much information is lost when one nerve transits electrical impulses to another. So according to this model, high intelligence (g) should be associated with a brain that processes information quickly and accurately. It is difficult to envisage a simpler theory, although Deary (2000) argues that it is perhaps *too* simple, in that the terms 'speed' and 'accuracy' are too broad, and could be taken to refer to anything from the time taken to complete an ability test, psychophysical performance or nerve conduction velocity at the physiological level. But how might a link between g and nerve conduction velocity be tested?

Direct Measurement of Neural Conduction Velocity

It is difficult to get access to neurones in the human brain. However, if one makes the assumption that the same forces that influence speed/accuracy of information processing in the brain also influence peripheral nerves, then it is possible to test this hypothesis directly by

(a) Measuring an individual's general ability, using a test such as Raven's Matrices (Raven, Raven & Court, 2003) or the Wechsler Adult Intelligence Scale (Wechsler, 2010).
(b) Applying two widely spaced electrodes to the skin above one of the nerves whose long axons run down the arm.
(c) Measuring the distance between these electrodes with a tape measure.
(d) Electrically stimulating the nerve by applying a small electric shock to one electrode.
(e) Timing how long it takes for the neural impulse to reach the other electrode.
(f) Repeating the process several times and averaging.

This process should be carried out for a sample of participants (typically 50 to 100 people) chosen to be representative of the general population.

It is then possible to estimate each individual's neural conduction velocity by dividing the distance between the electrodes by the time delay between the application of the shock to one electrode and its arrival at the other, although the measures are somewhat variable and may be influenced by a number of physical variables, including temperature that needs to be carefully controlled. Several studies have followed this pattern, some also correlating the neural conduction velocities (ncvs) with measures such as inspection time or reaction time (discussed later in this chapter). If the speed of neural conduction hypothesis is correct, and it does not matter that a peripheral (rather than cerebral) nerve is chosen and that there is no synaptic transmission involved, then one would expect a positive correlation between ncv and g. Vernon and Mori (1992) did indeed find a significant correlation of 0.42 to 0.48 between ncv and g.

However, a number of studies have failed to replicate this finding (including Barrett, Daum & Eysenck, 1990; Reed & Jensen, 1991; Rijsdijk, Vernon & Boomsma, 1995b; Wickett & Vernon, 1994), and a review of the area concluded that there was little evidence of any consistent link between peripheral ncv and intelligence (Vernon, Wickett, Bazana & Stelmack, 2000). However, many "replications" also introduced some methodological differences, particularly with relation to temperature control. Curiously, handedness also seems to play a part and the correlations in Vernon and Mori's data were much stronger for males than females. This has also been found in some replications: Tan (1996) found a positive correlation for men (as expected) but a negative correlation for women. The reasons for these effects are not well understood (Wickett & Vernon, 1994), but researchers now seem to have given up trying to discover a link between peripheral ncv and g.

These results do not provide good evidence for the neuronal conduction model of g—though given the caveats mentioned above (peripheral versus central nerves, so differences in myelinisation; lack of synaptic transmission) such failures are not necessarily fatal for the theory either. But it may suggest that it is necessary to measure neural conduction velocity indirectly through experimental designs where the dependent variable is thought to be highly correlated with neural conduction velocity. The rest of this chapter examines some indirect measures of neural conduction velocity.

Reflex Latency

A second way of estimating individual differences in nerve conduction velocity is by measuring how long it takes an individual to make some involuntary, reflex, response—e.g., withdrawing the hand from a painful stimulus. The beauty of this approach is that reflexes occur very quickly— the knee-jerk reflex reported below takes only about 0.09 seconds, which is several times faster than any conscious response can be. The response requires zero thought or reasoning, and there can be no real question about strategy use, which is something that poses considerable problems for some other experiments.

The modern literature on this is meagre. Margaret McRorie and I (McRorie & Cooper, 2001) have carried out three studies investigating whether the latency of the knee-jerk reflex, the withdrawal reflex and the eye-blink reflex are related to g, as the neural-processing-speed theory of intelligence would predict. The first experiment involved tapping the knee with a special spring-loaded hammer, the use of which started a timer. The nerve impulse travels up to the spine, across one synapse and back down to the leg, where it makes the lower-leg twitch: the movement of the ankle was detected by a micro-switch positioned behind the ankle, and the time interval measured. Careful control of temperature was needed, and limb length was measured and taken into account when analysing the results. The second experiment involved participants holding down two metal buttons using the first and middle fingers of one hand. After a variable pause, a strong and painful electric shock was applied across the buttons. This led the participant to rapidly withdraw their fingers from the buttons (generally cursing as they did so), and we measured the time taken between the shock being delivered and the fingers being removed from the buttons. This reflex is known to involve a great number of synaptic connections. The final experiment involved participants wearing a pair of goggles. These goggles were attached to equipment that can deliver a puff of air to one eye, which makes the participant blink involuntarily. The goggles used infra-red reflection to detect whether the other eye was open or closed: when the eyelid came down, the amount of infra-red light reflected from the cornea changed. A computer measured the time interval between the puff of air being delivered and the other eye closing. For all experiments we measured cognitive ability using two tests, one of which was untimed: that is, participants could take as long as they wished to solve the problems.

The first experiment did not work very well, possibly because measuring the movement of the leg was rather crude, and there may have been appreciable individual differences in the speed at which the muscle contracted as a result of fitness etc. With hindsight, it would have been better to have measured muscle activity in the hamstring muscle (using electrodes) instead of physical movement at the ankle. This study showed no significant correlation with tests measuring g. On the other hand, the task involving electric shock correlated significantly with tests of general intelligence, and with reaction time, as do preliminary data from the eye-blink study.

I think that this work is important because the reflex task (a) measures speed fairly unequivocally and (b) does not involve conscious thought, so there can be no question of correlations being due to strategy use. I hope that others extend this work.

Inspection Time

Vickers, Nettelbeck and Willson (1972) developed a useful paradigm for estimating neural conduction velocity. They argued that as the retina is essentially an outgrowth of the brain, if the neural conduction velocity interpretation of g is correct, high-g individuals might be able to see/take-in/apprehend simple visual stimuli faster than low-g individuals. They developed a simple task, called inspection time (IT), to measure how long it took individuals to see a simple image, and found that this did indeed have a substantial negative correlation with g, as expected.

The stimuli that they used are shown in Figure 6.1. Participants peer into a box (the tachistoscope). On a screen in front of them is a black dot on a white background. They push a button, and either the shape shown in Figure 6.1a or that in Figure 6.1b appears extremely briefly, and is immediately followed by the figure shown in Figure 6.1c, which stays on the screen for several seconds. Because of the short presentation times, it is very difficult to see which of the two figures (6.1a or 6.1b) was presented. But for each trial participants are asked to say whether they believed that the left leg or the right leg of the stimulus was the longer. This procedure is repeated many more times, normally using at least 30 exposures at each of several durations. The experimenter then works out the percentage of correct answers at each duration, and from this estimates how long the stimulus has to be presented in order for a particular individual to have a particular probability (e.g., 90%) of being able correctly to identify which of the two figures was presented. This is their inspection time.

It is important to note that participants can take as long as they like to decide which of the two stimuli was shown: the task does not measure speed of response. It instead measures how long a simple shape must be shown for on the screen in order for it to be correctly recognised.

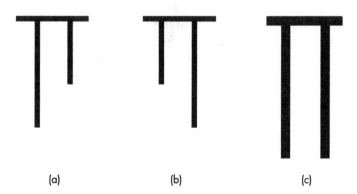

(a)   (b)   (c)

Figure 6.1 Two stimuli plus mask for an inspection-time task

Nettelbeck and Lally (1976) suggested that the correlation between IT and general ability was approximately −0.9. Such a substantial correlation suggested that conventional tests of general ability could perhaps be replaced by this simple experimental technique. However, the reason why this correlation was so large is because the authors used participants who varied enormously in their levels of general ability: the sample comprised a sample of university students plus some individuals with moderate to severe learning difficulties, and all of these people showed very long inspection times and very low scores on the test of general ability. The experiment has been repeated a great many times using better samples of people, however, and several good reviews of these findings have been published (e.g., Deary & Stough, 1996; Kranzler & Jensen, 1989; Sheppard & Vernon, 2008). The correlation between IT and general ability is in the order of −0.4 to −0.55, with Kranzler and Jensen's meta-analysis concluding that best estimate for the correlation is −0.54. Thus, it is probably fair to say that about a quarter (-0.54^2) of the variability in g can be explained by IT. The correlation is generally rather higher for tests measuring Gf than those with a verbal component Gc, and at the level of primary abilities, IT correlates best with perceptual speed (Cooper, Kline & MacLaurin-Jones, 1986; Sheppard & Vernon, 2008).

Other methods of measuring IT have been developed. These include changing the rate at which a light flashes to determine the point where an individual can just detect whether it is flickering or lit continuously (Nettelbeck, 1982), and a tactile version in which a person is invited to place two fingers on two metal plates. The plates are then made to vibrate, one marginally before the other, and the participant is invited to say which finger was stimulated first. It does not correlate very well with measures of ability (Nettelbeck and Kirby, 1983). We have also developed a task where people are shown a succession of coloured circles each in the same position on the screen. The duration of the first circle is varied, and participants are asked to simply identify which colour was shown first. McCrory and Cooper (2007) gave this, the Nettelbeck (1982) flashing lights task and the Nettelbeck and Lally (1976) task to a sample of students and found that the three intercorrelated substantially (approx 0.4) with each other and with tests of g ($r = -0.4$). Effective auditory IT tasks have been developed where two briefly presented tones differ in pitch (Deary, Head & Egan, 1989), loudness (Olsson, Bjorkman, Haag & Juslin, 1998) or phase, which determines whether tones of the same pitch and loudness presented through headphones appear to come from the left or right of centre (Parker, Crawford & Stephen, 1999). In each case, IT is defined as the duration necessary for the two stimuli to be reliably discriminated. As with the visual IT task, the three auditory tasks intercorrelated substantially, and also correlated −0.5 with g (McCrory & Cooper, 2005).

The whole point of IT studies is that they supposedly measure a very simple aspect of individual differences—the amount of time needed to interpret a very simple pattern that is projected on the retina, or that reaches the ear. The task is trivially easy if presented for long durations. For example, two lines differ *greatly* in length; two tones differ *greatly* in pitch. The key thing about the task is that it is thought to measure how much time is taken to correctly perceive which of several stimuli is being shown: it measures rate of information gathering. The tasks have deliberately been designed to be as simple as possible so that no meta-components (strategies) should be able to influence performance on this task. If it is found that it is possible to devise strategies to improve performance, then IT loses its theoretical appeal as an experimental measure of how long a person's nervous system takes to process a standard stimulus: the task becomes of less interest.

It has been claimed that scores on an IT task *can* be influenced by perceptual strategies, such as looking for flicker at the ends of the legs (Alexander & Mackenzie, 1992): the correlations between IT and g might thus arise because individuals with high g notice certain cues that make the task easier. However, this strategy cannot explain the correlation between IT and ability (Chaiken & Young, 1993; Egan, 1994) as there is a relationship between IT and g for both cue-users and non-cue-users. The outer parts of the retina are more sensitive to flicker than the central fovea, and so the 'flickering light' measure of IT becomes easier if individuals take advantage of this and look at the flickering lights out of the corner of their eyes. Or perhaps low-ability individuals will be less likely to concentrate hard throughout a gruelling bout of testing: a high error-rate will be interpreted as a slow IT. Perhaps practice is important: this could present problems if some of the high-ability participants (typically psychology students) are more used to taking part in cognitive experiments than are others. Strategies also seem unable to explain why auditory IT tasks show such substantial correlations with g (McCrory & Cooper, 2005). There is not space to discuss such issues in detail, and in any case Brody (1992) gives a good account of these problems, whilst White's (1996), Levy's (1992) and Burns and Nettelbeck's (2003) articles contain still-relevant discussions of how the IT paradigm fits in to theories of cognitive psychology and psychophysics. Ian Deary's reviews are also useful (Deary, 1997; Deary & Stough, 1996).

So is the correlation between IT

- Well-established fact?
- Likely to be due to some fairly basic neural processes?
- Large enough to be important?

The first point is not really in dispute: a wide range of inspection-time paradigms have been correlated with scores on many different ability tests in many different samples (ranging from young children to elderly people) worldwide, with a surprising unanimity of results: there really does seem to be a consistent correlation of about −0.5 between IT and general ability.

The heritability of IT is 0.45 (Edmonds et al., 2008), and multivariate genetic analysis shows that a substantial part of the correlation between IT and intelligence comes about because some genes influence performance on both tasks (a multivariate genetic correlation of 0.48 was found by Edmonds et al., 2008). Once again, the multivariate genetic analysis tells us that *some* feature(s) of the nervous system are shaped by our genetic makeup, and these genetic variations influence both performance on IT tasks and performance on cognitive ability tasks (even when the ability tasks are untimed). But identifying these characteristics experimentally is best described as challenging.

Do the same neural processes that are measured in the inspection-time task actually *cause* individual differences in ability, are they consequences of such individual differences, or are both influenced by some other variables? To answer this, Deary (1995) measured IT and general ability on two occasions, 2 years apart, in a sample of schoolchildren. His analysis allowed him to test whether the children's ability levels at age 11 determined their IT performance at age 13, whether their IT at age 11 determined their levels of ability at age 13, or whether the relationship was not causal. The second model fitted the data best, suggesting that whatever causes individual differences in IT at age 11 is likely to *cause* individual differences in general ability later on.

Finally, are the correlations between IT and ability large enough to bother about? Howe (1997) writes: "The correlations are found to be relatively low, typically around + .3 to + .4 or less,[1] which means that they 'account for' up to about 15 per cent of the variability in people's scores". It is clear that he does not regard such correlations (which are lower than the generally agreed estimates mentioned above) as particularly substantial. However, when one considers all the other variables that might influence general ability, finding one simple task that seems able to explain about 15% (Howe's figure) to 30% (Kranzler & Jensen, 1989) of the variation certainly seems to be a useful step forward. Statistical rules of thumb have, in any case, been developed to assess the 'effect size'. Here a population correlation of 0.5 is conventionally regarded as a 'large effect' and one of 0.3 a 'medium effect' (Cohen, 1988). Howe's assertion that correlations between inspection time and general ability are relatively low is thus surprising.

Reaction Time and g

If there are individual differences in the speed with which people's neurones process information, how else might this show itself? The IT task discussed above focused on the amount of time it took to perceive a stimulus. It should also be possible to measure the amount of time taken to respond to a stimulus—a measure known as reaction time. In the simplest possible reaction time task, a person may be given a button to hold, and asked to wait for some event (e.g., a light being turned on): when this happens, the person presses the button as quickly as possible. The delay between the onset of the light and the start of the response is known as the 'simple reaction time'. In a typical experiment, an individual's reaction time would be measured 50 or more times, and then averaged. It is also possible to calculate the variability of each person's reaction times, which shows how consistent the person's reaction times are.

The data from reaction times tends to be rather skewed. Figure 6.2 shows some typical data from two people. Few if any of the responses are faster than 0.15 seconds; you will notice that the second person has generally longer reaction times than the first (the graph is moved along to the right) and also shows a larger spread of scores (higher standard deviation): the range of reaction times is wider.

It is also possible to devise more complicated tasks. A choice reaction time apparatus used by Arthur Jensen is shown diagramatically in Figure 6.3. Eight electric push buttons have lights mounted on their tops, rather like those found on gaming machines. These are arranged equidistant from a ninth button, the 'home button', as shown in Figure 6.2. All eight lights are switched off, and participants are invited to hold down the home button with the index finger of their preferred hand. After a variable-length pause (typically 1 to 3 seconds) one of the eight buttons is illuminated; the participant is asked

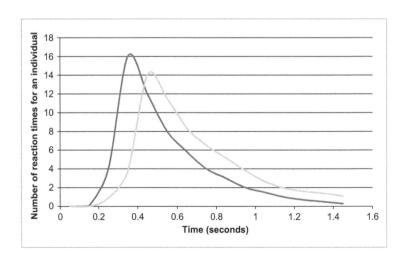

Figure 6.2 Distributions of reaction times from two people

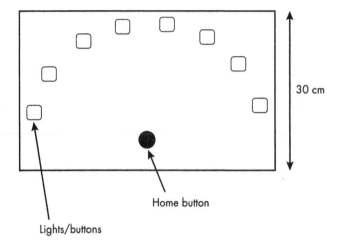

30 cm

Home button

Lights/buttons

Figure 6.3 Jensen's choice reaction time apparatus

to lift the finger from the home button and press the illuminated button as quickly as possible. Two measures are calculated from this experiment:

- The time that elapses between the button being illuminated and the participant lifting the finger from the home button ('reaction time' or RT).
- The time that elapses between lifting the finger from the home button and pressing the illuminated button ('movement time' or MT).

As before, this procedure is performed many times, and the individual's mean reaction time, mean movement time (and their variabilities) are calculated—normally after 'cleaning up' the data a little to ignore any trials where the RT or MT was very long or very short, suggesting a lapse of attention or lifting the finger then deciding where to move it.

The procedure is then repeated using the same participant after masking off some of the lights using metal plates, so that only one, two or four (usually adjacent) lights are visible. It is well known that people's reaction time becomes longer as the number of lights to be scanned increases—a phenomenon known as Hick's Law, which was studied extensively by cognitive psychologists in the 1960s. So if the participant's average reaction times are plotted against the number of lights, a graph similar to that shown in Figure 6.4 will be obtained, where a line is drawn through the various mean reaction times.

This graph shows two important things. The height of the line shows how slowly the person responded overall: if a second person took 0.05 seconds longer (on average) than the first to respond in each condition, then that

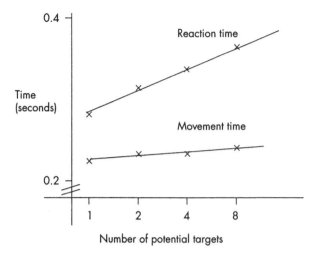

Figure 6.4 One individual's reaction time and movement time as a function of targets in a choice reaction time

person's line would be parallel to that shown in Figure 6.4, but somewhat higher. The slope of the line indicates the extent to which the reaction time slows down as the number of potential targets increases. The experiment would be repeated using other participants, whose level of general ability would also be assessed.

Both the height of the line and its slope should be related to general ability. The reaction time task is likely to involve two stages. The first involves scanning the lights, noticing which has come on, and deciding which way the finger should move. The second step involves actually initiating the movement.

We know from cognitive psychology that increasing the number of targets leads to longer reaction times. This implies that more cognitive processing (of some kind) is involved when carrying out a four-choice reaction time task than when carrying out a two- or one-choice task. Imagine that two people, Maud and Claude, sat the reaction time task described above. Suppose too that Claude's nervous system takes twice as long to process information as Maud's. We would expect their lines to be of different heights, as Claude takes longer to initiate the response than does Maud. We would also expect the lines to differ in slope if Claude takes twice as long (rather than a fixed amount longer) to scan the various lights, notice that one has lit up, and decide which way the finger should move. Claude's line will slope more steeply than Maud's, as shown in Figure 6.5. So we might expect both the height of the line (its 'intercept') and its slope to have a negative correlation with general ability.

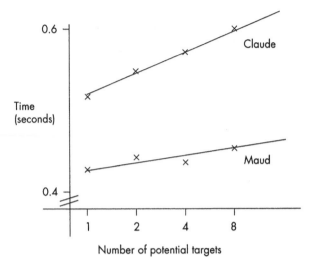

Figure 6.5 Hypothetical reaction times of two individuals differing in neural processing speed

Several such studies have been performed, the findings being summarised by Sheppard and Vernon (2008) and Jensen (2006). The results show that more intelligent people generally do have rather faster reaction times, but although correlations between g and the height of the Hick's Law line are usually statistically significant, they are not always large (about −0.2 for simple reaction time [one button, one light], rising to about −0.4 for the eight-light task). There is little convincing evidence that the slope of the Hick's Law line relates to reaction time at all (Barrett, Eysenck & Lucking, 1986; Beauducel & Brocke, 1993).

One of the problems with reaction time studies is that they confuse speed with consistency of performance. Rapid mean reaction times can be obtained only when individuals (a) respond quickly and (b) respond *consistently* fast. If participants in the reaction time experiment sometimes daydream or let their attention wander, then this may lead to some very long response times. This will increase the standard deviation of the individual's reaction times, and may also increase the mean reaction time appreciably. Thus, it is unsurprising to find that the standard deviation of people's response times is also related to g. It has been found that people with learning difficulties show distributions of reaction times that show a far longer "tail" of long responses, and where the modal reaction time is also rather longer than for students (Baumeister & Kellas, 1968).

A second problem with some studies is that some tests that are used to measure g are themselves speeded: that is, they have time limits. This means that only people who work quickly will achieve high scores on the ability test. It should be unsurprising that people who perform quickly when solving one type of problem (in the ability test) also perform quickly when performing another type of problem (e.g., the Odd Man Out task described below) that produces reaction time measures. Studies reporting links between reaction time and cognitive ability are far more interesting and potentially important when untimed tests are used.

Jensen (e.g., 2006) makes much of the need to distinguish reaction time (which is long, and correlates with g) from movement time (which shows little correlation with g) by using the apparatus shown in Figure 6.2. This equipment requires substantial hand/arm movements (in the order of 10 cm) to make a response, and so it obviously makes sense to eliminate movement time as Jensen suggests, But when measuring one- or two-choice reaction times, it is more usual to ask participants to hold a response button in their hand and press it with their thumb: the button has a very small amount of travel, and so movement time is minimised.

Other tasks may also be used to measure reaction time: the 'odd man out' paradigm (Frearson & Eysenck, 1986) uses Jensen's apparatus (Figure 6.2), but instead of just one light being illuminated, three come on together. Two of these are close to each other and another is further away. The participant is asked to push the illuminated button that is furthest from the other two. Reaction times from this task correlate about -0.48 to -0.62 with general ability (Frearson, Barrett & Eysenck, 1988; Frearson & Eysenck, 1986)—somewhat higher than Jensen's measures. And when several different measures of reaction time are used to predict general ability (using a technique known as multiple regression), the reaction time measures can explain between 10% and 50% of the variation in g within the samples of people tested (Vernon, 1990). It seems that the more complex that a reaction time task is, the better it correlates with g. This is important in the context of working memory research (see below).

As with inspection time, it is necessary to consider whether the correlation between general ability and reaction times is

- well established,
- likely to be caused by basic neural processes,
- large enough to be interesting.

The correlation between reaction time and g has been found often enough in the literature to make it a "safe" phenomenon, albeit not the largest one known to humankind. Jensen (1993b) talks about and tries to explain the -0.35 barrier, since it is rather difficult to find reaction time measures that correlate better than this with measures of g.

The second issue is more vexed: that is, whether reaction times really do measure simple speed-of-processing. For there have been some methodological criticisms of Jensen's work (Longstreth, 1984, 1986). For example:

- Jensen began by measuring RTs to one light, then two, four and eight of them, rather than varying the order in which the conditions were administered, and when Widaman and Carlson (1989) gave the eight-light trials first and then worked their way down to the one-light trials, they found a *positive* correlation between slope and g! However, this criticism cannot apply to the simple (one-choice) reaction time data, which still shows a correlation of about -0.19 with g (Jensen, 1987).

- Detterman and Daniel (1989) and Rabbitt (1985) argue that the reaction time task is far from being a simple measure of processing speed, but may instead involve a number of cognitive strategies—for example, in deciding which error rate is acceptable when performing the task. Some individuals may respond very rapidly but may often push the wrong button; others may respond slowly but make no errors. Perhaps high-g individuals respond rapidly but make many errors? However, this is not the case: high-g individuals make *fewer* errors than others (Jensen, 1987). In any case, diffusion models (described below) now allow us to separate the speed with which a person acquires or processes information from their chosen error rate.

- The Jensen task is quite gruelling, and participants need to concentrate hard throughout in order to achieve fast average reaction times, or RTs that show a small standard deviation. High-ability individuals may be better able to concentrate, and perhaps this is the real reason why some people tend to perform rather well on both tests. Larson and Alderton (1990) found evidence supporting this idea in cognitively complex cognitive tasks. Each person's reaction times were ranked, from shortest to longest. It was found that the length of each person's five longest reaction times correlated better with g ($r = -0.37$) than did their five shortest reaction times ($r = -0.20$), which might perhaps indicate that individual differences in focusing attention on the task may be important although Jensen (2006) argues that attention is too vague a term to merit much consideration.

- It is found that the response that is made following an error in a reaction time task is rather slower than normal and that participants who have very low scores on ability tests tend to slow down much more than others following a mistake on a reaction time task (Brewer & Smith, 1984). So perhaps this strategy explains the differences in mean scores? Brody (1992) argues that it cannot.

There seems to be a very real possibility that individual differences noted in the reaction time tasks may correlate with g because individuals high on general ability are more able than others to perform at a consistent level of performance. Although measures of reaction time do consistently show correlations with g, such correlations are both fairly modest in size, and may well reflect individual differences in attention rather than pure mental speed.

Finally, is the link between RT and g large enough to be interesting? Perhaps—but the relationships are generally rather small, and individual differences in strategy-use and attention may well complicate matters. More researchers now focus on inspection time, where the correlations are larger and the confounding variables fewer.

What are the practical implications of individual differences in reaction time? Once again, if a task requires someone to choose quickly and consistently between several different responses, high g is likely to facilitate performance of this task. So there may well be a correlation between g and scores on arcade games of the "shoot'em-up" variety, or perhaps driving or piloting aircraft. Whether this is due to the direct influence of g or the effect of concentration is another matter.

Reaction Times from More Complex Tasks

Several researchers have studied how individual differences in the performance of more complex cognitive tasks relate to g. Sometimes these tasks have been chosen so that there is a strong theoretical rationale for using them: sometimes tasks appear to have been chosen just because cognitive psychologists have studied them previously!

The obvious problem in using complex tasks is that such tasks will (by definition) involve several different cognitive processes to be executed. Suppose that someone is just shown two words on a screen (e.g., 'spoke' and 'said') and is asked to press a button in their right hand if they can mean the same thing, or a button in their left hand if they cannot mean the same thing. Even this apparently trivial task is quite complex. The words on a screen must be recognised, the meanings of the words must be recalled from memory, each meaning of the first word must be compared with each meaning of the second word, some decision is made about which response is appropriate, and then the physical movement of the thumb is made. Some of these operations (e.g., recalling every meaning of a word) might be performed in sequence, where one meaning of a word is recovered, followed by a second meaning etc. Or perhaps several meanings can be retrieved at the same time (parallel processing). Perhaps the meanings can all be compared in parallel too. Or perhaps some people perform some operations sequentially whilst others can perform them in parallel! Add to this, the problems of priming (a bicycle fanatic may retrieve the "wrong" meaning of 'spoke' first, whereas the rest of us may not), the willingness of some people to make a fast but incorrect response, whereas others may choose to be slow but 100% accurate, and you can see that even if people *do* differ in their overall reaction time on this task, it is not obvious why this is. It could be attributable to faster speed of lexical access. Or the ability to perform some operations in parallel. Or a strategy of responding based on minimal evidence (perhaps just the first meaning is examined) rather than an exhaustive analysis. Or a faster nervous system that speeds all cognitive operations. Or a memory store that can hold many different meanings of two words at the same time: the possibilities are almost endless.

There is also something of a logical error in correlating measures of *g* with performance on these tests. Tests measuring *g* themselves involve a huge number of different cognitive processes—visualisation, short and long-term memory, semantic processing etc. Thus *g* is really a measure of how well a person can perform cognitive operations in general. If the reaction time tasks are themselves are quite complex in terms of the cognitive operations that are involved, then it is unsurprising that they correlate substantially with tests measuring *g*: the more cognitively complex a reaction time task becomes, the closer it resembles an item in an ability test. There is a lot to be said for focusing on the simple reaction time tasks discussed above.

Cognitive Correlates and Cognitive Components

A number of tasks have been developed to measure processes thought to be of theoretical importance in cognitive psychology. Classic examples include the S. Sternberg (1969) memory scanning paradigm, or the Clark and Chase (1972) sentence verification task. Individual differences in performance on these tasks can be correlated with scores on ability tests, which is known as the cognitive correlates approach. Alternatively, performance on many cognitive tasks can be factor analysed, and scores on the factors may be correlated—the cognitive components approach Carroll (1980, 1983).

Earl Hunt was interested in individual differences in verbal ability, and how these related to memory process. He believed that speed of lexical access may be the key to understanding these individual differences. Perhaps some individuals are better able than others to retrieve the meanings of letters from memory. So Hunt (1978) asked participants to each perform two experiments. In one, they were shown pairs of letters and were asked to decide whether the two letters in each pair were physically identical (aa; BB) rather than different (ab; Aa) by pressing one button if a pair was identical, and another button if they were physically different. Their reaction times were recorded.

The same participants then took part in a second experiment that involved exactly the same pairs of letters. However, they were now asked to press one button if the letter pairs referred to the same letter of the alphabet (Aa; bB) or not (Ab; bA). The mean time that it took participants to recognise that a pair of letters was physically identical was then subtracted from the average time that it took them to recognise that the two letters referred to the same letter of the alphabet. This was thought to reflect the amount of time that it took to retrieve the meaning of the letter from memory—the speed of lexical access. So does speed of lexical access predict verbal ability? Unfortunately, although statistically significant, the link is not as strong as Hunt had expected; it has consistently been found that the correlation is in the order of −0.3 (Hunt, 1978). Thus, although speed of lexical access does seem to be an important component of verbal ability, other cognitive processes must also be involved. Carroll (1993) briefly summarises some other tasks that have been used to measure other mental processes. Here, too, correlations above 0.3 with abilities are rarely found.

Diffusion Models

I argued above that more sophisticated analyses of responses to fairly simple tasks may tell us more about the relationship between g and mental speed than will simple analyses of responses to complex tasks, because these complex tasks resemble the items in the tests used to measure g. In addition, the reaction time analyses discussed above are unrealistic because they focus on correct responses only: it seems plausible that some people will make mistakes when performing anything but the simplest cognitive task. Suppose that we gave someone two response buttons, and trained them to press the left button when a red square is shown on a screen and the right hand button when a yellow square is shown. Some people may respond slowly but with great accuracy, whilst others may make many mistakes. Some people may show a bias toward making a particular response: they may be more likely to respond correctly to the red square than the yellow square, for example. Some people may perform consistently, whilst others may show considerable variability in their reaction time. Traditional analyses cannot take any of this into account.

Diffusion models are mathematical models that have been developed to overcome these problems. They recognise that those parts of our nervous systems that make the decision how and when to respond to the stimulus must do so by gathering information from lower-level units/networks, and continue doing so until a decision can be made as to how to respond. The information coming from these lower-level units is thought to be "noisy", a term that will be discussed below.

An example may help—one where we gather information over days or possibly years rather than fractions of a second. Suppose that you are single and want to find a boyfriend or girlfriend. You will weigh-up people you meet, and for each person, you will eventually make a decision that either they are worth dating, or that they are not your type. This can be shown diagrammatically (see Figure 6.6).

The x-axis represents time, and the y-axis your opinion of a person. The point where the x-axis crosses the y-axis is the time that you first met each person. After a period, you start trying to evaluate each person's merits as a possible partner. The wiggly lines shows how you view each of three potential partners over time. You gather evidence on each person until he or she either meets the criterion for dating (top horizontal line) or not dating (bottom horizontal line).

The person represented by the light-grey line appears attractive for a very brief moment, then the negative evidence builds up—slowly at first and then faster. Thus you rather quickly have enough evidence to decide that

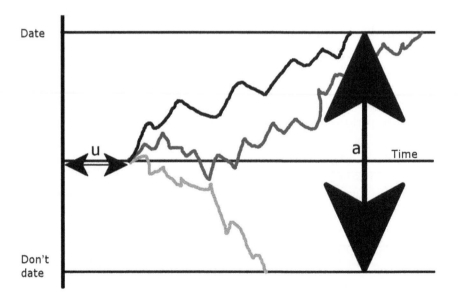

Figure 6.6 Diffusion model applied to dating

you definitely do not want to date them. (The light-grey line hits the bottom horizontal line after a fairly short time.) The person represented by the black wiggly line shows a fairly consistent upward trend—though with a few minor setbacks on the way, and you decide to date him/her. The person represented by the medium-grey line seems attractive at first, then you have a burst of negative evidence after which the positive evidence builds up steadily, and you decide to date him/her too. Oops.

The diagram suggests that people who are weighing up others as potential partners will vary in three ways. First of all, they will vary in how long they have known a person before they begin to even think about their potential as a girlfriend or boyfriend. This is time **u** on the diagram. Next, people will differ in the width between the top and bottom horizontal lines. Some people may want to gather an enormous amount of information and will only conclude that someone is or is not worth dating after they have amassed a lot of evidence: in other words, the distance **a** will be very large. Other people may arrive at a decision based on rather little evidence. Their value of **a** will be small. The **a** parameter is known as 'boundary separation'. Finally, the slope of the wiggly lines indicates how much information the person gathers in a particular amount of time. This parameter is known as the **drift rate**. Individuals who are skilled at evaluating potential partners are likely to gather a lot of information quickly. Their lines will slope sharply up or down, which means they will have a large drift rate. Those of us who are less skilled will show lines with much shallower slopes. They will take longer to reach a decision, assuming that boundary separation remains unchanged.

The key point is that if we know how long a person takes to decide whether or not to date potential partners, it is possible to estimate the person's **u, a** and drift rate parameters by means of some rather complicated mathematics, the detail of which need not concern us. These analyses are performed on individuals, not on groups of people. Thus we obtain values of **u, a** and drift rate for each person, and these can be correlated with any other information we may have about them.

You may have thought that you can also measure other things from Figure 6.6. For example, some people may be desperately keen to find a partner, and so they may require less evidence to decide to date someone than they would to reject them. In other words, the wiggly lines would start above the mid-point showing bias toward the decision to date. Or you could measure the variation in each person's drift rates, as well as their average drift rate. And so on. All these (and more) have been considered in the literature: a seven-parameter model has been developed (Vandekerckhove & Tuerlinckx, 2007) although the three-parameter 'EZ-diffusion model' developed by Wagenmakers, van der Maas and Grasman (2007) and discussed above is the most widely used—not least because estimating all seven parameters requires huge amounts of data from each person.

How can all this relate to intelligence and cognition? Instead of measuring decision time about partners in weeks or months, our nervous systems weigh up outputs from the sensory pathways and cognitive modules in fractions of a second. We can hypothesise that when asked to make a two-choice decision (e.g., "is 'floop' a real word?") a person will go through a process rather like that shown above. We can measure how long it takes them to react to a series of problems like this, and make the assumption that **u** represents the amount of time for the stimulus to be perceived (read) before any cognitive processing can take place, that each person sets their criterion **a** for determining how much evidence they need before responding, and that the drift rate too will vary each person—although there will be random variation for each item (the rate of uptake of information is represented by a wiggly line rather than a straight line).

It is possible just to measure reaction times from a task such as this, and estimate the drift rate, **a** and **u** parameters for each person. However in reaction time tasks, one must also consider that the amount of time taken to physically push the button once the decision has been made as to which button to push. It is not possible to separate this from **u**, and so the sum of these two is measured instead. One might expect that drift rate will be related to intelligence, as people with faster, more efficient nervous systems should be able to process information faster. And it is less obvious whether intelligence will relate to the **a** parameter—which determines how much evidence the person needs to amass before making a response.

Evidence shows that drift rate correlated 0.79 with a measure of g (Schmiedek, Oberauer, Wilhelm, Suss & Wittmann, 2007), and **a** (the distance between the boundaries) correlated −0.48 with g. That is, intelligent people gather more information in a given amount of time than less intelligent people, and also made the decision on the basis of less evidence.

It is also possible to show that the diffusion model can explain many of the other correlations between g and cognitive/perceptual variables—for example its correlation with inspection time, and the finding that the slowest reaction times are better predictors of g than the fastest ones (van Ravenzwaaij, Brown & Wagenmakers, 2011): this paper is well worth scrutinising. Research using diffusion models is in its infancy, but it looks as if these rather complex models might be a valuable tool for analysing reaction time and other data related to g.

At Belfast, Wilson and Cooper (in preparation) used the EZ-diffusion model parameters to investigate the relationship between inhibitory control and intelligence. Inhibitory control is a general term used to describe how well a person can identify a correct answer in the midst of distracters. We showed people the names of colours (e.g., the word RED) written in different colours of ink. The task was to identify the colour of ink, whilst trying to ignore the meaning of the word. In some trials, the colour of the word was the same as the colour of the ink ("congruent condition"): in others they were different ("incongruent condition").

Many old studies have examined the differences between mean RT and accuracy across the incongruent and congruent conditions. These "traditional" difference measures did not correlate significantly with g, suggesting inhibitory control is not related to intelligence (Hendrickson, 1982a). However, when the EZ diffusion model parameter changes across the two conditions were correlated with IQ, they showed a substantial correlation between the change in boundary separation parameter and performance IQ ($r = .58$; $n = 68$; $p < .0005$). The boundary separation parameter represents response caution and thus determines the trade-off between speed and accuracy of responses. This speed/accuracy trade-off is something that cannot be taken into account when mean RT and accuracy are considered separately—a major problem when using timed tasks to investigate individual differences in performance. The results show that high-IQ participants were more cautious when responding to incongruent stimuli, and less cautious in their responses to the easier congruent stimuli. Average-IQ individuals seemed to be equally cautious in both conditions (i.e., no change in the parameter), and low-IQ individuals were associated with a counterproductive strategy; where more caution was exercised in responses to the congruent stimuli. It can be seen that because it can separate the speed of information-gathering from the speed/accuracy trade-off, diffusion models show considerable promise for relating performance on cognitive and perceptual tests to intelligence, and preliminary results look encouraging.

Working Memory and *g*

There is one area where massive correlations have been found between a cognitive task and g: the area of working memory. Working memory (Baddeley & Hitch, 1974) is supposedly a form of short-term memory where information is stored and processed. Crucially, short term memory is conceptualised as a "central executive" that prioritises tasks and directs attention plus a phonological loop (which ensures that words are not forgotten) and a visio-spatial scratchpad (ditto for shapes); each of these can themselves be broken down into several cognitive components.

Thus it is clear that working memory is nowhere near as simple as (for example) Hunt's "speed of lexical access". Working memory performance depends on the operation of a host of processes and sub-processes. This is evident from the types of task used to measure it. Several of these have been devised: a popular one developed by Daneman and Carpenter (1980) involves people remembering the last word in sentences whilst also remembering the sense of a story told by the sentences. In other words the task is designed to have a heavy processing load (the meaning of the words) and memory load (the last words of the sentences) and the central executive presumably has to work hard to ensure that resources are switched between each of these operations.

Performance on working memory tasks correlates very substantially with g. Some researchers have claimed that the two concepts were virtually identical (Stauffer et al., 1996) although a widely cited meta-analysis suggests that the correlation is closer to 0.48 (Ackerman, Beier, & Boyle, 2005). However Oberauer, Schulze, Wilhelm and Suss (2005) identify several problems with the meta-analysis. Ackerman et al. included several studies that claimed to measure working memory, but which almost certainly did not. This means that the correlation of 0.48 is an under-estimate, as the tasks that were feeble measures of working memory had smaller correlations with g and so pulled down the average correlation. Second, the statistical analysis also looked at the correlation between individual working memory tasks and g, rather than averaging several different working memory tasks in order to obtain a more accurate measure of working memory for each participant. This too will lead to the underestimation of the true correlation. There are other statistical issues, too. Oberauer's work suggests that the true value for the correlation between working memory and g is 0.85: the two concepts are not quite identical, but they show massive overlap (72% of variance). Unfortunately some working memory researchers are keen to claim that they are studying something wonderful and new, and so make surprising comments about nature of intelligence ("in a typical IQ test, you might have to provide a definition of a word") and claim that working memory task are radically different. However the same researcher uses a scale from published intelligence tests ("backward digit span") claiming that it measures working memory, which rather undermines the logic of their argument (de Lange, 2012)!

I cannot see why cognitive psychologists are so excited about the correlation between working memory and intelligence. We know that working memory relies on a lot of cognitive components (the phonological loop, episodic buffer, articulatory loop and so on [Baddeley, 2000]. Thus a person's performance on a working memory task reflects the sum of scores on a lot of elementary cognitive operations, assuming that they add, rather than just interact. When one adds together the scores on a number of cognitive components, the overall score represents what all of the components measure in common: 'specific variance' from each component (attention-switching, rehearsal strategies and so on) and measurement error will tend to disappear. So if some individuals process information faster than other, performance on rather complex tasks will show a larger correlation with g than will performance on any simple component, because each simple component measures a substantial amount of 'specific variance' (such as ability to switch attention) and random error variance as well as g. We saw this earlier with the work of Frearson and Eysenck (1986) whose cognitively complex odd-man-out reaction time task correlated better with g than did a simple reaction time task.

There is thus excellent reason to suppose that working memory tasks will reflect a person's level of g because both g and working memory rely on combining scores from a number of rather different cognitive tasks/cognitive operations. Another way of looking at the issue is that a correlation of 0.85 between working memory and general intelligence corresponds roughly to a loading of 0.85 on the g factor. Hakstian and Cattell (1978) found that a memory factor loaded 0.51 on the g factor, and so the idea that memory is associated with g is hardly novel.

Which aspects of working memory (attention-switching, storage or both) are responsible for the correlation between working memory and g? This has been addressed by Colom, Abad, Quiroga, Shih and Flores-Mendoza (2008) who studied the relations between multiple tasks measuring speed of processing, short-term memory, working memory and executive functioning plus measures of general ability. They found that (a) short-term memory is rather closely related to working memory, and (b) when one controls statistically for individual differences in short-term memory and executive functioning, the correlation between working memory and intelligence declines. This shows that individual differences in short-term memory and executive functioning are the reason why working memory correlates with g. They concluded that "simple short-term storage drives the relationship between working memory and intelligence".

Physiological Correlates of *g*

If tests measuring general ability, g, reflect some aspects of activity in the nervous system (as suggested by behaviour-genetic studies, and work on inspection time and reaction time considered above) rather than a mere convenient description of the way in which we behave, then we might expect to find some links between scores on tests of g and various physiological measures of brain structures or brain activity.

g and Brain Structure

There used to be a lively debate about whether brain size (or head size) was related to *g*, but since the advent of magnetic resonance imaging scanning techniques the issue has been resolved. There is now good evidence that intelligence is positively correlated with brain size (Pennington et al., 2000; Willerman, Schultz, Neal Rutledge & Bigler, 1991) with McDaniel's (2005) meta-analysis concluding that the correlation is about 0.33. The volumes of the frontal and temporal areas are particularly important (Flashman, Andreasen, Flaum & Swayze, 1997) and changes in cognitive performance (e.g., due to age) are also correlated with changes in brain size (Tisserand & Jolles, 2003). Perhaps the more neurons that a person's brain contains, the more intelligent they are? Salthouse (2011) suggests that it may be facile to assume that there is such a simple causal relationship between brain volume and cognition, and that argues that other variables might mediate this relationship. However the finding that the relationship between brain size and intelligence in healthy adults is almost entirely genetically mediated (Posthuma et al., 2002) is of considerable interest as it provides yet more evidence that *g* has a strong biological basis.

Individuals with larger brains thus tend to have above-average levels of general ability (Rushton & Ankney, 2009) and more specifically the thickness of the cortex is related to *g* (Karama et al., 2011). The outermost layer of the cortex is made up of grey matter—cell bodies that cover a mass of myelin-coated axons known as white matter. Imaging studies show that the amount of grey matter in several areas of the cortex are linked to *g* (Colom et al., 2009), so *g* is not located in one area of the brain. It instead reflects the structure of sizeable areas of the cortex, and the link between brain volume and several abilities seem to come about because the genes that cause parts of the brain to grow larger in some people rather than others also affect levels of several cognitive abilities (Betjemann et al., 2010). Posthuma et al. (2002) also found that the same genes that coded for *g* influenced the volume of grey matter (cell bodies) in the cortex. The overlap was close to 100%. Thus it certainly seems probable that individual differences in the thickness of the grey matter at the top of the cortex (and particularly in the frontal lobes) results in higher levels of intelligence.

g and Brain Function

Scrutinising individual differences in brain structure does not tell us everything we need to know about the link between *g* and physiology. General ability might also be determined by individual differences in the way that systems of neurons are built up and operate. It is possible that high-ability individuals have developed highly efficient neural networks for performing cognitive tasks, whilst others might use larger, perhaps more error-prone or slower networks to achieve the same end. The problem is that it is not yet possible to measure this directly. For example, it could perhaps be the case that individual differences in neural pruning are important for g. This is the process by which nerve connections that are not useful disappear during development. It might perhaps be better for an individual to develop a nervous system containing many synapses that is then pruned hard, rather than develop and keep a system that requires little pruning. There is a literature on these issues (mostly based on computer simulation studies), but it is difficult or impossible to see how it can be directly related to theories of ability.

There are two main approaches to determining how general ability is related to brain function. It is now possible to determine which parts of the brain are active when an individual is performing cognitive tasks. Brain cells metabolise glucose; the more neural activity that takes place at a certain location in the brain, the more glucose is metabolised there. There are several techniques available for assessing how rapidly various parts of the brain are using glucose whilst an individual performs some mental activity. Functional magnetic resonance imaging (fMRI) is the most common. Magnetic resonance imaging (MRI), Computerised Tomography (CT) and Positron Emission Tomography (PET) scanning are older techniques. They show the rate of glucose metabolism at various locations, which are then related to g or other abilities, so it is possible to look for differences in the brain activities of low- and high-ability people.

The second, older, approach to the physiology of abilities rests on the study of how the brain and nervous system generates electrical signals—when resting, or processing information. Researchers use electrodes fixed to the scalp to measure electrical activity in the brain (the electroencephalogram or EEG). Some do so following some sort of stimulation (evoked potential recordings). This literature has a long history: it has been possible to measure brain electrical activity since the 1940s, whereas scanning technology to determine which parts of the brain are active when a person is thinking has only been around since the 1990s.

There are substantial individual differences in the extent to which individuals metabolise (radioactive) glucose whilst solving difficult abstract reasoning tasks, and there are very substantial negative correlations (in the order of -0.7 to -0.8) between the amount of glucose metabolised and g (Haier et al., 1988). People with high levels of general ability seem to have brains that are more efficient, in that they use less glucose when solving problems than do those low in g. This study was based on a sample of only eight participants, but other independent studies have found much the same finding with larger samples (Parks et al., 1988). Further studies have explored the role of practice. Do highly intelligent individuals show a greater drop in neural activity when they learn to perform a complex task? In other words, do they learn faster? Haier et al. (1992) carried out PET scans twice (4 weeks apart) on a sample of individuals who were learning to play a computer game. Sure enough, the participants with highest levels of general ability showed the greatest decline in glucose metabolism (e.g., greatest efficiency). The effects are most noticeable for tasks that are not very difficult and where the frontal lobes are monitored (Neubauer & Fink, 2009): where the task is difficult, there can be a positive correlation between glucose metabolism and g (Larson, Haier, Lacasse & Hazen, 1995).

The frontal lobes of the brain are particularly active when people complete intelligence tests (Duncan et al., 2000) and the precise areas that are involved in various types of reasoning are being explored in more detail (e.g., Krawczyk, McClelland & Donovan, 2011). A new technique called diffusion tensor magnetic resonance imaging now allows researchers to measure the efficiency with which information is transferred along nerves— white matter—from one area of the brain to another, in live humans. It seems that white matter tract integrity (the measure of how efficiently information moves) is broadly similar in all areas of an individual's brain, and individual differences in this physiological measure correlate approximately 0.3 with g (Penke et al., 2012). The four hundred participants in this study were given reaction time and inspection time tasks, as well as the MRI scan and intelligence test, and it was found that the correlation between neural tract integrity and g was entirely mediated by processing speed, as measured by the inspection time and reaction time tasks.

It is hard to overstate the importance of this work, which shows that processing speed is indeed the reason why g correlates with a physiological measure of brain function. This is a very new field, but one which is likely to develop considerably—perhaps using multivariate genetic techniques to determine whether the genes that influence g are the same as the genes that determine white matter tract integrity. However the early signs are that the simple theories linking g to efficiency and speed of neuronal transmission do receive some support at the physiological level.

The Electroencephalogram (EEG) and g

These techniques were used before scanning technology was developed, and now seems to be little used. As Deary and Carryl (1993) observe, "the enterprise was begun on little more than the premise that, since IQ tests and

EEG traces both have something to do with g and brain functioning, then aspects of the latter might correlate with the former." Attempts to discover which (if any) of the various aspects of the EEG are linked to general ability continue apace, with some important but complex theories emerging—for example, the work of Hendrickson (1982a), Robinson (1996) and Weiss (1986, 1989).

Measuring the EEG involves attaching a dozen or two electrodes to a set of standard locations on the scalp. These electrodes pick up electrical activity from various parts of the brain, and each is connected to a highly sensitive amplifier, and thence to a computer to allow the electrical activity to be recorded and analysed. It is found that the level of electrical activity at a particular electrode often rises and falls in a regular manner over time. For example, it may be found that the voltage "peaks" every 0.1 second or so. It is possible to analyse the pattern of electrical activity from an electrode, and work out how long there is between each peak—the frequency of the EEG. One of the most important types of brain activity is alpha activity. This corresponds to large swings in electrical activity that peak between 8 and 13 times every second (8–13 Hz) and is found when the person being tested is relaxed and awake.

So are individual differences in the EEG related to abilities? EEGs have been recorded from participants when doing nothing or performing some mental activity (e.g., solving multiplication problems). Various investigators have focused on different electrodes, and scrutinised different bands of EEG frequencies (some would look at activity in the whole alpha range of 8–13 Hz, whilst others focus on much narrower ranges of frequencies).

There is one good reason for not expecting any statistics derived from the EEG to correlate substantially with g: it has been found that the same individual can produce rather different results when tested on a different occasion and/or in a different setting (O'Gorman & Lloyd, 1985). This will result in low or inconsistent correlations between EEG measures and anything else. Giannitrapani (1985) measured 100 children's EEG whilst performing various tasks, and at rest. He found that the extent to which the children showed electrical activity of exactly 13 cycles per second correlated substantially ($r > 0.4$) and significantly with general ability. Other adjacent frequencies (e.g., 11 Hz) showed no such relationships: more recent studies also show that rather narrow bands of frequencies can be associated with g (Thatcher et al., 2005).

Older studies have focused on the broader ranges of frequencies in the alpha band. Children and adults who show most alpha activity tend to perform better at tests of general ability (e.g., Doppelmayr et al., 2002; Gasser, Von Lucadou-Müller, Verleger & Bächer, 1983; Giannitrapani, 1969; Mundy-Castle, 1958). These correlations can be quite substantial (in the order of

0.4 to 0.5) and some of these also found correlations between other frequency bands and general ability. As Deary and Caryl (1993) note, substantial correlations such as this "allow us to dismiss as uninformed authors such as Howe (1988a, 1988b) who have questioned whether *any* biological measures can be found which correlate with *g* once studies involving retarded subjects have been excluded."

It does indeed seem that general ability may be related in some way to brain electrical activity. Given that problem solving presumably involves some parts of the brain, and that neural transmission results in electrical activity it would be amazing if this were not the case. However as a psychologist, it is hard to know what to make of these findings, as it is difficult to be sure what they imply in terms of the mental processes that are involved in intelligence. It is not always obvious to me how complex theories of what the EEG traces might imply about the activities of the brain can be disproved.

Average Evoked Potentials (AEPs) and *g*

Evoked potential recordings examine the pattern of electrical activity at just one site of the brain following some form of sensory stimulation. This is often a tone or click presented via headphones or a flash of light, and the experiment is usually repeated 100 or so times and the results averaged (hence 'average evoked potential'). In essence, this approach examines how long it takes the individual's brain to react to the auditory stimuli. When the AEPs of a number of people are examined, the graphs generally have a similar shape. Immediately after presenting the tone, nothing happens for a few tenths of a second, and then a pattern of peaks and troughs emerges.

The various peaks and troughs have been given names, such as P-300 (P means that it is a positive voltage, 300 means that it occurs 300 milliseconds after the stimulus). So it is easy to measure how long after the stimulus is presented each of these parts of the waveform is found. Individual differences in the amount of time between the stimulus being presented and one of the characteristics of the AEP appearing can be measured, and correlated with the participants' levels of general ability. Several of the studies reviewed by Deary and Carryl (1993) and Stelmack and Houlihan (1995) report a negative correlation between general ability and the amount of time that elapses before various features of the AEP waveform are seen: that is, high levels of general ability are associated with rapid processing of information (e.g., Ertl & Schafer, 1969) that may be support for the "mental speed" hypothesis. However, there are also several studies that fail to find such relationships (Barrett & Eysenck, 1992; Rust, 1975) and some that find positive correlations! Most of the findings are non-significant, however, and so it is probably safe to conclude that individual differences in the time that it takes various parts of the AEP waveform to appear owe little to general ability. Likewise, whilst some researchers find that the *height* of the AEP waveform is positively correlated with general ability (Haier, Robinson, Braden & Williams, 1983), once again there are several notable failures to replicate this effect (Barrett & Eysenck, 1992; Rust, 1975). It also used to be thought that the 'spikiness' of the AEP was also related to g (Hendrickson, 1982a, 1982b) but this effect has proved difficult to replicate (Barrett & Eysenck, 1992)

Summary

The surprising thing about this chapter is how many different variables show sometimes-substantial correlations with g. Inspection time tasks, for example, do not involve any reasoning nor do they require any knowledge or speedy responding. Yet despite being very different from the tasks used to assess g, a wide range of different inspection time tasks all show similar substantial correlations with it. I find this much more exciting than the discovery that working memory tasks (which sometimes closely resemble tasks that are used to measure g) correlate with g. How could it be otherwise?

Even simple reaction time tasks can show very substantial correlations with g once the data are analysed properly using diffusion models. The simple idea that g reflects the speed with which the brain processes information receives substantial support from inspection time, reflex latency, reaction time and (some) EEG studies, although experiments relating direct measures of neural conduction velocity in the limbs to g have produced inconsistent results. However there is a considerable body of evidence suggesting that neural speed does influence g.

There is some suggestion that the speed of performing some elementary cognitive operations (e.g., lexical access) is related to mental abilities. However, the correlations are too small to suggest that the ability factors *just* reflect individual differences in the speed of these operations. Recently developed diffusion models greatly facilitate the analysis of data from reaction time tasks, and there needs to be a resurgence of interest in this area: initial results certainly seem to show that parameter estimates from diffusion models seem to have far more substantial correlations with ability measures than do means and standard deviations of reaction times.

The evidence from the physiological studies shows that several aspects of cortical structure and functioning are related to g: thick, highly convoluted layers of grey matter (particularly in the frontal lobe) seem to be linked to above-average levels of general ability, with the same genes that influence g

also influencing these individual differences in brain structure. But as a psychologist, I find it hard to know what to conclude from such studies: we do not know how all this additional scrunched up grey matter actually helps us to compute better, faster answers to problems.

Note

1   Presumably should read "−0.3 to −0.4".

7

APPLICATIONS

One of the delights of working with human intelligence is how applicable it is to everyday life. As we will see in this chapter, ability tests show surprisingly large correlations with real-life behaviours (such as job performance, or even whoever we select as a partner). Some of these relationships are fairly unsurprising. For example it probably comes as no great shock to learn that scores on ability tests correlate quite substantially with academic achievement and work performance. But there are some areas where the relationships are far less obvious. For example, who would have predicted that intelligence (measured in middle childhood) could predict how long people would live?

Finding correlations between scores on ability tests and real-life behaviours is not at all difficult, but interpreting what these correlations mean can be quite controversial. The problem is that a whole host of social variables tend to be associated with intelligence. Children of above-average intelligence are likely to come from families that are small, and with parents who are better-educated and more affluent. They may also attend better-quality schools. So it is hard to determine whether the reason why children who grow up in such a privileged environment then go on to shine at school or at work is because they are highly intelligent, or whether they excel because of their good fortune in having a supportive childhood environment.

Sociologists view individual differences in educational performance, work performance etc. as a symptom of social inequality. According to this view, the prime reason why some children perform better than others in school and/or go on to well-paid jobs is because of factors such as poverty, living in a crime-ridden neighbourhood, family background, or low expectations of success (e.g., Ensminger & Slusarcick, 1992; Gonzales, Cauce, Friedman & Mason, 1996) rather than anything to do with the child's cognitive capabilities. Indeed, they would not normally consider the possibility that children might possibly differ in cognitive ability. From a psychologist's perspective, this seems to be incomplete: surely anyone should admit that it is possible that a child's biological makeup may also influence his or her performance.

One reason that such researchers do not consider "intelligence" as a possible explanation might simply be ignorance. Those who are trained to explore the relationships between social upbringing and behaviour in society (sociologists, rather than psychologists) may simply be unaware that the correlation between intelligence and school performance is substantial, and might well be causal. A second possibility is that some non-psychologists (following Gould, 1996) view "intelligence" as a social construct: something that would not exist unless society decided to invent it. According to this view, we (as individuals, or as a society) may choose to categorise some people as "intelligent" or "less intelligent", but such categorisations cannot be causal.

On the other hand it is possible that scores on intelligence tests reflect something rather fundamental about the way in which a person's nervous system works. If the relationship is substantial, this means that it may be possible to use scores on intelligence tests as proxies for biological intelligence—"speed of neural processing", "grey matter density" or something similar. If this is the case, then it seems that arguments about the culture-specific nature of intelligence are essentially dismissed. This is why the biological issues discussed in the previous chapters are so important. They may, perhaps, help us to decide whether or not "intelligence" can be regarded as a true causal influence.

It is also possible to address such issues empirically—that is, by gathering and analysing data. Statistical techniques (multiple regression, partial correlation, path analysis, structural equation modelling) can show whether some variable—such as quality of schooling—causes the correlation between intelligence and real-life behaviour to emerge. One can specify several different models (perhaps one where intelligence influences both job performance and school performance, and another where school performance affects both intelligence and job performance) and perform analyses to determine which model fits the data better. But finding good fit is really only the first step of getting a good, scientific, grasp of what is going on. It is also important to gather more data to find out precisely why (for example) attending an excellent school *should* cause children to perform better at an ability test than those who receive a lower-standard education. Precisely what skills are being developed by the school? Might it be the case that admission to the high-quality school is influenced by a child's cognitive performance? If this is so, and only the most intelligent children are admitted, it is hardly surprising if the intelligence scores of those attending this élite school are higher than the norm! Making sense of data from real-life studies usually requires something more than simple correlational analysis.

If scores on intelligence tests are no more than arbitrary social constructions, then one would not expect them to perform consistently over time or across cultures. And in addition, if one controls (statistically) for variables such as social class, educational attainment, self-esteem and all the other variables that sociologists believe are the *true* causes of behaviour, then if scores on ability tests have some residual influence on (say) job performance or health status, then this indicates that intelligence is real rather than just a social construct. Such analyses essentially show whether or not g would be related to job performance (or whatever) if everyone had the same social background, the same level of education, the same amount of experience on the job and so on. Thus when we examine the real-world correlates of scores on ability tests, this can tell us something rather interesting about the fundamental nature of intelligence—as well as potentially providing predictors of performance that can be of use to personnel managers, educators, occupational psychologists and others. So as well as giving useful tools to occupational psychologists, educational psychologists and others, the careful analysis of data linking scores on ability tests to real-life behaviour can say reveal some rather important things about the nature of abilities.

There are two ways of viewing the relationship between performance on psychological tests (such as tests of g) and real-world performance (such as how well a person performs their job, at school, or their level of health). In Figure 7.1 and 7.2, a single-ended arrow implies that there may be a causal relationship in the direction of the arrow: for example, that a child's level of nutrition may potentially affect his or her level of g. The presence of an arrow does not mean that there *has* to be a relationship, or that relationship is large: you know from previous chapters that the influence of socio-economic status (SES) on g is small for older children, for example. Instead the arrow shows that there could potentially be a causal relationship, the size of which can be determined empirically through statistical analyses. A curve, with an arrow each end, indicates that two variables are correlated, but that there is no direct causal link between them.

The first model views general ability, g, as some real characteristic of people—reflecting individual differences in the makeup or function of the nervous system, for example. Genes, the family environment, nutrition and other environmental factors influence a person's level of g, and their level of

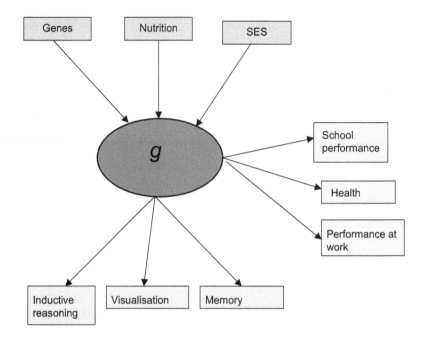

Figure 7.1   Model where genes, nutrition and SES influence g, and g influences both performance on ability tests (inductive reasoning, visualisation, memory etc.) and real-life behaviour (school performance, health, work performance etc.). Lines with arrows indicate causal links.

g might then influence (for example) how well a person performs at school, as well as their performance on other ability tests, via the hierarchical model of abilities discussed in Chapter 3. So according to this model some children perform better than others at school because they are more intelligent. This higher level of intelligence facilitates learning, memory, and so on. The parents' genes, the child's level of nutrition, SES and other environmental factors influence educational attainment via their effect on g. There is no arrow showing a direct influence between nutrition and school performance, for example.

The second model recognises that individual differences in g and other abilities exist—but the only thing that g influences is performance on other ability tests. So really, individual differences in cognitive abilities are completely irrelevant to real-world behaviour. They cannot explain anything, for as you can see from Figure 7.2 as there is no causal link between any cognitive ability and school performance, health or other real-world behaviours.

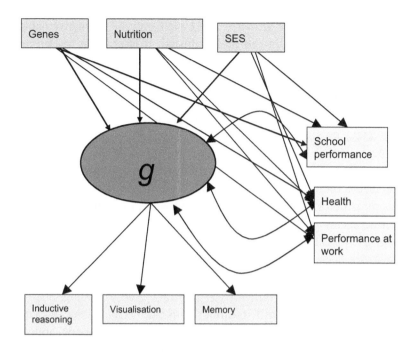

Figure 7.2 Model where genes, nutrition and SES influence real-life behaviour. *g* influences performance on ability tests but does not mediate the relationship between genes (etc.) and real life. (Curves with two arrows represent correlations.)

The cognitive abilities may be correlated with these outcomes (note the curves with an arrow at each end linking cognitive abilities and real-world behaviours) but this may just be because nutrition (for example) may affect both performance on cognitive tests and educational performance: note the arrows linking nutrition, genetic makeup and SES to education, work performance and health in Figure 7.2. But as there are no arrows leading from any cognitive ability to educational performance, health or occupational performance, it would be quite wrong to "explain" behaviour in terms of *g* or any other cognitive ability.

These are just two models: there are plenty of other variations (for example, we know from multivariate genetic analyses that some genes may influence both *g* and school performance). And in adults, *g* could well influence nutrition rather than vice versa, if only intelligent adults recognise the long-term benefits of healthy eating. However my purpose for showing the models is to demonstrate that just because there is a correlation between *g* and (say) school performance, it does not necessarily follow that high *g* is the direct cause of good school performance. There are plenty of alternative explanations that need to be explored and evaluated. It is possible to determine which of these models best fits the empirical data, using techniques known as structural equation modelling: see for example Loehlin (2004). However such analyses are rather technical and are beyond the scope of this book.

There is also one very important practical implication, which seems to confuse many people. If g does indeed influence job performance and so on, as shown in Figure 7.1, then in order to predict how well a job applicant is likely to perform if they are appointed, the sensible option is to choose the best-available measure of g, together with any other relevant information (e.g., a measure of experience of that sort of work, motivation, and perhaps personality factors such as conscientiousness or extraversion). The test used to measure g would simply be one that has a substantial loading on the g factor: it would not necessarily have to resemble what the job involves. According to this logic, it would be quite reasonable to give applicants for pretty much any job an appropriately difficult test having a high g loading, such as a non-verbal analogy test. Or if research shows that second-order or primary mental abilities may be important for a particular job (e.g., spatial ability for a budding architect) then the best-available tests of second-order or primary mental abilities should be used. But according to this logic, there is no need whatsoever for a test that is used to select architects (for example) to involve looking at architectural drawings, or anything else that is job related. Indeed, it is far better that it does *not* resemble anything that applicants may have encountered before, otherwise the score on the test will reflect a mixture of experience and ability. If one believes that experience is important, then it can of course be measured independently of the cognitive abilities—e.g., by a rating-scale derived from inspection of the candidates' employment histories. This is a difficult concept for many applied psychologists to grasp.

g and Education

There is excellent evidence that general intelligence, g, is strongly correlated with how well a child will perform in school, and the number of years of education that they undertake. This probably comes as little surprise. We observed in Chapter 3 that verbal comprehension, vocabulary, arithmetic skills and other abilities that are developed at school form a second-order factor of Crystallised Ability (Gc) that loads on the same g factor as second-order factors that have little or nothing to do with skills that are taught at school, such as memory, fluid ability, visualisation or creativity. The finding that all of these measures form a single g factor suggests that performance at the sorts of tasks that are assessed at school will also correlate with performance at tasks that are not specifically taught at school. The difficult question is whether intelligence influences school performance, whether school performance influences intelligence, or whether some other things (perhaps language skills, or parental behaviour) influence both school achievement and g.

The correlation between g and academic performance is large. A study by Calvin, Fernandes, Smith, Visscher and Deary (2010) used 178,000 children, and related ability scores obtained at age 11–12 to scores on a standardised test of educational attainment ("Key Stage 2"). It includes a thoughtful analysis: for example, the authors consider the possibility of overlap between the ability test content and the attainment scores, and it also considers the behaviour-genetic literature. The correlation between the cognitive test and Key Stage 2 performance was a massive 0.83.

Interpreting what this correlation actually *means* is however quite complex. Perhaps going to school (or being interested in schoolwork) increases intelligence. Or maybe some other variables (perhaps motivation or problems using language) might influence both performance on intelligence tests and performance at school. Or it could simply be the case that the more intelligent children find it easier to learn at school: the abstract thinking and problem-solving skills measured in IQ tests might be useful for helping students to understand and solve complex problems at school, identify what the key issues are, memorise effectively, think logically and so on.

Does Going to School Boost Intelligence?

Two sources of evidence suggest that exposure to school might make children become more intelligent. In such studies, it is obviously important to ensure that the tests that are used to measure intelligence do not contain content relevant to schooling—arithmetic ability, comprehension, vocabulary etc. If they do, it is rather obvious that younger children who have received more schooling will perform better at such tasks, and so may achieve higher intelligence scores. A hint that going to school might improve levels of intelligence came from de Groot (1951). Children in occupied Holland during World War II did not go to school for some years. When followed up later, they showed lower intelligence-test scores than one would expect, although other factors that also affected the children's lives (famine, etc.) might also account for these differences.

Several studies have examined children who are "young for their year" at school. Many countries operate a system where the year that children start school is determined by their birth date: for example, children born between 1st April 2012 and 31st March 2013 will start school in September 2018: a child who is born on 1st April 2013 will not go to school until September 2019. It is possible to compare the intelligence test scores of children who are born at the end of March with those who were born at the start of April. The two groups will be of very similar ages, but the first group will have enjoyed a year's more schooling than the second group. If going to school makes children more intelligent, you might expect the first group to outperform the second. There is a clear need to discover precisely why these increases are found: I know of no studies that have troubled to investigate this. It could be attributable to motivation, with younger members of the class recognising that they are underperforming at schoolwork, and so striving harder—which may also affect performance at ability tests. Perhaps the reason why education has an effect is that children who develop language and number skills a year earlier than their peers are better able to articulate and analyse problems—skills that may be relevant to solving IQ–type problems. It is also appropriate to ask what those children who entered school rather late actually did in the previous year. If most attended kindergarden, why did this experience not provide a similar level of intellectual advantage to school?

Plenty of studies show that an extra year's schooling boosts intelligence. Cahan and Cohen (1989) studied primary (elementary) school children and found that amount of schooling affected intelligence test performance over and above the effect of age, particularly in verbal tests. But there was good evidence from this study that the effects of schooling on IQ are also statistically significant for tests such as Raven's Matrices, which do not rely on language. Going to school a year earlier than your peers does make you a little smarter: a year's education boosts IQ by about a sixth of a standard deviation. The obvious problem with this sort of study is that the differences in the amount of schooling that any two children receive is quite modest (1 year), and it is found in practice that some young children (perhaps those identified as intelligent) enter schooling earlier than they should, whilst some children may re-take the same class a second time. These may both affect the results, and although Cahan and Cohen try to allow for these effects, they complicate the analyses. However it seems that the impact of going to school for a year is roughly twice the size of the impact of aging by one year: a year's schooling boosted performance on the non-verbal matrix task by 0.27 of a standard deviation, whilst merely being older by one year boosted it by just 0.13 of a standard deviation. There are other ways of addressing the issue, and Ceci's (1991) review is still relevant, although it is necessary to ensure that the IQ measures for each study that he discusses are not tainted by skills such as comprehension or vocabulary that are explicitly developed at school.

What no one seems to know is what, precisely, goes on within schools to boost g. It is possible that verbal and numerical skills may matter (helping children to conceptualise complex problems using words or mathematical notation). Perhaps a grasp of scientific principles helps too. But as far as I am aware, no one has studied precisely how schooling improves g, which is a great shame. A related issue is whether there is much variation between schools. Does going to a "good" school lead to a child developing a higher IQ score than if they had gone to a mediocre or poor quality school? One might expect that they should, if schooling provides the skills to allow children to conceptualise problems. Answering this question obviously requires some fairly careful analyses (because the "better" schools may be populated with higher-IQ children in the first place), but Jencks (1972) found that variations between schools have a negligible effect on IQ. So whilst going to school seems to boost IQ, the actual quality of teaching might not matter much. This is surprising, but the literature is sparse and more work needs to be done.

Do children who have received less schooling eventually catch up? One might expect that they should, if schooling boosts IQ because it teaches skills such as logical thinking, representation of problems using mathematics, and vocabulary. Perhaps children who have such skills do better at intelligence tests? If so it seems probable that by adolescence (when all children will have acquired these basic skills) the differences will disappear. Unfortunately, only one published study seems to examine this. Cliffordson and Gustaffson (2008) conclude that the advantage of receiving more education persists until at least age 18. They looked at the results of an Army admission test that was administered several times over the year: participants took this test as soon as they turned 18. Some 18-year-olds would have received slightly more education than others by the time that they were tested: the researchers worked out how many days at school each participant had received since their 18th birthday. Surprisingly, this was reflected in their IQ scores: an extra year of education at age 18 boosted IQ by about a sixth of a standard deviation in their sample. Given that attempts to boost intelligence through early-years intervention projects are ineffective (see Chapter 8) the idea that attending school a little longer than one's peers at age 18 will have a measurable influence on IQ is counter-intuitive, to say the least. This finding needs to be replicated, and once again it is necessary to try to discover what it is about going to school that causes this effect.

Not all the evidence supports the idea that schooling boosts intelligence. In Malawi, it is not unknown for some children to receive hardly any schooling, whilst others receive a considerable amount: the range of environments is far greater than in the Western world. Van de Vijver and Brouwers (2009) found that after the effects of age were controlled, schooling had little or no influence on the Raven's Matrices scores. These authors also reminded us that even in societies where children experience little or no formal education, they still develop skills of complex problem solving.

Do Some Other Variables Affect Both Schooling and Intelligence?

We saw in Chapter 5 that the quality of the childhood family environment—parental encouragement, nutrition, availability of books, crowding etc.—have zero influence on g in late adolescence and adulthood. If they do not influence g, then they cannot possibly moderate the correlation between g and academic performance. So I suggest that the interesting variables that might possibly influence both performance on ability tests and performance at school are likely to be psychological characteristics, rather than characteristics of the parental home.

Other, more direct, evidence for the limited influence of the home environment on educational performance comes from two sources: studies of the behaviour genetics of school performance, such as Haworth, Kovas, et al. (2009), and studies of the influence of social and psychological factors on school attainment analysed using structural equation modelling. As well as looking at learning disability, Haworth et al. report the effects of the common (shared) environment on school performance. They found that in a large sample of 12-year-olds, the influence of the shared environment on mathematics, language and reading ranged from 0.14 to 0.22. It is hard to see how such small influences can lead to correlations of 0.6–0.8 emerging between tests of g and school performance. The evidence from structural equation modelling will be discussed in more detail when considering the relationship between g and performance at work. However, the work of Duncan, Featherman and Duncan (1972) shows that the child's intelligence has a substantial causal influence on their academic performance (0.43), whereas the father's income and father's occupation have much lower influences (0.19 and 0.04).

There might well be other variables outside the home environment—self-esteem, teachers' expectations, ability to pay sustained attention, for example—which influence both school performance and performance at ability tests. For example, some children may simply feel that they are failures, and so will not try hard at school or at psychological tests. Some may have attentional problems that might affect their ability to concentrate whilst taking ability tests, and that may also affect school performance, and so on. Polderman et al. (2009) performed a multivariate genetic analysis to discover whether the genes that influence ability to pay attention are the same genes that influence intelligence: they found that there was indeed a modest overlap (0.25), though as they did not measure school performance, their study cannot say whether these same genes also influence educational outcome. But there are rather few good studies that have been specifically designed to discover whether some other psychological or social variables can explain all or part of the correlation between g and educational performance.

This is a shame, as it is frequently hard to discern what causes what. For example, does the boy who believes that he is not good at cognitive tasks and educational activities actually *develop* that belief because he is, in reality, not very good at cognitive tasks? In other words, does g influence educational performance and thereby lead to the correlation between self-esteem and educational performance emerging? Or is the child perfectly able, but their lack of self-esteem leads him or her to avoid or give up at such tasks? In this case self-esteem would *cause* the correlation between g and academic performance. Unfortunately, although there is a substantial literature on self-esteem, self-concept and educational attainment, few studies also measure g because social psychologists are generally unaware of the literature discussed in Chapters 5–6 and enjoy the fantasy that social factors alone are responsible for educational outcomes.

There are several studies exploring how self-esteem or self-concept affect educational performance. I think it is important to look at this in young children, as their self-esteem will not have been overly influenced by the feedback they have received on their academic performance. Helmke and van Aken (1995) found that prior levels of self-esteem said nothing about the academic achievement of elementary school children. Academic performance went on to influence academic self-concept: prior academic self-concept did not influence performance. Thus it would seem wrong to regard low academic self-concept as a cause of poor school performance (and possibly low scores on ability tests). In studies that find that self-concept etc. *does* influence academic outcome (e.g., Bachman & Omalley, 1977), the first assessment of self-esteem tends to be made much later (e.g., at age 14), after feedback on academic prowess is already likely to have affected self-esteem.

In order to tell whether social class is the explanation for the link between reasoning and education, Rehberg and Rosenthal (1978) ran some regressions. They found that scores on ability tests predicted educational performance far better than did measures of social class. So social class seems unlikely to be the sole explanation of the larger correlation between academic performance and scores on tests of cognitive ability. Though in any case, I think that one needs a clear model of why, precisely, social deprivation might be expected to affect children's educational performance, and how these factors might interact with g.

Do language skills matter? Language skills are taught and developed at school, and many measures of academic performance (e.g., performance at any subject which requires essays to be written) are likely to reflect language skills to some extent. A child with weak language skills is arguably unlikely to shine at a whole host of academic subjects. In addition, some (but not all) tests of general ability include sub-tests that involve language—for example, measures of comprehension, vocabulary or verbal analogies. So it is possible that children with weak language skills will also perform poorly at such tests. This could cause a correlation between g and academic performance to emerge: a child with excellent language skills will shine at both, whilst a child with weak language skills will flounder at both. There are of course a number of reasons why some children may not show strong language skills. The language used in school may be the second or third language to which some children have been exposed. Some children may be dyslexic. Or some may just fail to attend school sufficiently often to develop their language skills. Any or all of these could, in theory, lead to a correlation between educational outcome and tests measuring g.

In practice, it seems unlikely that this is the main reason why educational success is linked to g. Not all tests of g require participants to use language. Some, such as Cattell's Culture Fair scales (Cattell, 1951) or Raven's Matrices (Raven, Raven & Court, 1993) just ask participants to draw inferences about which shape should be used to complete a sequence. And other tests, such as the Wechsler scales (Wade et al., 1995; Wechsler, 1992, 2010) contain sections that do not require the use of language: e.g., those requiring participants to arrange coloured blocks so that they form a particular pattern, arrange cartoons in sequence so that they tell a story, or identify missing elements from pictures (e.g., a car without a wheel). The acid test is whether such tests also show a link to school performance. If they do, then the correlation between educational performance and g is likely to be genuine—and not just a statistical quirk that occurs because both variables are linked to language skill. A wealth of studies such as Rindermann and Neubauer (2004); Pind, Gunnarsdottir and Johannesson (2003) or Balboni, Naglieri and Cubelli (2010) show that scores on these nonverbal tests show impressive correlations with educational performance in a number of cultures. It does not seem that the correlation between tests of g and academic performance arises because some children have problems using language.

In science, it is impossible to prove a negative. That is, one cannot ever determine that no other psychological or social variable determines both a child's level of g and his or her level of academic performance. However the weak influence of the family environment (as determined by behaviour genetic studies) and the inability of self-concept measures to predict the academic performance of young children seem to suggest that these are unlikely to be powerful influences. The finding that genes that influence ability to pay attention also influence g is perhaps important, though we do not yet know whether these also influence academic performance.

Does Intelligence Influence School Performance?

There are two main ways of determining whether intelligence influences school performance. The first involves prospective studies, where children's intelligence is measured at an early age: their school performance is then assessed some years later. This sort of design is better than measuring school performance and intelligence at the same time, because if schooling improves intelligence those who have engaged more with their education may also achieve higher scores on intelligence tests because of this. If a child's intelligence is instead measured at an early age (ideally before they have decided whether or not to engage with the education system) any correlation between the test score and subsequent academic performance suggests that intelligence has a genuine causal influence.

The second way of examining this issue is to turn to behaviour genetics. Conventional univariate methods of behaviour genetics can show the extent to which the common (family) environment, the unique environment and genetic makeup each influence performance on various school subjects. If performance at several school subjects is substantially influenced by genetic makeup, multivariate genetic analyses are needed to show whether the same genes influence more than one school subject.

We have shown earlier that g is substantially influenced by individual differences in genetic makeup. If g also causes some children to perform better than others at all subjects at school, one would expect some of the "generalist genes" that influence g to also influence performance on a number of seemingly different school subjects. For example, some genes might affect performance on both mathematics and languages. If g does not directly influence performance on all subjects, then if mathematics and languages are influenced by genes at all, one might expect them to be influenced by different sets of genes. So a multivariate genetic analysis of performance at different school subjects can show whether children have specific "genetic aptitudes" for mathematics, music or other individual subjects, a genetic aptitude to perform well at all subjects, or a genetic aptitude to perform well at certain groups of subjects—for example the arts, or the sciences.

This gives a rather direct test of whether g has a causal influence on school performance. And by focusing on just the genetic aspect of g, it shows that social class and other variables that correlate with childhood intelligence are not responsible for the relationship between g and academic performance.

Prospective Studies Relating g to School Performance

There are several studies that relate measures of childhood intelligence— ideally taken at an early age—to subsequent performance at school. A correlation of 0.57 was reported by Benson (1942) using an old test (Haggerty, 1922) that required children to perform simple actions (e.g., "draw a circle around the picture of the cat"), use logic, identify the missing parts of pictures and so on. The test content was not closely linked to information or skills taught at school (there was no test of mathematics and only two of the 12 tests involved complex vocabulary). Thus it is unlikely that the skills measured in the ability test were the same as the skills assessed as part of academic performance. As school achievement was assessed some years after the children's intelligence was assessed, it seems likely that intelligence influences school performance, rather than vice versa.

There are plenty of other studies, too. Butler, Marsh, Sheppard and Sheppard (1985) predicted the reading ability of Australian children from an ability test administered when they were aged between 5 and 7. Their reading ability was assessed 1, 2, 3 and 6 years later. Strengths of this study include the large sample (396 initially of whom at least 296 were tested later), the use of a large number of ability tests that included measures other than language-related skills, a representative sample, and a long follow-up period. It showed a correlation of 0.46 between overall IQ and reading performance that was assessed 6 years later. The six factors that were extracted from the battery of ability tests each correlated between 0.37 and 0.48 with reading ability obtained 6 years later. Tasks involving copying shapes and reproducing a rhythm by tapping (for example) appear to have little to do with language skills, yet they were potent predictors of later language performance. This is precisely what one would expect if each of these ability tests measures g to some extent, and this g also influences language performance at school. All cognitive abilities (and thus g) seem to predict future language performance.

Likewise, Stevenson and Newman (1986) found that 21 of 25 cognitive tests administered to children aged 5 correlated significantly with both reading and mathematics performance at age 16. The correlations between the most obviously mathematical and verbal tests administered to the young children and school performance 11 years later are shown in Table 7.1. This study suggests that g influences academic performance. We can tell this

Table 7.1 Correlations between cognitive ability tests obtained at age 5 and school achievement aged 16. N = 105. (From Stevenson and Newman, 1986)

	Language Performance at Age 16	Numerical Performance at Age 16
Arithmetic at age 5	0.58	0.46
Word matching at age 5	0.38	0.42
Word recognition at age 5	0.25	0.35
Word reproduction at age 5	0.43	0.36

because the arithmetic and word-based tests that were administered at age 5 all predict both language performance and numerical performance some 11 years later. If children had specific skills, one might expect the arithmetic test to predict later numerical performance but not language performance, and the word-based tests to predict language performance but not arithmetic performance. Table 7.1 shows that this is clearly not so.

There are plenty of more recent studies, too. For example Siegler et al. (2012) found correlations of 0.42 and 0.46 between verbal and non-verbal IQ measured at age 10 and mathematics performance measured at age 16, whilst Duckworth, Quinn and Tsukayama (2012) found that IQ assessed at age 9 predicted school performance 5 years later, the correlation with grade-point average being 0.5, and the correlation with scores on a standard school achievement test being 0.74.

A meta-analysis by Jencks (1979) found that correlations between tests of *g* and amount of education received ranged from 0.4 to 0.63. These correlations are surprisingly large, when one considers that many other factors (economic hardship, pressure from family, pregnancy, disenchantment with school) might cause intelligent children to leave school early: despite all these factors, performance on cognitive ability tests is an excellent predictor of the amount of education received. (In practical settings, it is rare to find a correlation between any real-life behaviour and any psychological characteristic that is as high as 0.4: correlations above 0.5 are extremely exciting and correlations above 0.6 are virtually unknown.)

Finally an excellent study by Deary, Strand, Smith and Fernandes (2007) used intelligence-test scores of 70,000 English 11-year-olds to predict level of performance on public examination scores (GCSEs) taken at age 16. Intelligence predicted performance on each of the 25 subjects that were assessed, with correlations ranging from 0.44 (with art and design) to 0.77 (mathematics). A "*g*-factor" extracted from the ability test scores obtained 5 years earlier correlated 0.81 with a 'GCSE performance' factor obtained by aggregating performance on the six most popular GCSE subjects for 13,000 students who took this combination of subjects. This study is important because it was prospective, used a large, representative sample of students, performed supplementary analyses to check that language skills were not the cause of the relationship, and used multiple measures of academic attainment.

All of these relationships are enormous. To put them in context, there is a substantial literature on learning styles, which argues that identifying each child's preferred method of learning (e.g., visual, or verbal) and teaching in ways that match each child's preferred style will lead to enhanced performance in the classroom. A meta-analysis suggests that the effect size (essentially a correlation) is just 0.35 (Dunn, Griggs, Olson, Beasley & Gorman, 1995) to 0.37 (Lovelace, 2005) and it has been argued that even these figure are overestimated, as some studies were omitted from the analyses (Robbins, Oh, Le & Button, 2009). Huge amounts of money have been invested in exploring learning styles and implementing classroom programs, yet it is clear from the figures shown above that if you want to understand academic achievement, the thing to measure is g, not learning styles.

Overall, then, there is a consistent body of evidence showing that when IQ tests (measuring g) are administered to children, these can predict their future academic performance rather well. Where researchers report the correlations between several different tests and several different aspects of school performance, it seems that each of the tests predict all of the measures of academic achievement. This strongly suggests that g influences every aspect of school performance, and is evidence against their being specific abilities ("mathematics ability", "language ability" etc.) each of which is tied to a rather narrow area of academic performance. However these studies say nothing about the *mechanisms* that cause this to take place. It could be the case that some outside variables (e.g., social deprivation, self-confidence or motivation to do well) might in some yet-to-be-specified way influence scores on both the ability test and measures of academic performance. Given that we know that g is quite strongly biological in nature, checking whether the same biological mechanisms are at work for both tests of g and measures of academic performance allows such possibilities to be evaluated.

Do Genes Influence Performance at School?

This is an important issue, because if g is essentially biological, and if g influences school performance, one would expect school performance to also be inherited and the same genes that influence g should also influence school performance. If school performance and scores on IQ tests happen to correlate because both are influenced by environmental factors (e.g., social class), then one would not expect there to be any genetic influence on school performance. Thus discovering whether our genetic makeup influences school performance is an important first step toward understanding whether g really does *cause* some children to perform better than others at school.

It is a simple matter to discover the origins of individual differences in school performance using conventional methods of behaviour genetics. Behrman, Taubman and Wales (1977) reported data from 1900 pairs of twins, born from 1917–1927 in the United States. The number of years of schooling that the children received was moderately heritable (A = 0.44), although unlike studies that examine the heritability of intelligence in adolescents, the common environment (C) also had an appreciable influence (0.32) with the unique environment explaining the rest of the variance. The non-trivial influence of the family environment suggests that factors as parental encouragement, wealth and so on influence how long children stay at school/college.

Because some children might have to leave school early because they are expected to earn a wage, it might be better to examine how well children perform at school (before any have the chance to leave) rather than how long children stay within the education system in order to understand the link between g and educational performance. Bartels, Rietveld, Van Baal and Boomsma (2002) examined the heritability of a standard test of academic performance that is administered to 12-year-old children in Holland. This was another study of twins reared together, involving 691 pairs. Genetic effects explained 57% of the variance in academic attainment; the common environment explained another 27% and the unique environment 16%— results which are fairly similar to those of Behrman, Taubman and Wales (1977). A literature search will reveal other studies, too. The common findings are that

(a) genetic factors are more important than the family environment when predicting overall educational outcome, and
(b) the influence of the family environment is sometimes appreciable (unlike studies of the heritability of g in older children).

The presence of a clear and substantial genetic basis for overall school performance is consistent with the idea that g may directly influence academic attainment. Environmental factors also play a part, including the type of environment shared by both members of a pair of twins. This might include the quality of education, parental attitudes, parental income and so on.

Do the Same Genes Influence Performance
at Several Different School Subjects?

Now that we know that genetic makeup influences school performance, it is important to establish whether many of the genes that influence English performance (for example) also influence mathematics or science performance. If it is found that few of the genes that influence performance in one aspect of school work are responsible for performance in other areas, that would be conclusive evidence that biological g cannot directly influence school performance. On the other hand, if each aspect of school performance is heritable, and the genes that influence one aspect of school performance also influence all other aspects of school performance, then it is possible that g is the cause of this.

It is thus necessary to establish:

(a) whether performance at various school subjects is heritable,
(b) whether some of the genes that influence performance at one school subject (e.g., mathematics) to also influence performance at other, apparently quite different school subjects (e.g., languages).

Twin studies can show whether school achievement is inherited. For example, Haworth, Kovas, Dale and Plomin (2008) found the heritability of English, mathematics and science performance varied from 0.49 to 0.62 in a sample of 13-year-olds. Calvin et al. (2012) found that the heritability of English, mathematics and science performance in a sample of over 3000 English 11-year-olds were 0.81, 0.66 and 0.51. They also studied the heritability of mathematics and English performance in smaller samples of Dutch twins aged 8, 10 and 12: these too were appreciable (ranging from 0.36 to 0.74). We saw earlier that overall measures of school performance were heritable, and it seems that each individual aspect of school performance is moderately heritable too. This need not necessarily be the case: it could be argued that although the overall heritability of school performance was moderate or large, some areas might have zero heritability whilst others could be very large.

Multivariate genetic analyses of twin pairs show that the actual genes that influence performance at one school subject also influence performance at other subjects. Harlaar, Kovas, Dale, Petrill and Plomin (2012) found that a set of genes that was common to all three areas of performance explained all of the genetic variance in mathematics, half the genetic variance for reading comprehension, and 75% of the genetic variance for word decoding. This shows that some genes affect reading comprehension but not the other two variables, but all of the genes that influence mathematics performance also influence comprehension and decoding. Thompson, Detterman and Plomin (1991) found a 0.98 correlation between the genes that influenced mathematics and those that influenced language abilities in 12-year-olds.

It therefore seems clear that the same genes that influence performance at one subject (e.g., mathematics) also influence performance at other school subjects (e.g., language). Some studies find more overlap than do others: this may reflect differences in the tests used to assess performance, and the age or representativeness of the samples used.

Do Genes That Influence Intelligence Also Influence School Achievement?

This is, of course, the crucial issue. Multivariate genetic studies can show the extent to which the genes that determine g also influence performance at school: either in individually assessed subjects or in overall school performance. All the evidence with which I am familiar indicates that the genetic overlap between g and school achievement is appreciable: many of the genes that influence g also influence academic performance. This suggests that the biological element of g really does predict academic achievement to a substantial extent.

Calvin et al. (2012) report a study based on 2,500 pairs of twins in Holland and the United Kingdom for whom school achievement data and scores on an intelligence test were available. The heritability of g was substantial (0.7 in the United Kingdom; 0.43 in Holland): we mentioned the heritability of school attainment above. Standard methods of multivariate genetic analysis were used to determine whether the genes that influenced school performance were the same as the ones that influenced g. Many of them were. The genes that influenced school performance included many that also influenced intelligence (an overlap of 0.76 in the United Kingdom, 0.33 in Holland), so there is a clear relationship between the biological element of g and the biological determinants of school achievement. Gottschling, Spengler, Spinath and Spinath (2012) found a similar result with a smaller sample of German twins.

A critic might argue that children with language difficulties would necessarily perform weakly at the intelligence test and at school, and so language skills (rather than g) might be the reason for the genetic overlap between g and school performance. However in the UK study reported by Calvin et al. (2012), the overlap between the genes that influenced academic performance and those that influenced non-verbal ability was also substantial (0.94). Thus we can be confident that the overlap is not just caused by genes that influence language skills influencing performance on the IQ test and also influencing school performance.

Table 7.2 Multivariate genetic correlations between *g* and various aspects of school performance in a large sample of 12-year-olds. Adapted from Haworth, Kovas et al. (2009).

	g	*Mathematics*	*Language Use*
Mathematics	0.75		
Language use	0.82	0.65	
Reading	0.62	0.58	0.63

For mathematics, language use (comprehension etc.) and reading, the influence of genes is in every case much larger than the influence of either the shared or the unique environment—but more importantly, there is substantial overlap between those genes that influence *g* and the genes that influence each of these three aspects of school performance, as shown in Table 7.2. This table shows the extent to which the same genes that influence *g* or school performance also influence other aspects of school performance.

Table 7.2 shows that the generalist genes—those genes that influence performance on many tests of cognitive ability, even those that appear to involve completely different cognitive processes, such as creativity, memory and visualisation—clearly affect several aspects of academic performance. Multivariate genetic studies show that the same genes that influence performance on a number of very different tests of cognitive ability (and that, through their influence on brain structure and function, represent the biological basis of *g*) also influence performance at a wide range of subjects studied at school (Plomin, Kovas & Haworth, 2007). This implies that some children come to school with a predisposition to perform at a particular level at many academic subjects (Brody, 1997; Harris, 1940; Neisser et al., 1996).

Conclusions: *g* and Educational Attainment

From the results discussed above, it seems that the relationship between *g* and educational attainment is bi-directional. Schooling seems to affect levels of general intelligence to some extent, but as far as I know, no one really knows exactly what it is about the educational process that causes this to happen. Prospective studies also show that a child's level of *g* predicts their educational attainment many years later. It is therefore clear that *g* influences educational attainment. However, it is logically possible that some other factors (for example expectations of success) might affect both scores on the intelligence test and school performance. Scrutiny of the link between the purely biological aspect of g and school achievement is thus useful. Multivariate genetic studies show that the genes that influence g also influence school attainment. This provides conclusive evidence that g really does have a causal influence on educational attainment because of its link to the biology of the nervous system.

Most psychologists working in the field of individual differences take the view that g is an important causal influence on children's educational performance. Despite counterarguments from sociologists such as Byington and Felps (2010), I think that there are five sound reasons for believing that g influences school learning.

1. The proposal is theoretically coherent. The very existence of g implies that some children find it easier than others to think abstractly, grasp the links between theories and pieces of information, visualise things, memorise information, argue an articulate case, show creativity and so on. These are basic cognitive skills that are likely to influence performance on most tasks that involve thinking and learning. So it seems reasonable to hypothesise that children with high levels of g are more likely than others to excel at a most, perhaps all, subjects at school. This is not to say that g is the only determinant of academic performance: other factors such as motivation are doubtless also important: see for example Spinath, Spinath and Plomin (2008) whilst the personality trait of conscientiousness also affects performance at school (de Fruyt, Van Leeuwen, De Bolle & De Clercq, 2008). Furthermore, the evidence shows that school performance can be influenced by genes other than those generalist genes that represent g: performance at science is substantially influenced by some specific genes in addition to the generalist genes (Haworth, Kovas, Dale & Plomin, 2008).
2. Experimental evidence based on structural equation modelling (a statistical technique that determines which variables influence with other ones) shows that contrary to Ceci's (1991) assertions, mental speed influences g, and g then influences school performance (Rindermann & Neubauer, 2004). This type of model also fits in well with the biological approach outlined in previous chapters. This argues that g is substantially inherited and linked to brain structure and hence to low-level cognitive functioning (e.g., inspection time, reaction time, reflex latency).
3. Other studies also based on structural equation modelling (e.g., Duncan, Featherman & Duncan, 1972) reveal a direct link between g and subsequent educational performance: the father's educational and occupational background are far weaker influences.

4. There are major problems with the hypotheses that the correlation between education and *g* comes about because education influences *g* or that both *g* and school performance are influenced by other variables. If a child's level of *g* was essentially determined by social factors (quality of school attended, family income, and so on), it is reasonable to assume that each of these factors would affect all children in the same family similarly. All children in a family are likely to attend the same school, for example. Yet the behaviour genetic studies discussed in previous chapters show that such factors have zero influence on adult levels of *g*.

5. We will mention in Chapter 8 that early environmental interventions such as the Milwaukee Project on school performance (and *g*) suggest that environmental and cognitive stimulation, no matter how intensive, have just a modest influence on school performance—just as one would expect if biological *g* also exerts a potent influence on school learning. The effect of the common family environment on academic performance at age 12 is also modest. In the Haworth, Kovas et al. (2009) study, the influence of the family environment on mathematics, language and reading ranged from 0.14 to 0.22: the genetic influences ranged from 0.45 to 0.62. This is another example of how social factors simply do not show a substantial relationship with school performance.

Overall, although there is some evidence suggesting that schooling can raise intelligence to some extent (Cahan & Cohen, 1989), there is a wealth of strong evidence indicating that high levels of *g* also facilitate performance at school.

Ability Tests in Personnel Psychology

Ability tests are big business. Many businesses and other organisations have found that ability tests provide a cost-effective means of selecting employees, identifying individuals who might most benefit from a training course, and so on. And so a great number of tests have been developed for this purpose. They are generally used following some sort of job analysis (for instance involving interviews with current employees to determine the skills that are necessary for the post, or where an occupational psychologist will 'shadow' an employee and note what they do). Occupational psychologists (called 'organizational psychologists' or 'I/O psychologists' in the United States) are major users of ability tests—although they frequently develop bespoke tests for their clients rather than using tried and trusted measures available cheaply "off-the-shelf".

The United States military developed and administered two ability tests to recruits in World War I, assessing 1.7 million recruits (Yerkes, 1919) in order to "increase military efficiency and to lessen the cost of training and maintenance" by identifying recruits who had learning difficulties, and who should therefore not be taken into the army and identifying those whose above-average abilities suited them for officer training or specialised roles such as aviation. Although it is uncertain how effective such tests actually proved (as the war ended soon after testing began) psychological assessments of workers and job applicants became extremely popular as shown by reviews such as Viteles (1930). Some employers used tests of general ability, whilst others tried to assess a range of different abilities, sometimes attempting to match applicants' patterns of abilities to the demands of various jobs. For example, those with good language skills might be encouraged to take up a secretarial post; those with good spatial skills might be routed toward air traffic control. Personnel selection—using psychological ability tests as part of the selection process—started to be commonplace, although many test users seem not to have checked whether the use of tests actually led to better selection decisions. Issues such as the difficulty of establishing accurate measures of work performance were starting to be understood: criteria such as sales performance or the number of electric lamp bulbs produced per day were used as well as the more error-prone supervisors' ratings of performance. Viteles' works shows that many of these early studies are based on small samples, tests of unknown worth, dubious measures of performance in the workplace and meagre statistical analysis. So although there was great enthusiasm for selection testing, it was less than obvious that it actually helped employers to select the candidates who would perform best in employment. Nor did these early studies attempt to find out whether selection tests worked because they measured specific skills, or whether they worked because each test measured g to some extent.

Selecting Individuals Based on an Ability Profile

The most obvious way to use ability tests as part of the selection procedure is to analyse the job that is to be filled, and draw up a list of abilities (and probably also personality characteristics) that would lead to good performance. The list of required abilities and personality traits could come from an analysis of what current employees actually do, performed by an occupational psychologist. For example, they might observe air traffic controllers at work and deduce that they require above-average performance at several spatial tests, verbal skills, inductive reasoning and so on—as well as other characteristics such as the ability to work well under stress. The psychologist could then locate (or possibly devise—at huge expense to the employing organisation) tests to measure each of these abilities, and administer them to applicants.

The second way of identifying which abilities are important would involve measuring a wide range of abilities in people who are already doing the job, and either comparing their scores with the population average or else gathering performance data. For example, it might be found that the spatial ability scores of air traffic controllers (ATCs) who are highly rated by their peers and managers are much higher than he spatial ability scores of students who were asked to leave the ATC training course because of poor performance. This suggests that spatial ability is probably linked to performance, and so should be assessed in job applicants. Multiple regression might be used to determine how much weight should be given to each ability. For example, it might be found that spatial ability is twice as important as inductive reasoning for performing this job.

All that one then needs to do is measure the relevant abilities (and personality factors, attitudes etc.) in applicants, and select those applicants whose profile of skills best matches the "ideal" profile. One problem is knowing how to analyse such data. Do applicants require a certain mimimum level of competency in each of these areas? Or can exceptional spatial ability (for example) compensate for mediocre performance in another area or two?

A second problem is that as all abilities measure g to some extent, they will all be quite highly correlated. People will tend to perform at a similar level at all abilities, and it will be rather rare to find someone who performs well above average at spatial ability (for example) who does not perform at least at an average level on other abilities too. This can present problems for organisations such as the armed forces that have a pool of individuals for whom they have to recommend roles: the high ability individuals are likely to excel at everything and so could probably fill any role, whereas some individuals will be quite hard to place. So whilst matching profiles sounds sensible in principle, it is not easy to perform in practice.

Work Baskets

Some employers prefer to assess applicants on precisely the tasks they would be performing, if appointed. A customer service applicant might be given a letter of complaint to answer, or a "standard" role-played telephone conversation with a supposedly irate customer. The people who perform best are hired. Who needs any understanding of the psychology of abilities for this? Although appealing, this process is fraught with difficulties. First, it will confuse potential to perform well with experience. An applicant with plenty of experience may outperform someone with more ability in the short term, but the person with more ability may go on to perform better in the long term: this has been shown to be the case by Hunter and Schmidt (1996). So it would be better to select applicants using ability tests (which assess future potential) rather than work-baskets, and assess experience separately from ability—perhaps by scrutinising the individual's employment history. Second, as no theory is involved, selectors would be impotent if the in-basket technique stopped being able to select adequate employees: they would not be able to determine whether one test was no longer effective and needed to be modified, for example. Finally, a work-basket that predicts how well a person might perform in a particular role would not be expected to work if that person's role within the organisation were to change—through promotion, or a redefinition of the tasks to be performed. A test of g, on the other hand, should predict how a person would perform on a wide range of tasks.

Do Specific Abilities or g Predict Job Performance?

You might think that the obvious way to test this is to design a test carefully, so that it only measures a single primary mental ability, or a single second-order ability, and then correlate test scores with work performance. Unfortunately this is just not possible: every task that involves thought measures g to some extent. But it is possible to perform statistical analyses to answer this question, using techniques such as partial correlation, multiple regression, path analysis or structural equation modelling. Thorndike (1985) wrote an enormously important paper that explored this issue. He found that g predicted how well people performed at work better than a measure based on multiple regression (which would perform better if some abilities were more important than others for job performance). Likewise Jensen (1998) observes that the size of the correlation between a test score and job performance mirrors how well the test measures g. Tests that have a fairly low g loading predict job performance worse than those that have a substantial g loading. (These analyses controlled for variations in the reliability of tests, which would also affect their predictive power). Jensen also "partialled out" g—a statistical procedure that allows one to tell whether it is general intelligence or narrow abilities that predict performance. General ability correlated 0.76 with job performance in a sample of 78,000 airmen (p. 284); after controlling for this, the narrow abilities unrelated to g correlated a mere 0.02 with job performance. So when a test measuring a primary mental ability (digit span, say) correlates with job performance, it does so because the primary mental ability is measuring g

to some extent—and not because there is anything special about digit span that is important for the job. Other work on the topic includes Ree and Earles (1991), Kuncel, Hezlett and Ones (2004) and Schmidt and Hunter (2004). Kuncel et al. (2004) additionally show that the g that predicts performance at work is virtually identical to the g that predicts performance at school—even though both are usually measured by different tests.

There is a lot to be said for making selection decisions on the basis of tests of general intelligence. It overcomes the problem of predicting performance when the person shifts to a different role within the organisation, and furthermore there is excellent evidence that tests that predict job performance work because they each measure g to some extent—not because the narrower abilities are important. The problem is that employers do not seem to understand this literature, and prefer (quite wrongly, in my opinion) to use ability tests that look as if they are highly relevant to the job for which the applicant is being selected. The evidence mentioned above seems to show that this is not a sound decision. Also, rather than using a simple "off-the-shelf" tried and trusted test of g that may have been around for years, I have seen some horrible examples of occupational psychology firms developing new tests for employers—to make money, one assumes—when a cheap test of g would probably have been more effective. All the theory and empirical results seem to show that tests work in occupational psychology because they each measure g to some extent. It is hard to see why one would choose to develop anything more exotic for an employer than a good, solid test of g.

Many tried-and-tested tests turn out to be substantially correlated with tests of g. The Watson Glaser Critical Thinking Appraisal (WGCTA: Watson & Glaser, 2008) is a test much beloved of personnel managers. It claims to measure how well a person can identify the assumptions underpinning arguments and other skills that seem to be highly relevant to senior managers. Yet when one looks at the correlation between the WGCTA and a test of verbal analogies (the Miller Analogies Test) in the WGCTA manual, the correlation is 0.7. This is high—but when one considers that scores on the WGCTA are not particularly accurate (its reliability is only 0.76: that of the Miller test is approximately 0.90). It can be shown that the correlation would be 0.85 if both tests were free of measurement error. It is hard to argue that two tests that correlate 0.85 measure different things! So why not strip out the pretence, and instead say that one is using a test of g?

Because the work by Thorndike (1985), Jensen (1998) and Schmidt and Hunter (2004) and others shows beyond doubt that g is far more important than narrower primary or second-order abilities when predicting job performance, we ignore primary and second-order abilities and focus almost entirely on the predictive role of g in the following sections.

Intelligence and Occupation

Ability tests were used extensively for selection purposes in World War II. The mass testing of conscripts gave psychologists access to huge random samples of individuals from various walks of life, and some evidence emerged that performance on the military intelligence tests was related to occupation. Harrell and Harrell (1945) found that the IQ's of professional people in civilian life were high (accountants and lawyers had an average IQ of over 125) whilst miners, farmhands and other labourers had IQs below 100 and electricians, clerks, sales staff etc. were somewhere in the middle. The labourers also showed larger standard deviations, showing that whilst it was rare to find a low-IQ lawyer, some labourers were well above average in intelligence.

It is tempting to assume from this that the professions may require more abstract thought and other cognitive skills than do labouring jobs, and so only the brightest and best can succeed at them. Perhaps those who cannot shine at cognitively demanding jobs end up labouring—alongside some intelligent individuals who might perhaps have taken a menial job rather than train for a trade or profession. However Harrell and Harrell's (1945) data do not necessarily imply this.

Suppose that it was decreed that in future only the very best singers could train to be accountants. After a few years, all accountants would be far better singers than the rest of us: they had to be able to sing well in order to get onto a training course. But this does not imply that accountants *need* to be able to sing well to do their job. Their above-average scores would come about merely because some crazy bureaucrat decided that they should be selected by this means.

It could be the same with intelligence. Perhaps the results noted by Harrell and Harrell (1945) only come about because only those applicants with the best academic achievements are accepted onto professional training courses. We have seen (above) that academic achievement is linked to intelligence. So it follows that accountants, etc. will end up with above-average intelligence if they are selected in the basis of their examination scores. But it may not follow that one *needs* to be intelligent in order to be a lawyer or an accountant. Perhaps anyone could excel if they were allowed into the training course. If this is the case, it would clearly be wrong and arbitrary to use ability tests to select applicants. So whilst Harrell and Harrell's data are consistent with the thesis that high levels of intelligence are necessary for professional careers, there are other explanations too.

In one attempt to get round this problem, Strenze (2007) reports a meta-analysis of longitudinal studies, where children's intelligence was assessed and their eventual level of SES was also measured some years later (rather than measuring the intelligence of people who are working in various trades and professions). The clearest results were found when intelligence was measured after age 10, and when adult SES was measured after age 25, when most had finished education and had started a career. The analyses show that "the scientific research on the topic leaves little doubt that people with higher scores on IQ tests are better educated, hold more prestigious occupations, and earn higher incomes than people with lower scores". He noted that intelligence was at least as good a predictor of adult SES as were parental SES and education. However such an analysis cannot really consider whether intelligence affects adult SES via its influence on education: once again, high intelligence might help children obtain good educational qualifications, and these (rather than intelligence itself) may lead to their achieving a high SES in later life. To investigate whether intelligence (or other abilities) ready lead to better levels of job performance, we need to consider some rather more subtle analyses.

More recent research seems to suggest that intelligence really does have a causal influence on the type of job that one obtains—even after controlling statistically for variables such as one's parents' social class and educational qualifications. Von Stumm, MacIntyre, Batty, Clark and Deary (2010) looked at the social class, intelligence, educational attainment and behavioural problems of 6,000 Scottish boys aged 11, and followed them up when they were aged 46–51. Social class was assessed by looking at income, housing status, number of cars and occupational status. Intelligence was measured using a standard test: this comprised two long verbal reasoning tests (VI and VII) consisting of 30 scales, an arithmetic test (AR) and an English test (EN). Figure 7.3 summarises what was found. The straight lines indicate causal relationships (in the direction of the arrow): the curve indicates a correlation. The numbers on the lines/curve indicate the size of each relationship; they are all statistically significantly different from zero. Thus the model shows that g has a substantial influence on level of educational qualifications (0.46), and that the level of educational qualifications obtained goes on to influence SES 25 or so years later (.32). The influence of educational qualifications (0.32) on SES is stronger than the influence of the parents' social class (0.20). But the interesting part of this analysis is that there is a substantial direct link (0.29) between intelligence measured at age 11 and the social class that these children go on to reach 25 or so years later. It is clear that intelligence has a direct causal influence on social class in adulthood. It is clearly not just the case that intelligence influences school qualifications, and these school qualifications influence SES in later life. Indeed, if one looks at the size of the direct influence of intelligence and parental social class on

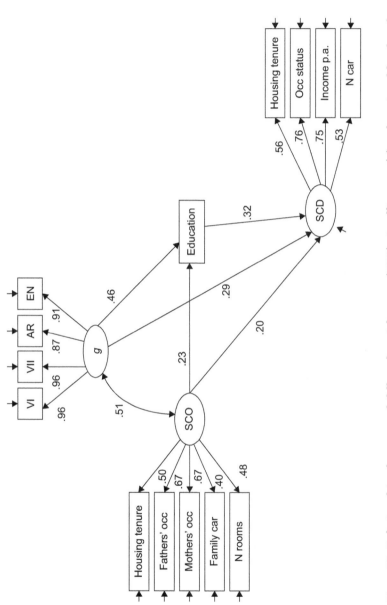

Figure 7.3 Relationships between childhood social status (SCO), intelligence (g), educational level and adult social status (SCD) in a sample of Scottish men. Adapted from von Stumm, MacIntyre, Batty, Clark and Deary (2010).

adult social class, it seems that it is better to be born smart than born rich in order to attain wealth and status in adulthood.

I have discussed this study in some detail because it is methodologically sound and relatively easy to read for those who are unfamiliar with the statistical methodology and terminology. However it builds on a number of previous studies that had similar aims. For example, Thienpont and Verleye (2004) also examined the relationships between IQ, social class and education, but unfortunately what they call "IQ" is an odd mixture of scores on four mathematics and comprehension tests (at ages 11 and 16) plus one IQ test administered at age 11. One might therefore expect that their "IQ" measure (which comprises far more school attainment tests than IQ tests) will show a stronger correlation with educational qualifications than in the von Stumm study. This is what they found. The path linking "IQ" to educational qualifications was 0.7, and the link between their "IQ" and SES was close to zero—so in this analysis there was little evidence of a direct link between IQ and SES, though IQ did also influence educational attainment that in turn influenced SES (0.24). However as their "IQ" measure contained even more mathematics and English attainment tests than in von Stumm's study, it is hardly surprising that these correlated substantially with school qualifications.

A classic study by Duncan, Featherman and Duncan (1972) found results similar to von Stumm et al. (2010): intelligence influenced educational attainment (0.43), educational attainment influenced SES (0.53) and intelligence also influenced SES (0.22). The influence of the father's SES and level of education on the child's SES were again far more modest. All of these studies show that intelligence influences job performance—both directly, and via its influence on educational attainment. This implies that it should be appropriate to select individuals for jobs using ability tests.

Such studies also have powerful implications for social policy, which are generally ignored by policy makers. For example, sociologists assume that parents' low SES (and other social/environmental factors) leads to their children's underachievement at school (Sirin, 2005): according to his view, poverty causes poor educational performance, which leads to the children entering low-status jobs. We have however seen that there is a clear causal influence (direct and indirectly via school achievement) between intelligence and adult SES. Therefore it seems probable that the lower-than-average SES of the parents is in many cases itself a consequence of their lower-than-average IQ. Given the high heritability of intelligence, although some children may be lucky and inherit intelligence-facilitating genes from both parents, on average the children's IQ will be below average, like that of their parents. And this lower-than-average IQ will predispose many of them to perform below average at school, and enter low SES careers. Thus it is possible that the direct causal influence of intelligence on school behaviour, coupled with its substantial heritability, may explain why socially deprived children tend not to excel at school (Miller, 1970; White, 1982) and also why they may not enter cognitively demanding careers. However the sociologists whose research on such issues inform government policy (e.g., Connor & Dewson, 2001) typically never consider the possibility that anything other than social factors can influence academic performance: this should be a matter of some concern to psychologists who are aware of the very causal link between g and academic outcomes.

It is also common for researchers to identify some behaviour (such as reading performance, age of learning to read, mathematics performance) as a predictor of later academic or vocational success (e.g., Crawford & Cribb, 2013) without ever considering whether the "predictor" may work just because it measures g to some extent. The danger is that many researchers will assume that a narrow ability (such as reading skill) causally influences how the child will perform later in life, and will advise governments to pour money into improving reading standards (or whatever) in the hope that this intervention will improve educational outcomes. In reality, there might be little or no evidence for a direct causal link between childhood reading performance and educational outcome. The two may well be correlated just because intelligent children read well and also do well at school. Unless social researchers get into the habit of routinely administering tests of general ability as well as gathering social data, they will simply not be able to determine whether any of their relationships are truly causal. Assuming that all children are equally intelligent (which is what social science researchers typically do) seems to be naive, at best.

Intelligence and Performance Within a Particular Job

Rather than looking to see whether intelligence is related to career choice, it is also possible to determine whether higher levels of intelligence lead to better performance of *any* job. Such analyses are important because although studies such as von Stumm et al. (2010) show that intelligence affects adult SES independently of the effects of educational qualifications and parental social class, there are some problems with such analyses.

First, the amount that society decides to pay various workers is fairly arbitrary. Bankers (in the United Kingdom) and government employees (in Canada) are popularly perceived as being overpaid relative to the skills they require, whilst care assistants are seen as underpaid. So although we have seen that intelligence influences SES, it is not obvious that SES is the most appropriate index of occupational success. This will lead to the correlation between SES and g being underestimated. Second, we noted earlier that some highly capable people may have to leave the education system early because they cannot afford college, and so will not be able to enter training for many careers. Correlations between g and SES will also be underestimated because of this. It might thus be more useful to look at the relationship between intelligence and performance *within* each occupation, rather than *between* occupations. For example, are the best salespersons, managers and truck drivers the most intelligent salespersons, managers and truck drivers?

Schmidt and Hunter (2004) reported the following results when correlating g with how well people performed in their chosen occupation or profession.

It can be seen from this Table 7.3 that high g is an asset for every job. The average correlation between tests that measured g and job performance was 0.51: the correlation was larger for more professional/managerial jobs (r = 0.58) and lowest for the few completely non-skilled jobs that were examined (r = 0.23). When one considers that a non-skilled job is (by definition) a job that anyone should be able to undertake, such as collecting litter or lifting boxes from a production line, it is perhaps surprising to find that there is *any* correlation between g and job performance. Schmidt and Hunter (1998) argue that when compared to other selection techniques such as interviews, performance during a "probationary period", or measures of job experience, measures of g have "the highest validity [correlation with job performance] and lowest application cost": it is easy to see why employers frequently use cheap but effective cognitive ability tests as part of the selection procedure.

Table 7.3 Correlations between tests of general ability and job performance. From Schmidt and Hunter (2004).

Job Category	Correlation Between Job Performance and g
Clerical work	0.52
Law enforcement	0.38
Technical proficiency of enlisted soldiers	0.63
General soldiering proficiency	0.65
Supervisors	0.64
Clerks	0.67
Computer programmers	0.73
Oil refinery workers	0.31

Rather than reporting results for individual jobs, some researchers have extended this work by categorising jobs as "high complexity" (e.g., chemists, engineers, managers), "medium complexity" (e.g., sales staff, police, clerical staff) or "low complexity" (machine operator, driver, carpenter) to allow them to combine the results of hundreds of studies, based on thousands of workers. Salgado et al. (2003) found that the correlations between tests of general ability and performance in these categories of jobs were 0.64, 0.53 and 0.51 (after allowing for measurement error, restriction of range and so on). This study again showed that intelligence is related to how well a person performs a particular job: the relationship seems to be a little stronger for the more cognitively demanding and complex jobs, but a strong relationship exists even for quite undemanding jobs—for example, 0.45 for drivers, 0.54 for electricians. High g helps workers perform better, no matter what their job is.

However it would be premature to infer from this that there is a direct causal relationship between g and job performance. It could be that literacy is important, for example. One would expect that drivers, electricians etc. will need to read and write; if some people have problems doing so, they are unlikely to perform well at their job, and will also perform poorly on an ability test *if this test is one that involves language*. Of course, some tests (such as Raven's Matrices) do not involve language, and so it is important to explore which tests were used, a topic that is well beyond the remit of this book! In addition, if language problems explained the correlation between tests of g and job performance, it seems more likely that the correlation would be large for jobs requiring little cognitive complexity as individuals with poor language skills are perhaps less likely to be accepted for training in high-level jobs. As similar relationships are found between tests of g and performance for all classes of job, it is perhaps unlikely that language deficit is the sole explanation.

Some Practical Considerations

The financial savings incurred by using selection tests can be huge. When selecting individuals for posts where there is an expensive training period where not everyone can reach the minimum required standard—flying a military jet aircraft, or training to become a doctor for example—a test that has even a modest correlation with success or failure on the training course can prove cost-effective, even if it costs a huge amount to administer it to job applicants. On the other hand, if an organisation wants to select employees for a low-skilled post, there would be no good financial justification for expensive selection procedures (a) because the relationship between g and job performance is likely to be lower than for highly skilled workers, and

(b) because if no intensive training is involved, the costs to the organisation of someone leaving because they cannot perform effectively will be minimal. Thus in practice, the most sophisticated assessment measures tend to be used with individuals whose training costs are high, or where the consequences of making a bad decision can be catastrophic: for example, appointing an inept chief executive or vice chancellor.

What of the role of experience? Perhaps scores on ability tests might be of some use when selecting raw, unexperienced applicants for a job—but that on-the-job experience will soon take over, so that after a few years ability tests might show no relationship to job performance. It is an appealing idea—and like many appealing ideas in the psychology of intelligence, it is incorrect. Schmidt, Outerbridge, Hunter and Goff (1988) studied how job experience and g both influenced job performance in a sample of 1,400 military personnel (cooks, logistics specialists, engineers and artillery soldiers). They followed up high- and low-ability individuals over a period of 5 years and found that the difference in performance between the high-g and low-g workers (the quality of performance between the low-g and high-g cooks, for example) did not diminish over the years. Selection tests seem to be able to predict who will perform well in their post, even after many years. g seems to predict job performance, even after years of experience.

Conclusions: g in the Workplace

Kanfer, Ackerman and Goff (1995) suggest that

> Companies have unarguably saved billions of dollars by using ability tests to assure a merit-based selection process. . . . Overall, tests of intellectual abilities are the single most predictive element in employee selection . . . and certainly more valid than the use of personal interviews . . . in predicting training and on-the-job success.
>
> (p. 597)

Thus, there is good reason to regard occupational selection testing as one of the most useful practical achievements of psychology.

g and Health

Ian Deary and his colleagues at Edinburgh and Aberdeen universities have developed a new branch of psychology that they term "cognitive epistemology". It explores how g, measured in childhood, goes on to influence health status and longevity throughout life. Almost all Scottish children who were born in 1921 were given an intelligence test in June 1932, and the 87,000 or so results of this "Scottish Mental Survey" were found in a basement in the 1990s. Deary and his colleagues set about tracing and following up as many of these now-elderly individuals as possible, with the aim of discovering whether intelligence (measured at age 11) was related to the types of lives that these people had led. Of course the methodological problems were extreme. One cannot assume that the sample of people he located formed a random sample of those tested at age 11 (for example, they tended to be the ones who still lived in the same area). They had participated in a world war: perhaps the smarter individuals managed to find ways of surviving this? Social class differences, amount of education received and similar variables might also affect health and longevity. It is to the great credit of these researchers that they made determined efforts to control for all of these variables as much as possible (using structural equation modelling), so that their analyses show what the relationship between childhood intelligence and adult lifestyle would be if all children had been raised similarly. They have also found some other similar sets of data to boost the sample size.

We have already seen that intelligence at age 11 is an excellent predictor of intelligence age 77: intelligent children tend to become intelligent pensioners (Deary, Whalley, Lemmon, Crawford & Starr, 2000). The actual correlation was 0.63, which rose to 0.73 after correcting for test unreliability and restriction of range in the older group. This is important, because it shows that people's levels of g are not hugely influenced by the vicissitudes of their lives. Because these children's lives will have varied in many ways after age 11 (e.g., the amount of education they received, exercise, diet, drinking, illnesses, self-esteem, hobbies, other aspects of lifestyle) one might expect that these will each impact on their levels of intelligence as adults. Deary's work shows that this is simply not the case: intelligent children usually become intelligent adults. So if it is a constant characteristic of the individual, it is reasonable to ask whether it can influence behaviour across the lifespan.

Childhood intelligence was significantly related to survival until age 77 in a sample of 2000 (Whalley & Deary, 2001) the effect being slightly larger for women, probably because higher-IQ men tended to die on active service during World War II (Whalley & Deary, 2001). The effect is quite substantial: a girl in the top 25% of her class in terms of IQ when tested age 11 had a 70% chance of living until age 77; a girl in the lowest 25% in terms of IQ only had a 45% chance of surviving that long. For men the figures were 50% and 37%.

Correcting for crowding in childhood (a measure of social deprivation) and father's occupation did not reduce this relationship. A meta-analysis including other studies showed similar results (Calvin et al., 2011b). Childhood intelligence is quite a potent predictor of mortality, quite independently of social deprivation.

The picture becomes more complex when one examines whether 79-year-olds will survive until age 89. IQ measured at age 11 does not predict this. The amount of decline in IQ between ages 11 and 79 does however predict who will fail to live another 10 years (Murray, Pattie, Starr & Deary, 2012). This relationship remained even when controlling for social class and health status. This shows that the decline in g over the lifetime did not predict mortality in very old age because of its association with poorer health or living conditions.

Why should childhood IQ predict survival to age 77? The authors consider four possible explanations for the relationship.

(a) In the early part of the 20th century when poverty was rife, it is possible that childhood IQ may have been reduced by environmental problems such as childhood illnesses, poor diet or antenatal care, and these might also affect longevity.
(b) If IQ has a biological basis, it is possible that the biological factors associated with having a high IQ have a direct influence on lifespan.
(c) High IQ individuals may enter occupations that are relatively safe (e.g., becoming accountants rather than deep sea fishermen).
(d) High IQ individuals may pay more heed to health information, and lead healthier lives.

Much of the authors' later work explores the merits of these approaches, and exploring other correlates of childhood IQ. For example, it was found that IQ is not just related to longevity, but to quality of life (Starr, Deary, Lemmon & Whalley, 2000); it predicts the extent to which the surviving 77-year-olds could look after themselves ($r = 0.24$, $N = 211$, $P < 0.001$), and IQ has a larger influence on quality of life in old age than do optimism and levels of anxiety and depression (Bain et al., 2003). This is important because it is often claimed that physical activity in older age influences cognition: in truth, the relationship seems to be the other way round. Modest correlations were found between cognition scores at age 77 and the number of social/cultural activities undertaken—e.g., visiting friends, or reading a book. However these correlations disappeared when IQ at age 11 was controlled for. This shows that childhood IQ is the cause of the correlation between cognitive ability and activity level in old age. The amount of social

and cultural activities that one chooses to undertake as they get older probably does not directly boost one's intelligence. Social activity happens because
some older adults are intelligent; the evidence suggests that it does not make
them intelligent.

Data from another study also show that low childhood intelligence predicts self-reported chronic pain in middle age (Gale, Deary, Cooper & Batty,
2012), a relationship that was partly (but not completely) mediated by adult
social-class and being overweight. The more intelligent children tended to be
thinner adults with higher SES—but there was also a direct link between low
childhood intelligence and experiencing pain in middle age. (Educational
attainment, smoking status and psychological distress did not mediate the
relationship.) However it is not entirely clear why the relationship arises, and
the difference between the IQ scores of the group who experience pain and
those who did not is only 3 IQ points (0.2 of a standard deviation). This difference is statistically highly significant because of the large sample size (N =
7,000), but it is not a huge effect.

Low intelligence also predicts the likelihood of developing dementia after
age 65 (Whalley et al., 2000), but although statistically significant, the effect
size is once again small.

Environmental Factors Affecting Both g and Health Status

It has been found that birth weight, social class, illegitimacy etc. did indeed
predict IQ at age 11 to some extent (Shenkin et al., 2001) although the
relationship was modest. Five such variables together explained only 15%
of the variance in IQ: parental social class was the largest influence. This
estimate of 15% is an overestimate. This is because parents' IQs will influence both their own social class (because of the links between the parents'
IQ and occupations, discussed earlier in this chapter) and their children's
IQ (because of genetic effects). Thus, it may not be appropriate to consider
parental social class as a purely environmental influence when predicting
children's IQ, as both it and the children's IQ will be influenced by the parents' IQ. In an ideal world, it would be better to study adopted children, for
as Plomin, Loehlin and DeFries (1985) have shown with younger children,
one cannot simply use checklists such as the HOME inventory (Bradley &
Caldwell, 1979) to measure "environmental" influences, as a substantial
amount of the variance in the HOME score is genetically determined.

Whether or not any of these variables also predict health status later in life
is unknown. Furthermore some theoretical rationale is needed to explain
why this might happen. It is plausible that early exposure to toxic chemicals
might affect childhood IQ and also lead to health problems later in life: it is

less obvious how some life events might be expected to affect both IQ and health.

Of course, it is always possible that some variables that were not included in Shenkin's study might influence childhood IQ. It is probably impossible to assess what degree of ante-natal care the children in this sample received almost a century ago or the number, nature and timing of childhood illnesses (in an era before vaccination was commonplace) let alone what their mothers' diets, stress levels, smoking and drinking habits were. Indeed, it might not be possible to discover the influence of comparatively uncommon events. For example, we know that environmental insults such as pre-natal exposure to chemicals such as PCBs can have a substantial influence on children's IQ (Stewart et al., 2008). The problem is that if children in the sample are exposed to arrange of different environmental insults—e.g., one or two to PCBs, one or two to lead, a couple to organo-phosphates—it will be difficult or impossible to identify these as influencing IQ because the number of children exposed to each of them is so small.

As it stands, there is not much evidence to suggest that individual variables such as birth weight have a massive influence on childhood IQ. In addition, behaviour genetic studies show that environmental factors that are shared by all members of the family (such as social class, or availability of books or educational games) are unlikely to have substantial links to childhood IQ. Those environmental factors that do influence IQ will therefore need to be different for each child in the family. We know that environmental influences outside the family are important—nearly as important as genetic influences—however not much is known about which individual environmental factors influence intelligence at age 11, or whether/how they go on to affect health status later in life.

Biological Factors Affecting Both *g* and Health Status

Deary's point (b) suggests that some individuals may have better-functioning nervous systems (and other physical systems) than others. This "system integrity" may lead to both in higher scores on tests of cognitive ability (and possibly measures of general health) at any point in the lifespan, and in better physical health and cognitive functioning in older age. The key point about this hypothesis is that the integrity of the nervous system can be detected at an early age. The theory does not just suggest that the gradual breakdown of nervous system functioning as one ages results in both cognitive decline and illness. It suggests a direct biological link between childhood intelligence and health and cognition later in life. Deary (2012) explores this concept: system integrity has also been linked to how symmetric a person's body is, how well coordinated one is, and so on, and so these variables might perhaps be linked to both IQ and health status. He also explores similarities and differences between system integrity and other concepts, such as cognitive reserve and allostatic load; he concludes that it is probably different from these.

Evidence for system integrity could come from the discovery of a direct link between the biological correlates of intelligence early in life and their link to physical and cognitive functioning in older age. We have seen that processing speed seems to be consistently correlated with performance on intelligence tests throughout life, and with measures of health and brain physiology. So it is just possible that this could be the neural basis of system integrity. However this work is extremely speculative at this stage and the question arises about why some individuals develop more resilient nervous systems than others.

One way to determine whether g has a direct causal biological link to health is to use multivariate genetic analysis to check whether the genes that influence g also influence health status in later life (assuming that health status is determined genetically rather than environmentally, which might be unlikely). The second possibility is to eliminate all possible social and environmental confounds—the influence of chemicals on the developing nervous system etc.—but because there may be a great number of these influences, each affecting a fairly small number of children in any sample it might be difficult or impossible to identify and assess these influences. The third possibility is to try to identify other signs of system integrity other than those related to intelligence or health. There has been speculation that bodily symmetry (for example, the degree to which one side of the face resembles a mirror image of the other) might reflect system integrity (Bates, 2007; Furlow, Armijoprewitt, Gangestad & Thornhill, 1997) though the theoretical rationale for this is rather tenuous. Little is known about whether bodily symmetry is related to health outcomes as well as to IQ. The concept of system integrity, and its possible role in predicting health outcomes, need further work.

Childhood Intelligence and Accidents, Death and Injury

Do intelligent people tend to enter safe jobs? And if so, could this explain the link between intelligence and health? This possibility is appealing: the life of a chartered accountant is arguably far less perilous than that of a miner, and so it is possible that longevity is linked to living a safe life, rather than anything to do with IQ. It is hard to research this directly, as the number of fatalities at work is low in the Western world—an average annual rate of 3.5 per 100, 000 in the United States (Bureau of Labor Statistics, 2012). This means that even if huge numbers of people were IQ-tested at an early age, only a tiny number would later die at work. Thus it would be difficult to determine whether choice of occupation is the reason for a link between childhood intelligence and mortality.

There is, of course, a substantial literature on occupational hazards and their effect on health in later life: exposure to asbestos, organic solvents, aluminium and heavy metals is known to affect health, and it is plausible to suspect that those with lower educational qualifications may gravitate toward jobs (such as welding or labouring) where exposure to toxins is greater. On the other hand, research chemists (high-IQ individuals who deal with toxic chemicals) did not seem to have a high rate of cancer when compared with members of a control group in an old study that was performed before the dangers of chemical reagents were well understood (Hoar & Pell, 1981). If the only reason why high-IQ individuals survived longer was that they entered safe occupations, high-IQ individuals in this unsafe occupation would be expected to die early.

One way of exploring whether the link between mortality and intelligence comes about because less intelligent people enter dangerous occupations is to look at accidents outside the workplace. A correlation between g and the incidence of these accidents indicates that any link between g and accident-proneness is direct, rather than being entirely mediated by riskiness of occupation. O'Toole and Stankov (1992) followed up 46,000 Australian ex-servicemen, of whom 389 died from "external causes" rather than illness. Over half of these were motoring accidents, whilst 76 were suicides. They expected to find that prior medical history and personality predicted such deaths, but to the authors' surprise, g was the best predictor of death: someone with an IQ of 85 was twice as likely to die as someone with an IQ of 115. This is a very substantial relationship.

There was little difference between those with IQs between 100 and 115 and those with IQs above 115, suggesting that low IQ is the "problem", rather than high IQ being a protective factor. The reasons for this are not known: it may well have something to do with risk-taking behaviour (e.g., recognising that reaction time is at least half a second, and so one will crash into the car in front if one tailgates it), or recognising the circumstances when this is particularly dangerous (high speed, wet roads) and modifying one's behaviour accordingly.

It would be surprising if these findings did not generalise to the workplace: perhaps higher-IQ workers might be better at identifying potential risks and/or more attentive to safety warnings and protocols. We saw earlier that IQ (and educational qualifications) influence occupational status. So one might expect that those working in manual jobs might tend to suffer more accidents and injuries as a consequence of their lower IQ, and not solely as a consequence of entering a riskier trade.

As far as coping is concerned, Deary, Whiteman, Starr, Whalley, and Fox (2004) found that for every standard deviation decrease in childhood intelligence, there was a 12% increase in the likelihood of a person having psychiatric contact at some stage of their life, which may again suggest that individuals with higher intelligence may be better able to develop coping mechanisms to help them deal with stress. Some of the basic elements of cognitive coping mechanisms—self-monitoring to recognise that there is a problem, thinking creatively and abstractly about possible options for dealing with the problem and their likely consequences—may be facilitated by g. However the empirical literature on how g influences coping is sparse (e.g., Bailey & Hailey, 1983).

Some years ago I looked at the relationship between stress and coping mechanisms in prisoners, expecting to find that some coping strategies were more effective than others with helping prisoners adjust to life "inside" (Cooper & Berwick, 2001). This project was a failure because very few of the prisoners (average IQ about 87: Hayes, Shackell & Mottram 2006) seemed to appreciate that they could do anything to influence the impact of life events. The whole concept of coping mechanisms was too abstract for many of them to appreciate, which ties in with Deary's findings.

There are plenty of other studies, too, which show that IQ is linked to injury and death later in life. Whitley et al. (2010) report Swedish data from over a million men that also show that intelligence predicts injuries caused by falling, road accidents, poisoning, medical complications and fire—though not drowning. Overall, it seems that accidents probably do not occur as randomly as we think, and that IQ has a causal influence. Given that there are strong relationships between IQ and death/injury in contexts other than work, it seems unlikely that the sole reason why high-IQ individuals tend to live longer, healthier, lives is because they enter safer occupations.

Childhood Intelligence and Lifestyle

We have seen that there seems to be a fairly strong, direct relationship between childhood intelligence and accidents. But do intelligent people also tend to live healthier lives (for example, paying more heed to warnings about smoking and diet, or better adhering to guidelines for taking prescribed medication)? If so, this could explain at least part of the link between childhood intelligence and health in later life.

Whether or not a person starts to smoke tobacco seems to be unrelated to their childhood IQ. This is unsurprising given the lack of information linking smoking and cancer in the 1930s–1950s. However the more intelligent smokers tend to give up the habit in adulthood (Taylor et al., 2003), a clear example of how higher-IQ individuals may pay more heed to health warnings and so lead a healthier life.

The amount of C-reactive protein (CRP) in the blood is associated with heart disease. In a study of 77-year-olds (Hagger-Johnson et al., 2012), it was found that childhood intelligence and childhood SES were both correlated with levels of this protein—but intelligence appeared to be the causal influence because intelligent children moved to a higher SES in adulthood, which resulted in less obesity, healthier lifestyles and a better quality of life. However the analyses are complex, and although intelligence also appeared to have a direct influence on levels of CRP (in addition to those that came about because intelligence influenced adult SES) the direct effect was very small. Although this study suggests that there may be a physiological causal link between childhood intelligence and coronary proneness, it is small. There is also a link between childhood intelligence and markers such as CRP in middle age (Calvin, Batty, Lowe & Deary, 2011a): here too childhood intelligence seems to influence whether a child adopts a healthy lifestyle in adulthood that in turn influences CRP levels. However these relationships are complicated.

Conclusions: *g*, Health and Wellbeing

It is clear from Deary's work that intelligence, measured in childhood, seems to have an influence on several aspects of adult health and functioning. It is surprising to find that scores from a simple intelligence test can predict who survives 66 years later, even after controlling for the effects of social deprivation. Finding that *g* also predicts quality of life in old age is also unexpected, and potentially important. For whilst it is known that there is a correlation between physical activity and cognitive ability in old age, Deary's work may suggest that high intelligence leads to more physical activity in old age, rather than vice versa. Disentangling the role of intelligence from other possible confounding variables (social class, lifestyle and so on) is not a trivial issue, but although some of the effects are rather small, Deary's attempts to do so show that *g* appears to have an enduring influence on health.

Summary

This chapter considered whether tests of ability are able to predict real-life behaviour, or whether they are merely of interest to academic psychologists. The answer seems to be clear. Intelligence seems to predict how people behave in a variety of real-life settings. It influences how well children perform at school: although there is some evidence showing that the amount of education that a child of a certain age receives influences g, g itself is a potent predictor of school achievement, even when factors such as social class are controlled.

Intelligence also predicts performance at work—both directly, and via its influence on educational qualifications: Gottfredson (1997) considers the links between the skills measured by intelligence tests and those that are required in the workplace. Once again, these links are very substantial indeed, and general intelligence seems to predict performance at just about all levels of all occupations—from manual workers to senior management. One very unexpected finding is that it is general intelligence rather than primary or second-order abilities, which seems to predict job performance. This is counter-intuitive as the primary or second-order abilities often look as if they are more closely related to the demands of the job than are tests of g.

Surprisingly, perhaps, intelligence has also been linked to health, longevity and accidents—perhaps through "biological fitness", better awareness of risks to health (e.g., smoking) or better judgement (e.g., when driving) or better ability to cope with stress—an area that has been woefully unresearched.

A strong case can be made that g seems to be an important causal influence on performance in many spheres of life. What other psychological variable that can be assessed cheaply in less than an hour can tell us so much about how a person will behave?

8

REFLECTIONS AND CONCLUSIONS

This chapter is a little more self-indulgent than the previous ones. In it, I shall outline what seem to me to be the most interesting and important issues to emerge from research into human intelligence, and muse about their implications. It basically tries to put the rest of the book in some perspective: the previous chapters have been quite heavily referenced and linked to empirical studies, and so having looked at the minutiae of modern research into g, it might be useful to step back a little and reflect on what it all implies, what we do *not* know, and some practical applications of the theories developed above.

One reason I enjoy working with human intelligence is because ability tests allow intelligence to be assessed directly. To perform well at an intelligence test, you actually have to *be* intelligent: there is no other way of obtaining a good score (apart from cheating). Perhaps this sounds obvious. However when assessing personality, measurements are almost invariably based on self-report, or assessments made by other people. When someone answers a question such as "do you enjoy lively parties" (a question that measures extraversion), the person does not actually *need* to be extraverted in order to say yes. People could be deluded about their own behaviour. They could be deliberately lying—perhaps trying to cover up what they perceive as a weakness in their character, or to obtain a job where they feel that a sober, boring person is more likely to be appointed. They may not know with whom they are supposed to compare themselves: if an introvert surrounds himself or herself with friends who are even more introverted, then relative to this circle of friends, they will be the most extraverted, and so might feel that they should answer yes to the question. There are plenty of other well-documented problems with self-assessment scales, too. But with the exception of Gardner's theory, intelligence researchers actually measure behaviour rather than ask for opinions. To solve an inductive reasoning problem correctly, one really does have to possess a certain level of inductive reasoning. We are not interested in asking how well the person thinks that they can solve such problems (e.g., by asking them to rate statements such as "I am better than most people at solving an abstract problem that requires logic", using a 1–5 rating scale). Instead, we give them a sample of problems (of varying difficulty, so that just about everyone will get some correct, whilst very few will get them all correct) and measure how good people actually are at solving them.

Basics

In individual differences, I always pay far more attention to findings that involve different methods of assessment.

It concerns me that in psychology, many concepts are conceptually highly similar to each other. For example, a lot has been written about the fine distinctions between hopelessness and depression. The most widely used scale to measure hopelessness (the Beck Hopelessness Scale) asks people to rate themselves on statements such as "I might as well give up because there's nothing I can do to make things better for myself" and "I never get what I want, so it's foolish to want anything". A widely used scale measuring depression (the Patient Health Questionnaire) asks how often the person "feels down, depressed or hopeless" or "feels bad about himself/herself". If a person agrees with the two hopelessness items, surely they are bound to also endorse the two items from the depression scale? How could a person who feels that he or she might as well give up *not* reporting feel down/depressed/ hopeless? So it follows that the two scales are bound to be correlated to some extent, just because some of the items in the two scales have similar meanings. And just because a person says he or she feels hopeless (etc.), it by no means follows that he or she really is. The person may be out of touch, or may not know how hopeless other people feel, or may be trying to project an image of himself or herself and so on. So it is really no great surprise to find that hopelessness is correlated with depression—partly because the concepts are similar, and partly because both are measured using self-report questionnaires. I would find it hard to get excited enough by such correlations to spend much time researching this area, though many people do.

Cognitive abilities are very different. Why *should* a person's level of vocabulary ("surely" something that is developed at school) correlate with his or her memory, the powers of creativity, spatial skills, the ability to identify which shape comes next in a sequence or their reaction time? It is not at all clear why such relationships should exist, as each task should involve rather different cognitive processes or modules, and many of the items in ability tests (particularly those involving abstract shapes) are unfamiliar to everyone taking part in the study, and are unlikely to depend much on knowledge or skills taught in school. So the finding of substantial correlations between tasks that look as if they ought to measure completely different things is both unexpected and intriguing.

Finding that scores on these tests has a strong correlation with inspection time (in the order of -0.5) is another intriguing issue. After all, the inspection time task does not even require people to think—but just report what they can see. So why should it correlate so closely with g? Large, unexpected correlations such as this are clues that something interesting and important is going on.

The often-substantial correlations between scores on these pencil-and-paper ability tests and real life behaviours are also interesting. Why should performance on tests that involve reasoning about geometric shapes go on to predict success in school? And why should a simple ability test adminis-tered once in childhood go on to predict longevity, health etc.? Most telling of all, why should performance on these tasks prove better predictors than tasks that seem to resemble the job that the worker will perform in post, and continue to have a substantial influence over the lifespan? It is all terribly counter-intuitive, and therefore interesting.

Then there is the behaviour-genetic evidence. If g was moulded by the fam-ily environment, these analyses would show it. But the reality is that adults' levels of intelligence owe virtually nothing to the way that their parents raised them. Unrelated adults who are brought up in the same environment are no more similar than a pair of randomly selected strangers by adulthood—although they do resemble individuals to whom they are biologically related. This is again counter-intuitive and so interesting. Finally, multivariate genetic analyses show that the genes that influence a person's level of g are pretty much the same genes as those that influence performance at school.

All of these findings seem to me to be unexpected in a way that much research in psychology is not. In addition, the correlations between abil-ity tests and real-life behaviour are frequently substantial: correlations in the order of 0.5 are not uncommon. There are very few other areas of psy-chology where seemingly dissimilar variables (such as job performance and performance on tests of general intelligence) correlate so substantially. Where variables do correlate substantially in psychology (e.g., depression and hopelessness, as mentioned above), there is frequently a nagging concern that the two variables share things in common (such as the way a person uses a rating scale, or the content of the questions) pretty much guaranteeing that two variables will be correlated. For these reasons, I believe that research into the nature and origins of human cognitive abilities are interesting, important for psychology, and also of considerable practical use.

Issues That I have Not Covered

There are several issues that I have not explored in this book, and it seems only fair to explain why this is the case.

Group Differences

The most obvious omission is that of group differences. A substantial literature shows that members of some minority groups (such as black Americans) perform less well than white Americans on most ability tests. So if ability tests are used to select black Americans for college or jobs, black students or employees will be underrepresented. The key question is whether the lower scores that some minority groups obtain are caused by some problem with the test, or whether the difference is genuine.

Apart from its political sensitivity, this is a hard problem to address empirically. Rather obviously, some ability tests include items that require some familiarity with the culture or language. A person from the tropics who is shown a picture of a snowy scene in which he or she supposed to realise that a set of footprints is missing is likely to find the item harder than a Canadian would. It is possible that social deprivation, cultural issues ("cool to flunk", "bad manners to outperform friends"), poorer education and so on might lead members of minority groups to underperform on some or all ability tests: the test score might well underestimate the true intelligence of a member of a minority group. This is known as bias. On the other hand, it might be the case that after considering all of these issues, there might still be some differences in test performance that are genuine.

My main reason for not discussing these issues in detail is because it is very hard to distinguish between bias and genuine group differences. For example, it is well known that the Japanese outperform Westerners on tasks involving spatial performance, visualisation and so on. But why is this? It could be due to eating fish, familiarity with a different form of alphabet (Kanji characters etc.), better attitudes toward learning, different teaching methods and a whole host of other possibilities. One author (Lynn, 1987) has even suggested that natural selection was responsible; because Asians were hunters in the ice ages, natural selection may have led to those with good spatial skills catching prey and avoiding being eaten. How can one control for all of these factors? Attempts have been made to do so, for example by looking at first, second and third-generation Japanese immigrants in the United States, but it is almost impossible (in my view) to be sure that everything has been taken into consideration.

One possibility (some have argued) is to compare scores on tests with how people perform at work or at school. If the tests are biased against members of a minority group, members of the minority group should perform better at work/school than their test scores should lead one to expect. But this assumes that it is possible to measure work performance in an unbiased way, which is at best questionable. If the test is biased and measures of work performance are also biased, then it will appear that lower-than-average test scores of the minority group are also reflected in below-average work performance: in other words, it will appear that there is a genuine group difference rather than biased measurements.

Some have suggested that techniques such as trans-racial adoption studies might help to solve this issue. White children adopted by black families (and black children adopted by white families) might be compared with black children adopted by black families and white children adopted by white families. It might be possible for such data to show whether there is any genetic basis for group differences. However the only such study of which I am aware suffers major design flaws, and small number of participants in some groups (only 25 adopted white children) so that even the authors admit that the results are inconclusive. There is also the problem that the adopted children may well not be representative of the population, given that adoption agencies normally take pains to adopt within the same culture. This limits the extent to which the results may be generalised.

The political right has also developed an interest in racial issues and eugenics—the proposal that society would benefit if less able (less intelligent) individuals were discouraged or prevented from having as many children as more intelligent individuals. Richard Lynn argues that differences in earning power of countries may be linked to the average IQ of its citizens (Lynn & Vanhanen, 2002) and that a policy of eugenics may have some merit (Lynn, 2001). The evidence on which the first proposition is based seems to be shaky at best and assumes that tests can be used in cultures very different from the ones in which they were devised without loss of validity. The eugenics argument is based more on political ideology than science and is repugnant to many of us who work in the area. Regarding racial differences as real rather than consequences of biased tests could have far-reaching political consequences were such views to become popular. In addition, it is tempting to apply stereotypes. Even if there *was* a difference in intelligence between black and white Americans, many black Americans would be more intelligent than the average white American, though social psychology teaches us that humans tend to overuse stereotypes and assume that group differences apply to all members of the group (Abrams, 2010). Hunt and Carlson (2007) suggest that because the social implications of group differences in intelligence can be so devastating, the quality of evidence required should be much greater than is normally required in psychology (where P < 0.05 holds sway).

There is also a literature on sex-differences in intelligence. This tends to be complicated by the fact that girls enter puberty rather earlier than boys that may impact upon their rate of cognitive development: studying sex-differences in adolescents is unwise for this reason. In adulthood, there is scant evidence for sex-differences in g, although women tend to perform men in verbal tasks, whilst men outperform women slightly in spatial tasks. But once again, the effects are small and (to my mind) rather uninteresting, as we cannot easily discover why they emerge (apart from perhaps speculating that some genes on the Y chromosome may perhaps influence spatial ability, whilst those on the X chromosome might influence language). A meta-analysis by Irwing and Lynn (2005) found a sex difference in adults favouring males. However all of the studies examined by Irwing and Lynn used Raven's Matrices as a measure of intelligence—a test where all of the items are similar in format. It is quite possible that the sex-difference that they observe arises because of the "specific variance" attributable to this type of problem, rather to g—that is arguably better assessed by calculating factor scores, or averaging performance across a number of disparate tasks, as with tests such as the WAIS. Unpublished data of my own (where a good population sample took some 12 different tests with approximately 10 items in each as part of the pilot testing for the BBC "Test the Nation" IQ tests) show no hint of any sex difference. This echoes the consensus view that has long been that sex differences are trivial or non-existent (Brody, 1992). Given Hunt and Carlson's (2007) concerns, it is probably premature to assert otherwise.

The Flynn Effect

James Flynn (1984) made a surprising discovery: the ability scores obtained by Americans had increased gradually from generation to generation. This "Flynn Effect" applied to tests of g and fluid ability, and not to crystallised ability. The effect is quite substantial—about a fifth of a standard deviation per decade. Thus an "average" 20-year-old in 2014 would achieve a very much higher score on a test of fluid intelligence than did her "average intelligence" grandfather when he was 20 in 1964. By today's standard, the average grandfather would be in the bottom third, as regards intelligence. The Flynn Effect has been found all round the globe, and using a wide range of tests (Flynn, 1987, 1999). The finding that the Flynn Effect is associated with abstract reasoning, Gf rather than Gc, suggests that it is not a simple consequence of better education, or access to knowledge (e.g., through cheap paperback books, radio, television and the internet); it is found in both prosperous and less prosperous countries too, which also argues against this explanation (Van de Vijver & Brouwers, 2009). The finding that the phenomenon appears worldwide (Flynn, 1984, 1987) also argues against the possibility that change in teaching methods within one culture enhances student thinking and learning.

Can it really be the case that intelligence is increasing at such a rate? If so, we would expect inspection time, reaction time, job performance, educational attainment etc. to change as well. There is not much evidence available, because it would obviously be necessary to check that both samples of participants was were drawn from the same population—and this is not easy. However Nettelbeck and Wilson (2004) looked at inspection time and intelligence scores in similar samples of children in 1981 and 2001 They found that whilst there was an increase in intelligence test scores between the two samples (the Flynn effect) there was no decrease in inspection time. This suggests that biological intelligence may not be increasing. Instead, people might just be getting better at problem solving because they live in a more cognitively demanding world than did their parents or grandparents.

There are other possible explanations, such as increased familiarity with solving the types of problems used in the ability tests, together with various theories as to why peoples intelligence may have improved, such as improved nutrition (Lynn, 1990), or better education (but why does Gc then not increase?). Flynn's current suggestion (Flynn, 2007) is that individuals with a genetic advantage are now better able to take advantage of this, through greater access to knowledge, intellectually demanding activities, and clever people—a suggestion originally made by Plomin, Loehlin and deFries (1985). But these are really just plausible post-hoc rationalisations of the observed facts, rather than proper theories that can be disconfirmed. This is why I did not explore these issues in the main text.

Age-Related Changes

Scores on tests of fluid ability increase through childhood, peak in one's early 20's and then plateau. They start to decline from the age of 40, and this decline speeds up as one gets older. Tests of crystallised ability do not decline so much as we age: our vocabulary, knowledge of French grammar and so on will probably be preserved into late old age, long after our ability to reason quickly has deteriorated (Ryan, Sattler & Lopez, 2000). I have not explored this literature in detail because it is hard enough to understand the processes that underpin cognition in "normal" adults, without bringing in the additional complexity of developmental trends. A wide range of factors might cause cognitive decline to happen faster in some individuals than others (e.g., contusion from playing sport; loss of brain cells from heavy drinking) and the effects of these, in terms of which areas of the brain are affected, may well vary from person to person. So whilst these issues are of obvious interest to developmental psychologists, it might further complicate the picture to introduce a developmental thread. Individual difference psychologists have always been more interested to examine the correlations between scores at different ages, without paying much attention to the average score for each age group. This is probably something that should be rectified.

Abnormal Psychology

I have avoided the literature on abnormal psychology—for example the effects of developmental disorders or open and closed head injury on cognitive functioning—partly because it is not always clear what light they can shed on "normal" cognitive functioning, and partly because to do it justice any such treatment would have to be so lengthy as to change the focus of the book.

Interventions to Boost IQ

Children from socially deprived backgrounds tend to underachieve at school. There have been several interventions where very young, socially deprived children have been given a massive amount of environmental stimulation, starting at a young age (e.g., 3 months) and lasting several hours a day for many years. These children received just about every intervention which developmental psychologists believed might help their cognitive development. The aim of such studies was to try to boost the school performance of these children relative to that of a control group. I have not explored this literature in the text for two reasons. First, the interventions did not appear to be particularly successful. Although the IQ scores of the children who took part in the Milwaukee project (Garber, Begab & American Association on Mental Retardation, 1988) did improve relative to the scores of the control group, these supposedly superior IQs were not reflected in better school performance (Jensen, 1989). So it seems likely that the children just got better at solving the sorts of problems that are used to measure g, rather than enjoying a genuine improvement in intelligence.

The Carolina Abecedarian Project (Ramey, 1992) was no more clear-cut. Here there was a difference between IQ scores of the children who received the intervention and those who did not until the children started school. But when the children started school, the cognitive scores obtained by the children in the enhancement group declined quite appreciably, whilst those of the control group improved. There is another problem, too. The difference between the enhancement and control groups was found after just a few months—and before the enhancement group had received very much of the 4-year enhancement programme. So whilst one possibility is that whatever happened in the first few months was all that mattered, it is more likely that through sheer bad luck, the children in the enhancement group were probably more intelligent in the first place (Spitz, 1997, 1999). So it is very hard to know what to conclude from these studies. There is certainly not much evidence that even a massive intervention (the Abecedarian study was for 8 hours per day, 50 weeks per year for 4 years) led to a large increase in intelligence that endured and was reflected in other aspects of the children's life (e.g., school performance). These results are just not clear enough to draw any firm conclusions from them.

Neural Plasticity

Neuroscientists study the plasticity of the neural system following damage and are at pains to stress the flexibility and resilience of the human nervous system. When one area is damaged, some other areas of the brain can (sometimes, to some extent) take over the function of the damaged part of the brain. Surely according to this model, the brain is almost infinitely flexible, with neural networks rewiring themselves when necessary (e.g., following a stroke) so as to process information efficiently. This seems to be at odds with the traditional models of ability that treat cognitive ability as a trait that is a stable characteristic of each person, remaining fairly constant from youth to old age. Intelligence research is largely ignored by neuroscientists who focus almost entirely on the regenerative potential of the brain.

It at first seems surprising that childhood IQ is very strongly correlated with IQ in late adulthood—even when childhood IQ is assessed whilst neural pruning is still very much in progress (Deary, Whalley, Lemmon, Crawford & Starr, 2000). (Neural pruning is the elimination of rarely used synapses that continues up to adolescence.) However there might be less conflict between these viewpoints than first appears. If the genes that largely determine an individual's level of IQ influence the speed/efficiency with which all the neurones in the cortex operate, then the study of this is quite distinct from the study of how neural networks are built, maintained and modified. It is a shame that neuroscientists generally regard the study of human intelligence as hopelessly old-fashioned, without recognising that models are complementary.

Myths

Scientists and commercial bodies sometimes promote interventions to boost IQ that almost invariably fail to stand up to independent scrutiny, and usually lack any sensible theoretical rationale. Unfortunately commercial providers frequently seem to target teachers and educators with "magic bullets": interventions that will (somehow) improve their children's performance in the classroom through boosting their intelligence.

Much was made of the Mozart Effect—a claim that listening to Mozart boosts children's IQ—following a popular book (Campbell, 1997). There was scant evidence to support this notion at the time (merely one study claiming that listening to music had a short-term influence on performance on a spatial task), and a wealth subsequent research has shown that the notion is of little value (Pietschnig, Voracek & Formann, 2010).

So too is the idea that humans only use 10% (or some other percentage) of their brains. According to Geake (2008) this originated when a 19th century Italian psychiatrist scooped out parts of the brain of psychiatric patients until he noticed changes in behaviour. It has no foundation in modern science, and it is not obvious to me how one could even test such a claim empirically.

The concept that some people use one hemisphere of the brain more than others is also popular. According to this, persons who use their right hemisphere more are creative and intuitive, whilst "left-brain" thinkers are more analytical and logical. The obvious problem with this idea is that the hierarchical model of intelligence shows that people who perform above average on the second-order creativity factor (Gc) also tend to perform well at tasks requiring relentless logic (Gf). This could not be the case if the world were divided into left-brain thinkers and right-brain thinkers. The original notion came from early studies of people whose corpus callosum (the neural pathway connecting the left and right hemispheres) had been surgically severed because of epilepsy. It seems to have little support in modern-day research.

Despite some earlier claims to the contrary (and a huge industry that develops and markets brain-training exercises to the public), there is little evidence that even undertaking massive amount of "brain training" exercises actually makes adults smarter. Performance at the various tasks that were trained improves with practice, but there was no evidence that performance on the task that was being trained generalised to other (cognitively similar) tasks in a huge study of over 11,000 participants (Owen et al., 2010). If brain-training actually improved g, a person whose performance improved on one type of exercise should also perform better on other tasks (as g influences performance on all cognitive tasks).

The Bell Curve

I have not mentioned this book by Herrnstein and Murray (1994) that caused something of a furore when it was published. There are several reasons for this. First, it seems to have been written with a political agenda in mind: that a "cognitive underclass" in the United States is responsible for what the authors perceived to be the woes of society (crime, single parenthood, high welfare expenditure etc.). Second, there are numerous problems with the analysis and interpretation of the statistical analyses: for example, regression lines for different groups are shown but without a R^2 statistic to show how well the model fits the data, it is impossible to interpret the analyses: the same regression line could indicate a R^2 of 0.01 (virtually no relationship between the variables) or 0.9 (a massive relationship). Because the analyses were published in a popular book the analyses and inferences had not gone through the rigorous process of peer review to which journal articles are subjected before publication. Finally, the book has a right-of-centre approach to racial differences in g, affirmative action and so on which has been widely criticised by commentators (e.g., Fraser, 1995; Jacoby & Glauberman, 1995).

Important Failures to Consider Intelligence Research

Chapter 7 explored some of the relationships between intelligence and everyday life—education, health, occupational performance and so on. To conclude this chapter I will consider a few examples where professionals, policy-makers and researchers could usefully be exposed to modern research in intelligence, but where this does not happen.

Many non-psychologists (and some psychologists who should know better) feel that it is "obvious" that because the problems in IQ tests do not resemble the problems that people solve in everyday life, scores on IQ tests must be valueless. Or if there is a correlation between g and educational performance, work performance etc. this must be due to some other factor (social class being a favourite) that influences performance on each of them. Ignorance of the literature outlined in the previous chapters (especially that pertaining to the biological basis of g and the methods of multivariate genetic analysis) coupled with a commendable desire to view human behaviour as determined entirely by social factors means that many professionals are not exposed to these issues as part of their training.

Teachers' Knowledge of Human Cognitive Abilities

Having scrutinised syllabi for a number of teacher-training courses in the United Kingdom, it seems that trainee teachers are taught virtually nothing about human cognitive abilities. Teachers will emerge from such courses with little idea that children differ in general intelligence, that intelligence tends to be fairly stable over the lifespan, that it is substantially influenced by genetic makeup, that probably influences performance at school, that going to school also influences intelligence, that it has clear links to brain structure and function, and so on. On the other hand (to give examples from one highly rated university department) teachers will be well aware of vital issues such as "the radical version of relativism sometimes held to be implied by postmodernism" and "some of the central philosophical problems in the social sciences", whilst their training in research methods considers only interviews and case studies, questionnaires and surveys and observational methods—with nothing on the assessment of cognitive abilities. It is not obvious that graduate teachers from this course will even know what IQ is, let alone that that it influences academic performance. Teachers will be completely in the dark about the structure of human abilities and the links between cognition and brain function.

Why teachers are kept in ignorance about one of the largest influences on normal students' educational outcomes is a mystery. One might have thought it would be useful for a teacher to know what IQ is, and how it can affect school performance, and that generally speaking, children without diagnoses of dyslexia etc. will probably perform at a similar level at tasks requiring quite different cognitive abilities, despite Gardner's vociferous and unfounded claims to the contrary. And they should be taught that whilst both genetic makeup and the family environment are important influences on educational attainment, family background has far less influence on IQ than might be expected, provided that children are exposed to a "normal" environment that allows them to learn, develop language skills and so on. They might be surprised to learn that the genes that influence verbal skills and numerical skills are the same as those that influence school performance. On a more positive note, they should be aware that genetic variation means that low-IQ parents who provide little in the way of educational stimulation at home will sometimes produce a highly intelligent child who will go on to perform well at school. Instead it seems that these trainee teachers are exposed to a syllabus devised by social scientists and sociologists that seems to suggest that all concepts are relativistic/culturally determined, that a wealthy and supportive family background guarantees educational success, and that plays down the inconvenient truth that thinking and learning involves the brain and that brains differ in their structure and function.

Personnel Managers' Use of Ability Tests

Occupational psychologists and personnel managers tend to have a much more balanced view of the subject, probably because they can see the practical benefits of assessing cognitive abilities for selection and prediction of training outcomes. That said, firms of occupational psychologists tend to develop specialised tests for selection purposes, despite a wealth of evidence showing that cognitive tests generally predict performance because they measure g to some extent. According to this logic, firms could use an "off-the-shelf" test of general intelligence for most personnel selection purposes, rather than something developed at huge cost for a specific application (Thorndike, 1985). Older tests will also have a wealth of validation data to support them, whereas any newly developed test cannot have such good psychometric credentials.

Why then do personnel psychologists select staff based on tests that appear to be relevant to job content, rather than using sound, validated tests of g? I suspect that in part this is a commercial decision, for a test development company can presumably make far more money by producing a tailor-made test for a customer, rather than selling an existing test. But managers too need to understand that although it seems counter-intuitive, the actual content of the test need not resemble the types of tasks that the employees will be performing in order for the test to be useful. General intelligence, by definition, is an ability that is correlated with performance at most tasks at work, and that also correlates with performance at just about any psychological task that requires thought. So the choice of which task should be used to measure g should be guided by how much g (and how little of other, narrower abilities and measurement error) each task measures. The actual *content* and *look* of the task (whether it measures memory, spotting patterns in matrices or whatever) is completely irrelevant, and need bear no relationship whatsoever to the sorts of activities that the employee would perform if appointed. This is a hard point for non-psychologists to grasp: personnel managers instead seem to think of a psychological test as being a mere selection of the tasks that the person will perform if appointed, with no great theoretical underpinning.

Government Briefing Papers

Research that is commissioned by government, and that thereafter informs policy, frequently fails to consider individual differences in intelligence and their implications. I feel uncomfortable writing this section, as I strongly agree with wealth redistribution and the reduction of poverty: however I am concerned that many writers go beyond the data when arguing that child-hood poverty is a direct cause of below-average educational achievement. If parental income is a direct cause of academic underachievement, then

(a) It is necessary to understand what the underlying mechanisms for this are. What are the critical experiences of children from lower-income families that so seriously affect their education? How do these combine and interact to explain academic underachievement?

(b) By boosting the income of the poorest families, the educational perfor-mance of their children is likely to rise. On the other hand, if lower-than-average intelligence is the cause of such academic underperformance in socially disadvantaged families, it is less obvious that reducing pov-erty will produce a direct increase in academic performance, although it might be desirable for other reasons.

Most studies seem to be carried out by sociologists who (by definition) assume that social problems have social causes, and who will know little or nothing about the pivotal role of intelligence in human functioning. I will give just two recent examples, although others can be found in the press just about every week.

Universities

UK universities have been criticised by governments because children from economically disadvantaged families are underrepresented: e.g., "Universi-ties should target working-class white boys, minister says" (Press Association, 2013). This is interpreted as a problem with the universities' admissions procedure unfairly favouring middle-class applicants. And of course it is vital to consider that admissions processes are fair: those involving inter-views etc. may well not be. However this position fails to acknowledge the possibility that although there will be plenty of individual exceptions, lower socio-economic status (SES) students may well tend have lower intelligence (and worse academic credentials) than high-SES applicants. This suggestion may sound shocking, but it follows logically from the empirical literature discussed in the previous chapters.

(a) Parental income is a major determinant of each family's SES (by definition).
(b) Parental intelligence will influence the parents' level of education and hence their income, as discussed in Chapter 7. So parents in low-SES families will, in general, tend to have lower intelligence than those in high-SES families.
(c) Because intelligence has a substantial heritability, children of low-SES parents will also generally tend to have lower intelligence than children of high-SES parents (although there will be plenty of individual exceptions, because of genetic variability).
(d) The children's lower intelligence will tend to lead to weaker academic performance at school (e.g., worse examination performance, lower probability of staying at school until age 18) as discussed in Chapter 7.
(e) As school examination performance at age 18 is a major factor in universities' admission decisions, it follows that fewer students from low-SES families will be admitted.

The problem, of course, is whether universities should attempt to identify and admit intelligent and academically able applicants who have the best potential to perform well in the future (in which case low-SES individuals will almost inevitably be underrepresented) or whether universities should apply a policy of positive discrimination so that academically weaker, less intelligent, applicants from low-SES backgrounds are accepted. If positive discrimination is used and such applicants tend to underachieve, the universities will doubtless be blamed for not providing sufficient support to such students, failing to provide a culture of inclusiveness, etc.

From a psychologist's perspective, it is truly amazing that the economists and sociologists whose research informs governments on such issues (e.g., Marcenaro-Gutierrez, Galindo-Rueda & Vignoles, 2007) never even mention the word intelligence let alone consider the possibility that children differ in cognitive ability and that this might affect their performance. Instead, low wealth is seen as the key influence on educational performance although we showed in Chapter 7 that intelligence has a far greater influence on educational performance than does family income or SES. The underrepresentation of low-SES adolescents at university is viewed as a failing of the education system.

Schools

The Save the Children charity's (2013) report "Too Young to Fail" (Warren & Paxton, 2013) was written to encourage UK political parties to develop their education policies in this direction. It points to a clear link between childhood poverty and educational underperformance; its authors argue that "whether a child is born into a poor or better-off family still largely determines how well he or she is likely to do at school" (a statement that is well supported by data, and with which no one would argue). But the authors then suggest that this link is causal, and that improving resources for deprived children can bring them up to the level of performance of their peers: "it is possible to make broad estimates of the likely impact on Britain's economic growth of making further progress in improving the education of the poorest children" that examines what would happen if "the poorest pupils achieved the same levels as others" as a result of extra funding for early education. Whilst it would be wonderful if these interventions could improve school performance, the report once again makes not a single mention of intelligence. The naive reader would assume that all children have the same academic potential, and that only social factors can lead to underachievement at school.

There is excellent evidence that controlling for social class and educational attainment does not remove the link between childhood intelligence and occupational status in mid-life (e.g., von Stumm, MacIntyre, Batty, Clark & Deary, 2010). These authors found that intelligence had twice as much influence on educational attainment as did parental social class. Intelligence and education went on to have similar-sized influences on social class in mid-life: the influence of parental social class was smaller. Intelligence is potent determinant of a person's social class in middle age—both directly, and because it leads to better educational qualifications. Its effect is larger than parental social class. To ignore it completely when advising ministers about social policy seems reckless, at best. For findings such as this suggest that economic benefits of reducing child poverty are likely to be far less than expected—although a case can obviously be made for reducing child poverty for other reasons.

The Take-Home Message

Few theories in psychology have stood the test of time as well as the psychology of human abilities. Since Spearman's seminal paper, psychoanalysis and other depth theories of personality have blossomed and been forgotten; so too have behaviourism, drive reduction theories of learning

(Hull, Spence and their ilk) and expert systems. Part of the reason is probably that it is so easy to replicate Spearman's results. Even when collections of cognitive tasks were put together to measure quite different aspects of cognitive functioning in order to diagnose damage to different parts of the brain (Wechsler, 1939), correlations between the tasks were very substantial. And whenever theorists (e.g., Gardner, 1983; Guilford, 1967) claimed that g was unnecessary, subsequent empirical analyses (Chen & Michael, 1993; Visser, Ashton & Vernon, 2006) showed them to be incorrect.

Despite the problems with the old behaviour-genetic studies, there is now huge amount of modern evidence showing that as long as they are brought up in a "normal" first-world environment, people's levels of g will be influenced more by their biological makeup than their home environment. And one of the most interesting recent discoveries is that the genes that influence one's ability also influence other abilities that look as if they involve quite different cognitive processes. These generalist genes also influence other behaviours (e.g., school performance) that makes it clear that g is a genuine causal influence.

The biological origins of g also are also evident in its correlations with some biological, cognitive and physiological measures (e.g., brain volume, reaction time, inspection time, Event Related Potentials) even if these involve little or no conscious thought or reasoning. There is also excellent evidence that a person's level of intelligence is fairly stable over time and is linked to work performance, school performance and (to a lesser degree) health. It is difficult to determine whether all of these relationships are causal, but the review of the literature in Chapter 7 strongly suggests that many of them are: g often seems to influence real-life behaviour, even when social deprivation, the effects of education etc. are allowed for, and these correlations are frequently large; Schmidt and Hunter (2004) found them to be over 0.5. One of the most counterintuitive findings is that narrower abilities (such as memory or visualisation) have little rather impact on job performance etc. once the effects of g are controlled for. Arthur Jensen spoke of g as being the "active ingredient" that makes cognitive tests useful for making predictions about how a person will behave at work or elsewhere. The more a test correlates with g the better it predicts performance in all sorts of areas. Narrower abilities such as visualisation or memory have almost no predictive power once the effects of g are statistically removed, a finding that has powerful implications for personnel selection—implications that are generally ignored by test designers even though Thorndike's seminal work on occupational selection was published in 1985. Because g seems to be the most potent predictor of behaviour, the latter chapters of this book have focused on it rather than the primary or second-order abilities discussed in Chapter 3.

Because g seems to have such a pervasive influence on performance in areas such as health, work and education as well as in cognitive and developmental psychology, I think it would make great sense for researchers to routinely administer a quick test of g alongside their preferred dependent variables whilst carrying out research—if only to check that any effects that they find are not caused by individual differences in g. At the very least, treating g as a covariate, rather than a factor that increases the size of the error term in a statistical analysis, will lead to more sensitive experimental designs.

Furthermore, any studies of behaviours involving relatives (e.g., mother–child interactions) really must consider that biological relatives will tend to have similar levels of g, and this might influence the behaviour of both the relatives. This is a huge problem for any study that simply measures parental behaviour rather than randomly assigning parents to an experimental or a control condition. For example, a researcher who measures how much a mother reads aloud to their child really must perform the analysis using adopted children or else measure g and use structural equation modelling in order to determine whether it is reading per se or the similar levels of intelligence of the mother and child that influences later academic outcomes.

The major issues for further research are clear. As well as the more technical work in identifying the genes that influence g and the biological mechanisms that allow them to do so, there is plenty of scope for psychologists to discover how individuals build their unique environments. Plomin has showed that this influenced by g and other abilities, though the actual processes do not seem to have been studied. There is also a need to further examine low-level correlates of g in order to further evaluate the speed of information processing theories; for example, our work on reflex latency needs to be replicated and extended. And finally, the processes that underpin the correlations between g, occupational performance, educational attainment, health and other real-life behaviours need to be understood. For example, what is it about g that makes some sales-people more successful than others? Or better delivery drivers? Then there is the issue of working memory. For a start, it is necessary to check whether the tasks that cognitive psychologists claim to measure working memory all do so; that is, validate them. Then structural equation modelling needs to be used to establish the size of the relationship between multiple working-memory tests and multiple tests of cognitive ability (g)—and ideally measures of inspection time, reaction time etc. as well.

Whenever intelligence is mentioned in the popular press, there is often a knee-jerk reaction against it; comments such as "the idea of general intelligence has been superseded", "intelligence tests do not measure anything of value" "intelligence might matter in childhood, but it is irrelevant after we grow up" and so on are often made in response to such articles. I am not sure why. Part of it may stem from the hope that cognitive abilities would be influenced by social factors, rather than biology. I would have hoped this myself, but the fact is that family background has next to no influence on g, whereas the particular combination of genes that one inherits has a huge influence. Then there are theorists such as Gardner or Sternberg who propose alternatives to intelligence theory without always ensuring that the theories are supported by firm empirical evidence. Perhaps these theories sow confusion? Having read this far you will appreciate that the topic of human intelligence (and other cognitive abilities) is far from moribund: modern physiological, psychological and statistical techniques are being used to discover how g is linked to human behaviour. The surprising thing is just how many aspects of behaviour it touches. Spearman's venerable theory still has much to offer psychological theory and practice.

REFERENCES

Abrams, D. 2010. *Processes of prejudice: Theory, evidence and intervention.* Canterbury, UK: University of Kent, Equality and Human Rights Commission Research Report Series.

Ackerman, P.L., Beier, M.E. & Boyle, M.O. 2005. Working memory and intelligence: The same or different constructs? *Psychological Bulletin,* 131, 30–60.

Ackerman, P.L. & Wolman, S.D. 2007. Determinants and validity of self-estimates of abilities and self-concept measures. *Journal of Experimental Psychology: Applied,* 13, 57–78.

Aiken, L.R. 1971. *Psychological and educational testing.* Oxford, UK: Allyn & Bacon.

Alexander, J.R.M. & Mackenzie, B.D. 1992. Variation of the 2-line inspection time stimulus. *Personality and Individual Differences,* 13, 1201–1211.

Alloway, T.P. 2010. Working memory and executive function profiles of individuals with borderline intellectual functioning. *Journal of Intellectual Disability Research,* 54, 448–456.

Anderson, M. 1998. Mental retardation general intelligence and modularity. *Learning and Individual Differences,* 10, 159–178.

Armstrong, T. 1994. *Multiple intelligences in the classroom.* Alexandria, VA: Association for Supervision and Curriculum Development.

Asbury, K., Wachs, T. D. & Plomin, R. 2005. Environmental moderators of genetic influence on verbal and nonverbal abilities in early childhood. *Intelligence,* 33, 643–661.

Bachman, J.G. & Omalley, P.M. 1977. Self-esteem in young men—longitudinal analysis of impact of educational and occupational attainment. *Journal of Personality and Social Psychology*, 35, 365–380.

Baddeley, A. 1986. *Working memory.* New York: Clarendon Press/Oxford University Press.

Baddeley, A. 2000. The episodic buffer: A new component of working memory? *Trends in Cognitive Sciences*, 4, 417–423.

Baddeley, A.D. & Hitch, G.J.L. 1974. Working memory. In: Bower, G.A. (ed.), *The psychology of learning and motivation.* New York: Academic Press.

Bailey, L.A. & Hailey, B.J. 1983. The influence of intelligence on coping style selection. *Journal of Clinical Psychology*, 39, 901–908.

Bain, G.H., Lemmon, H., Teunisse, S., Starr, J.M., Fox, H.C., Deary, I.J. & Whalley, L.J. 2003. Quality of life in healthy old age: Relationships with childhood IQ, minor psychological symptoms and optimism. *Social Psychiatry and Psychiatric Epidemiology*, 38, 632–636.

Baker, L. & Daniels, D. 1990. Nonshared environmental influences and personality differences in adult twins. *Journal of Personality and Social Psychology*, 58, 103–110.

Baker, L.A., Vernon, P.A. & Ho, H.Z. 1991. The genetic correlation between intelligence and speed of information-processing. *Behavior Genetics*, 21, 351–367.

Balboni, G., Naglieri, J.A. & Cubelli, R. 2010. Concurrent and predictive validity of the Raven Progressive Matrices and the Naglieri Nonverbal Ability Test. *Journal of Psychoeducational Assessment*, 28, 222–235.

Baron-Cohen, S., Leslie, A.M. & Frith, U. 1985. Does the autistic child have a "theory of mind"? *Cognition*, 21, 37–46.

Barrett, P.T., Daum, I. & Eysenck, H.J. 1990. Sensory nerve conduction and intelligence: A methodological study. *Journal of Psychophysiology*, 4, 1–13.

Barrett, P.T. & Eysenck, H.J. 1992. Brain evoked potentials and intelligence: The Hendrickson paradigm. *Intelligence*, 16, 361–381.

Barrett, P.T., Eysenck, H.J. & Lucking, S. 1986. Reaction time and intelligence—a replicated study. *Intelligence*, 10, 9–40.

Bartels, M., Rietveld, M.J.H., Van Baal, G.C.M. & Boomsma, D.I. 2002. Heritability of educational achievement in 12-year-olds and the overlap with cognitive ability. *Twin Research*, 5, 544–553.

Bates, T.C. 2007. Fluctuating asymmetry and intelligence. *Intelligence*, 35, 41–46.

Bates, T. C., Lewis, G. J. & Weiss, A. 2013. Childhood Socioeconomic Status Amplifies Genetic Effects on Adult Intelligence. *Psychological Science*, 24, 2111–2116.

Baumeister, A.A. & Kellas, G. 1968. Intrasubject response variability in relation to intelligence. *Journal of abnormal psychology*, 73, 421–423.

Beauducel, A. & Brocke, B. 1993. Intelligence and speed of information processing: Further results and questions on Hick's paradigm and beyond. *Personality and Individual Differences*, 15, 627–636.

Behrman, J., Taubman, P. & Wales, T. 1977. Controlling for and measuring the effects of genetics and family environment in equations for schooling and labor market success. In: Taubman, P. (ed.), *Kinometrics: Determinants of socioeconomic success within and between families.* Amsterdam: North-Holland Pub. Co.

Beloff, H. 1992. Mother, father and me: Our IQ. *The Psychologist,* 5, 309–311.

Bennett, G.K., Seashore, H.G. & Wesman, A.G. 1978. *Differential aptitude tests.* Orlando, FL: The Psychological Corporation.

Benson, V.E. 1942. The intelligence and later scholastic success of sixth-grade pupils. *School & Society,* 55, 163–167.

Betjemann, R. S., Johnson, E. P., Barnard, H., Boada, R., Filley, C. M., Filipek, P. A., . . . Pennington, B. F. 2010. Genetic covariation between brain volumes and IQ, reading performance, and processing speed. *Behavior Genetics,* 40, 135–145.

Bouchard, T.J., Lykken, D.T., McGue, M., Segal, N.L. & Tellegen, A. 1990. Sources of human psychological differences: The Minnesota study of twins reared apart. *Science,* 250, 223–228.

Bouchard, T.J. & McGue, M. 2003. Genetic and environmental influences on human psychological differences. *Journal of Neurobiology,* 54, 4–45.

Bouchard, T.J. 1993. The genetic architecture of human intelligence. In: Vernon, P.A. (ed.), *Biological approaches to the study of human intelligence.* New York: Ablex.

Bouchard, T.J. 1995. Longitudinal studies of personality and intelligence: a behavior genetic and evolutionary psychology perspective. In: Saklofske, D.H. & Zeidner, M. (eds.), *International handbook of personality and intelligence.* New York: Plenum.

Bouchard, T.J. & McGue, M. 1981. Familial studies of intelligence: A review. *Science,* 212, 1055–1058.

Bower, G.H. 1981. Mood and memory. *American Psychologist,* 36, 129–148.

Bradley, R.H. & Caldwell, B.M. 1979. Home Observation for Measurement of the Environment—Revision of the Pre-school Scale. *American Journal of Mental Deficiency,* 84, 235–244.

Brewer, N. & Smith, G.A. 1984. How normal and retarded individuals monitor and regulate speed and accuracy of responding in serial choice tasks. *Journal of Experimental Psychology: General,* 113, 71–93.

Brody, N. 1992. *Intelligence.* San Diego: Academic Press.

Brody, N. 1997. Intelligence, schooling, and society. *American Psychologist,* 52, 1046–1050.

Brody, N. 2003. Construct validation of the Sternberg Triarchic Abilities Test: Comment and reanalysis. *Intelligence,* 31, 319–329.

Brody, N. 2007. Barriers to understanding racial differences in intelligence: Commentary on Hunt and Carlson (2007). *Perspectives on Psychological Science,* 2, 214–215.

Brody, N. & Crowley, M.J. 1995. Environmental (and genetic) influences on personality and intelligence. In: Saklofske, D.H. & Zeidner, M. (eds.), *International handbook of personality and intelligence*. New York: Plenum.

Bureau of Labor Statistics 2012. *Census of Fatal Occupational Injuries Summary, 2011*. Washington, DC: United States Department of Labor.

Burns, N.R. & Nettelbeck, T. 2003. Inspection time in the structure of cognitive abilities: Where does IT fit? *Intelligence, 31*, 237–255.

Bus, A.G., Vanijzendoorn, M.H. & Pellegrini, A.D. 1995. Joint book reading makes for success in learning to read—a meta-analysis on intergenerational transmission of literacy. *Review of Educational Research, 65*, 1–21.

Butler, S.R., Marsh, H.W., Sheppard, M.J. & Sheppard, J.L. 1985. 7-year longitudinal-study of the early prediction of reading-achievement. *Journal of Educational Psychology, 77*, 349–361.

Byington, E. & Felps, W. 2010. Why do IQ scores predict job performance? An alternative, sociological explanation. In: Brief, A.P. & Staw, B.M. (eds.), *Research in organizational behavior: An annual series of analytical essays and critical reviews, Vol 30*. New York: Elsevier.

Cahan, S. & Cohen, N. 1989. Age versus schooling effects on intelligence development. *Child Development, 60*, 1239–1249.

Calvin, C.M., Batty, G.D., Lowe, G.D.O. & Deary, I.J. 2011a. Childhood Intelligence and Midlife Inflammatory and Hemostatic Biomarkers: The National Child Development Study (1958) Cohort. *Health Psychology, 30*, 710–718.

Calvin, C.M., Deary, I.J., Fenton, C., Roberts, B.A., Der, G., Leckenby, N. & Batty, G.D. 2011b. Intelligence in youth and all-cause-mortality: Systematic review with meta-analysis. *International Journal of Epidemiology, 40*, 626–644.

Calvin, C.M., Deary, I.J., Webbink, D., Smith, P., Fernandes, C., Lee, S.H., . . . Visscher, P.M. 2012. Multivariate genetic analyses of cognition and academic achievement from two population samples of 174,000 and 166,000 school children. *Behavior Genetics, 42*, 699–710.

Calvin, C.M., Fernandes, C., Smith, P., Visscher, P.M. & Deary, I.J. 2010. Sex, intelligence and educational achievement in a national cohort of over 175,000 11-year-old schoolchildren in England. *Intelligence, 38*, 424–432.

Campbell, D.G. 1997. *The Mozart effect: Tapping the power of music to heal the body, strengthen the mind, and unlock the creative spirit*. New York: Avon Books.

Carragher, T.N., Carragher, D. & Schliemann, A.D. 1985. Mathematics in the streets and in schools. *British Journal of Developmental Psychology, 3*, 21–29.

Carroll, J.B. 1980. *Individual difference relations in psychometric and experimental cognitive tasks*. Chapel Hill, NC: The L.L. Thurstone Psychometric Laboratory.

Carroll, J.B. 1983. Studying individual differences in cognitive abilities: Through and beyond factor analysis. In: Dillon, R.F. & Schmeck, R.R. (eds.), *Individual differences in cognition, Vol. 1*. New York: Academic.

Carroll, J.B. 1993. *Human cognitive abilities: A survey of factor-analytic studies*. Cambridge, UK: Cambridge University Press.

Carroll, J.B. 1995. Reflections on Stephen Jay Gould's 'The Mismeasure of Man' (1981): A retrospective review. *Intelligence*, 21, 121–134.

Cattell, R.B. 1951. Classical and standard score IQ standardization of the I.P.A.T. Culture-Free Intelligence Scale 2. *Journal of Consulting Psychology*, 15, 154–159.

Cattell, R.B. 1971. *Abilities, their structure growth and action*. New York: Houghton Mifflin.

Ceci, S. 1996. *On intelligence*. Cambridge, MA: Harvard University Press.

Ceci, S.J. 1991. How much does schooling influence general intelligence and its cognitive components—a reassessment of the evidence. *Developmental Psychology*, 27, 703–722.

Chaiken, S.R. & Young, R.K. 1993. Inspection time and intelligence: Attempts to eliminate the apparent movements strategy. *American Journal of Psychology*, 106, 191–210.

Chen, C.Y. & Michael, W.B. 1993. Higher-order abilities conceptualized within Guilford's structure-of-intellect (SOI) model for a sample of United-States-Coast-Guard-Academy cadets—a reanalysis of an SOI data-base. *Educational and Psychological Measurement*, 53, 941–950.

Child, D. 2006. *The essentials of factor analysis*. London: Continuum.

Chipuer, H.M., Plomin, R., Pedersen, N.L., McClearn, G.E. & Nesselroade, J.R. 1993. Genetic influence on the family environment: The role of personality. *Developmental Psychology*, 29, 110–118.

Cianciolo, A.T., Grigorenko, E.L., Jarvin, L., Gil, G., Drebot, M.E. & Sternberg, R.J. 2009. Practical intelligence and tacit knowledge: Advancements in the measurement of developing expertise. In: Kaufman, J.C., Grigorenko, E.L. & Sternberg, R.J. (eds.), *The essential Sternberg: Essays on intelligence, psychology, and education*. New York: Springer Publishing Co.

Clark, H.H. & Chase, W.G. 1972. On the process of comparing sentences against pictures. *Cognitive Psychology*, 3, 472–517.

Cliffordson, C. & Gustafsson, J.E. 2008. Effects of age and schooling on intellectual performance: Estimates obtained from analysis of continuous variation in age and length of schooling. *Intelligence*, 36, 143–152.

Cohen, J. 1988. *Statistical power analysis for the behavioral sciences*. Hillsdale, NJ: Hove, Lawrence Erlbaum.

Colom, R., Abad, F.J., Quiroga, M.A., Shih, P.C. & Flores-Mendoza, C. 2008. Working memory and intelligence are highly related constructs, but why? *Intelligence*, 36, 584–606.

Colom, R., Haier, R. J., Head, K., Alvarez-linera, J., Quiroga, M.A., Shih, P.C. & Jung, R. E. 2009. Gray matter correlates of fluid, crystallized, and spatial intelligence: Testing the P-FIT model. *Intelligence*, 37, 124–135.

Comrey, A.L. & Lee, H.B. 1992. *A first course in factor analysis*. Hillsdale, NY: Lawrence Erlbaum Associates.

Conners, F.A. 1992. Special abilities of idiots savants, hyperlexic children, and phenomenal memorizers: Implications for intelligence theory. In: Detterman, D.K. (ed.), *Is mind modular or unitary?* Westport, CT: Ablex Publishing.

Connor, H. & Dewson, S. 2001. Social class and higher education. *U.K. Department of Education Research Reports*. London: UK Department of Education.

Cooper, C. 1998. *Individual Differences*. London: Arnold.

Cooper, C. 2010. *Individual differences and personality*. London: Hodder Education.

Cooper, C. & Berwick, S.A. 2001. Factors affecting psychological well-being of three groups of suicide-prone prisoners. *Current Psychology*, 20, 169–182.

Cooper, C., Kline, P. & MacLaurin-Jones, L. 1986. Inspection time and primary abilities. *British Journal of Educational Psychology*, 56, 304–308.

Cox, T.H., Lobel, S.A. & McLeod, P.L. 1991. Effects of ethnic-group cultural differences on cooperative and competitive behaviour on a group task. *Academy of Management Journal*, 34, 827–847.

Craig, C.M., Goulon, C.D., Berton, E., Rao, G., Fernandez, L. & Bootsma, R.J. 2009. Optic variables used to judge future ball arrival position in expert and novice soccer players. *Attention, Perception, & Psychophysics*, 71, 515–522.

Crawford, C. & Cribb, J. 2013. *Reading and maths skills at age 10 and earnings in later life: A brief analysis using the British Cohort Study*. London: Institute for Fiscal Studies and CAYT.

Croft, C., Beckett, C., Rutter, M., Castle, J., Colvert, E., Groothues, C., Hawkins, A., Kreppner, J., Stevens, S.E. & Sonuga-Barke, E.J.S. 2007. Early adolescent outcomes of institutionally-deprived and non-deprived adoptees. II: Language as a protective factor and a vulnerable outcome. *Journal of Child Psychology and Psychiatry*, 48, 31–44.

Cronbach, L.J. 1957. The two disciplines of scientific psychology. *American Psychologist*, 12, 671–684.

Daneman, M. & Carpenter, P.A. 1980. Individual differences in working memory and reading. *Journal of Verbal Learning and Verbal Behavior*, 19, 450–466.

Davies, G., Tenesa, A., Payton, A., Yang, J., Harris, S.E., Liewald, D., … Deary, I.J. 2011. Genome-wide association studies establish that human intelligence is highly heritable and polygenic. *Mol Psychiatry*. 16(10). 996–1005.

Davis, O.S.P., Haworth, C.M.A. & Plomin, R. 2009. Learning abilities and disabilities: Generalist genes in early adolescence. *Cognitive Neuropsychiatry*, 14, 312–331.

De Fruyt, F., Van Leeuwen, K., De Bolle, M. & De Clercq, B. 2008. Sex differences in school performance as a function of conscientiousness, imagination and the mediating role of problem behaviour. *European Journal of Personality*, 22, 167–184.

De Groot, A.D. 1951. War and the intelligence of youth. *The Journal of Abnormal and Social Psychology*, 46, 596–597.

De Lange, C. 2012. Tracy Packiam Alloway: Working memory is a better test of ability than IQ. *The Observer*, December 16, 2012.

Deary, I. 1995. Auditory inspection time and intelligence: What is the direction of causation. *Developmental Psychology*, 31, 237–250.

Deary, I.J. 1997. Intelligence and information processing. In: Nyborg, H. (ed.), *The scientific study of human nature*. Oxford: Pergamon.

Deary, I.J. 2000. *Looking down on human intelligence: From psychometrics to the brain*. Oxford: Oxford University Press.

Deary, I.J. 2012. Looking for 'system integrity' in cognitive epidemiology. *Gerontology*, 58, 545–553.

Deary, I.J. & Carryl, P.G. 1993. Intelligence, EEG and evoked potentials. In: Vernon, P.A. (ed.), *Biological approaches to the study of human intelligence*. Norwood NJ: Ablex.

Deary, I.J., Head, B. & Egan, V. 1989. Auditory inspection time, intelligence and pitch discrimination. *Intelligence*, 13, 135–147.

Deary, I.J., Johnson, W. & Houlihan, L.M. 2009. Genetic foundations of human intelligence. *Human Genetics*, 126, 215–232.

Deary, I.J. & Stough, C. 1996. Intelligence and inspection time: Achievements, prospects and problems. *American Psychologist*, 51, 599–608.

Deary, I.J., Strand, S., Smith, P. & Fernandes, C. 2007. Intelligence and educational achievement. *Intelligence*, 35, 13–21.

Deary, I.J., Whalley, L.J., Lemmon, H., Crawford, J.R. & Starr, J.M. 2000. The stability of individual differences in mental ability from childhood to old age: Follow-up of the 1932 Scottish mental survey. *Intelligence*, 28, 49–55.

Deary, I.J., Whiteman, M.C., Starr, J.M., Whalley, L.J. & Fox, H.C. 2004. The impact of childhood intelligence on later life: Following up the Scottish mental surveys of 1932 and 1947. *Journal of Personality and Social Psychology*, 86, 130–147.

Demetriou, A., Kui, Z.X., Spanoudis, G., Christou, C., Kyriakides, L. & Platsidou, M. 2005. The architecture, dynamics, and development of mental processing: Greek, Chinese, or Universal? *Intelligence*, 33, 109–141.

Detterman, D.K. & Daniel, M.H. 1989. Correlations of mental tests with each other are highest for low IQ groups. *Intelligence*, 13, 349–359.

Dilalla, L.F., Thompson, L.A., Plomin, R., Phillips, K., Fagan III, J.F., Haith, M.M., . . . Fulker, D.W. 1990. Infant predictors of pre-school and adult IQ: A study of infant twins and their parents. *Developmental Psychology*, 26, 759–769.

Doppelmayr, M., Klimesch, W., Stadler, W., Pollhuber, D. & Heine, C. 2002. EEG alpha power and intelligence. *Intelligence*, 30, 289–302.

Duckworth, A.L., Quinn, P.D. & Tsukayama, E. 2012. What no child left behind leaves behind: The roles of IQ and self-control in predicting standardized achievement test scores and report card grades. *Journal of Educational Psychology*, 104, 439–451.

Duncan, J., Seitz, R.J., Kolodny, J., Bor, D., Herzog, H., Ahmed, A., . . . Emslie, H. 2000. A neural basis for general intelligence. *Science*, 289, 457–460.

Duncan, O.D., Featherman, D.L. & Duncan, B. 1972. *Socioeconomic background and achievement*. Oxford, England: Seminar Press.

Dunn, R., Griggs, S.A., Olson, J., Beasley, M. & Gorman, B.S. 1995. A meta-analytic validation of the Dunn and Dunn model of learning style preferences. *Journal of Educational Research*, 88, 353–362.

Edmonds, C.J., Isaacs, E.B., Visscher, P.M., Rogers, M., Lanigan, J., Singhal, A., . . . Deary, I.J. 2008. Inspection time and cognitive abilities in twins aged 7 to 17 years: Age-related changes, heritability and genetic covariance. *Intelligence*, 36, 210–225.

Egan, V. 1994. Intelligence, inspection time and cognitive strategies. *British Journal of Psychology*, 85, 305–316.

Ekstrom, R.B., French, J.W. & Harman, H.H. 1976. *Manual for the kit of factor-referenced cognitive tests*. Princeton, NJ: Educational Testing Service.

Ensminger, M.E. & Slusarcick, A.L. 1992. Paths to high-school graduation or dropout—a longitudinal-study of a 1st-grade cohort. *Sociology of Education*, 65, 95–113.

Ertl, J.P. & Schafer, E.W.P. 1969. Brain response correlates of psychometric intelligence. *Nature*, 223, 421–422.

Eysenck, H.J. 1953. The logical basis of factor analysis. *American Psychologist*, 8, 105–114.

Eysenck, H.J. 1962. *Know your own IQ*. Harmondsworth: Penguin.

Eysenck, H.J. 1967. Intelligence assessment: A theoretical and experimental approach. *British Journal of Educational Psychology*, 37, 81–98.

Fancher, R.B. 1985. Spearman's computation of *g*: A model for Burt? *British Journal of Psychology*, 76, 341–352.

Farrelly, D. & Austin, E.J. 2007. Ability EI as an intelligence? Associations of the MSCEIT with performance on emotion processing and social tasks and with cognitive ability. *Cognition & Emotion*, 21, 1043–1063.

Finkel, D., Reynolds, C.A., McArdle, J.J. & Pedersen, N.L. 2005. The longitudinal relationship between processing speed and cognitive ability: Genetic and environmental influences. *Behavior Genetics*, 35, 535–549.

Flashman, L.A., Andreasen, N.C., Flaum, M. & Swayze V.W. 1997. Intelligence and regional brain volumes in normal controls. *Intelligence*, 25, 149–160.

Floyd, R.G., Shands, E.I., Rafael, F.A., Bergeron, R. & McGrew, K.S. 2009. The dependability of general-factor loadings: The effects of factor-extraction methods, test battery composition, test battery size, and their interactions. *Intelligence*, 37, 453–465.

Flynn, J.R. 1984. The mean IQ of Americans—massive gains 1932 to 1978. *Psychological Bulletin*, 95, 29–51.

Flynn, J.R. 1987. Massive IQ gains in 14 nations-what IQ tests really measure. *Psychological Bulletin*, 101, 171–191.

Flynn, J.R. 1999. Searching for justice—The discovery of IQ gains over time. *American Psychologist*, 54, 5–20.

Flynn, J.R. 2007. *What is intelligence? Beyond the Flynn effect.* New York: Cambridge University Press.

Fodor, J.A. 1983. *The modularity of mind: An essay on faculty psychology.* Cambridge, MA: MIT Press.

Fraser, S. (ed.) 1995. *The bell curve wars.* New York: Basic Books.

Frearson, W.M., Barrett, P.T. & Eysenck, H.J. 1988. Intelligence, reaction time and the effects of smoking. *Personality and Individual Differences*, 9, 497–517.

Frearson, W.M. & Eysenck, H.J. 1986. Intelligence, reaction time and a new 'odd man out' paradigm. *Personality and Individual Differences*, 7, 807–817.

Furlow, F.B., Armijoprewitt, T., Gangestad, S.W. & Thornhill, R. 1997. Fluctuating asymmetry and psychometric intelligence. *Proceedings of the Royal Society B-Biological Sciences*, 264, 823–829.

Gale, C.R., Deary, I.J., Cooper, C. & Batty, G.D. 2012. Intelligence in childhood and chronic widespread pain in middle age: The National Child Development Survey. *Pain*, 153, 2339–2344.

Galton, F. 1883. *Inquiries into human faculty and its development.* London: Macmillan.

Garber, H.L., Begab, M.J. & American Association on Mental Retardation. 1988. *The Milwaukee project: Preventing mental retardation in children at risk.* Washington, DC: American Association on Mental Retardation.

Gardner, H. 1983. *Frames of mind (1st ed.).* New York: Basic Books.

Gardner, H. 1993. *Frames of mind (2nd ed.).* London: Harper-Collins.

Gasser, T., Von Lucadou-Müller, I., Verleger, R. & Bächer, P. 1983. Correlating EEG and IQ: A new look at an old problem using computerised EEG parameters. *Electroencephalography and Clinical Neurophysiology*, 55, 493–504.

Geake, J. 2008. Neuromythologies in education. *Educational Research*, 50, 123–133.

Giannitrapani, D. 1969. EEG average frequencies and intelligence. *Electroencephalograpy and Clinical Neurophysiology*, 27.

Giannitrapani, D. 1985. *The electrophysiology of intellectual functions.* Basel: S Karger.

Glutting, J., Adams, W. & Sheslow, D. 2000. *WRIT: Wide Range Intelligence Test manual.* Wilmington, DE: Wide Range.

Goleman, D. 1995. *Emotional intelligence.* New York: Bantam Books.

Gonzales, N.A., Cauce, A.M., Friedman, R.J. & Mason, C.A. 1996. Family, peer, and neighborhood influences on academic achievement among African-American adolescents: One-year prospective effects. *American Journal of Community Psychology*, 24, 365–387.

Gordon, E.E. 1989. *Advanced measures of music audiation: Manual.* Chicago, IL: GIA Publications, Inc.

Gorsuch, R., L. 1983. *Factor analysis.* Hillsdale, NJ: Lawrence Erlbaum Associates.

Gottfredson, L. 1997. Why g matters: The complexity of everyday life. *Intelligence,* 24, 79–132.

Gottfredson, L.S. 2003. Dissecting practical intelligence theory: Its claims and evidence. *Intelligence,* 31, 343–397.

Gottschling, J., Spengler, M., Spinath, B. & Spinath, F.M. 2012. The prediction of school achievement from a behavior genetic perspective: Results from the German twin study on Cognitive Ability, Self-Reported Motivation, and School Achievement (CoSMoS). *Personality and Individual Differences,* 53, 381–386.

Gould, S.J. 1981. *The mismeasure of man.* New York: Norton.

Gould, S.J. 1996. *The mismeasure of man: Revised and expanded edition.* New York, W.W. Norton.

Guilford, J.P. 1967. *The nature of human intelligence.* New York, McGraw-Hill.

Gustafsson, J.-E. 1981. A unifying model for the structure of intellectual abilities. *Intelligence,* 8, 179–203.

Gustafsson, J.-E., Collis, J.M. & Messick, S. 2001. On the hierarchical structure of ability and personality. *Intelligence and personality: Bridging the gap in theory and measurement.* Mahwah, NJ: Lawrence Erlbaum Associates Publishers.

Hagger-Johnson, G., Mottus, R., Craig, L.C.A., Starr, J.M. & Deary, I.J. 2012. Pathways from childhood intelligence and socioeconomic status to late-life cardiovascular disease risk. *Health Psychology,* 31, 403–412.

Haggerty, M.E. 1922. *Haggerty Intelligence Examinations: Delta I and Delta 2: Manual of Directions . . . Catalog of Standard Tests.* Yonkers, NY: World Book Company.

Haier, R.J., Robinson, D.L., Braden, W. & Williams, D. 1983. Electrical potentials of the cerebral cortex and general intelligence. *Personality and Individual Differences,* 4, 591–599.

Haier, R.J., Siegel, B., Nuechterlein, K.H., Hazlet, E., Wu, J., Paek, J., . . . Buchsbaum, M.S. 1988. Cortical glucose metabolic rate correlates of abstract reasoning and attention studies with positron emission tomography. *Intelligence,* 12, 199–217.

Haier, R.J., Siegel, B., Tang, C., Abel, L. & Buchsbaum, M.S. 1992. Intelligence and changes in regional cerebral glucose metabolic rates following learning. *Intelligence,* 16, 415–426.

Hakstian, A.R. & Vandenberg, S.G. 1979. The cross-cultural generalizability of a higher-order cognitive structure model. *Intelligence,* 3, 73–103.

Hakstian, R.N. & Cattell, R.B. 1976. *Manual for the Comprehensive Ability Battery.* Champaign, IL: Institute for Personality and Ability Testing (IPAT).

Hakstian, R.N. & Cattell, R.B. 1978. Higher stratum ability structure on a basis of 20 primary abilities. *Journal of Educational Psychology*, 70, 657–659.

Halford, G.S., Baker, R., McCredden, J.E. & Bain, J.D. 2005. How many variables can humans process? *Psychological Science*, 16, 70–76.

Harlaar, N., Kovas, Y., Dale, P.S., Petrill, S.A. & Plomin, R. 2012. Mathematics is differentially related to reading comprehension and word decoding: Evidence from a genetically sensitive design. *Journal of Educational Psychology*, 104, 622–635.

Harrell, T. & Harrell, M. 1945. Army General Classification Test scores for civilian occupations. *Educational and Psychological Measurement*, 5, 229–239.

Harris, D. 1940. Factors affecting college grades: A review of the literature, 1930–1937. *Psychological Bulletin*, 37, 125–166.

Haworth, C.M.A., Dale, P.S. & Plomin, R. 2009. Generalist genes and high cognitive abilities. *Behavior Genetics*, 39, 437–445.

Haworth, C.M.A., Kovas, Y., Dale, P.S. & Plomin, R. 2008. Science in elementary school: Generalist genes and school environments. *Intelligence*, 36, 694–701.

Haworth, C.M.A., Kovas, Y., Harlaar, N., Hayiou-Thomas, M.E., Petrill, S.A., Dale, P.S. & Plomin, R. 2009. Generalist genes and learning disabilities: A multivariate genetic analysis of low performance in reading, mathematics, language and general cognitive ability in a sample of 8000 12-year-old twins. *Journal of Child Psychology and Psychiatry*, 50, 1318–1325.

Haworth, C.M.A., Wright, M.J., Luciano, M., Martin, N.G., De Geus, E.J.C., Van Beijsterveldt, . . . Plomin, R. 2010. The heritability of general cognitive ability increases linearly from childhood to young adulthood. *Molecular Psychiatry*, 15, 1112–1120.

Hayes, S., Shackell, P. & Mottram, P. 2006. Identifying intellectual disability in a UK prison. *Journal of Applied Research in Intellectual Disabilities*, 19, 256–256.

Heim, A.W., Watts, K.P. & Simmonds, V. 1970. *AH4, AH5 and AH6 Tests*. Windsor: NFER.

Helmke, A. & Van Aken, M.A.G. 1995. The causal ordering of academic achievement and self-concept of ability during elementary school: A longitudinal study. *Journal of Educational Psychology*, 87, 624–637.

Hendrickson, A.E. 1982a. The biological basis of intelligence. Part I: Theory. In: Eysenck, H.J. (ed.), *A model for intelligence*. Berlin: Springer-Verlag.

Hendrickson, D.E. 1982b. The biological basis of intelligence. Part II: Measurement. In: Eysenck, H.J. (ed.), *A model for intelligence*. Berlin: Springer-Verlag.

Herrnstein, R.J. & Murray, C. 1994. *The bell curve: Intelligence and class structure in American life*. New York: The Free Press.

Hoar, S.K. & Pell, S. 1981. A retrospective cohort study of mortality and cancer incidence among chemist. *Journal of Occupational Medicine*, 23, 485–94.

Hogan, H.W. 1978. IQ self-estimates of males and females. *The Journal of Social Psychology*, 106, 137–138.

Horn, J. L. & Cattell, R. B. 1966. Refinement and test of the theory of fluid and crystallised intelligence. *Journal of Educational Psychology*, 57, 253–270.

Howard, B., McGee S., Shin, N. & Shia, R. 2001. The triarchic theory of intelligence and computer-based inquiry learning. *Educational Technology Research and Development*, 49, 49–69.

Howe, M.J.A. 1988a. The hazard of using correlational evidence as a means of identifying the causes of individual ability differences: A rejoinder to Sternberg and a reply to Miles. *British Journal of Psychology*, 79, 539–545.

Howe, M.J.A. 1988b. Intelligence as explanation. *British Journal of Psychology*, 79, 349–360.

Howe, M.J.A. 1989. *Fragments of genius*. London: Routledge.

Howe, M.J.A. 1997. *IQ in question: The truth about intelligence*. London: Sage.

Hunt, E. & Carlson, J. 2007. The standards for conducting research on topics of immediate social relevance. *Intelligence*, 35, 393–399.

Hunt, E.B. 1978. The mechanics of verbal ability. *Psychological Review*, 85, 109–130.

Hunter, J.E. & Schmidt, F.L. 1996. Intelligence and job performance: Economic and social implications. *Psychology Public Policy and Law*, 2, 447–472.

Irwing, P. & Lynn, R. 2005. Sex differences in means and variability on the progressive matrices in university students: A meta-analysis. *British Journal of Psychology*, 96, 505–524.

Jacoby, R. & Glauberman, N. (eds.) 1995. *The Bell Curve debate: History, documents, opinions*. New York: Times Books.

Jencks, C. 1972. *Inequality: A reassessment of the effect of family and schooling in America*. New York: Basic Books.

Jencks, C. 1979. *Who gets ahead? The determinants of economic success in America*. New York: Basic Books.

Jensen, A.R. 1987. Individual differences in the Hick paradigm. In: Vernon, P.A. (ed.), *Speed of information-processing and intelligence*. Norwood, NJ: Ablex.

Jensen, A.R. 1989. The Milwaukee-Project—Preventing Mental-Retardation in Children at Risk—Garber, Hl. *Developmental Review*, 9, 234–258.

Jensen, A., R. 1993a. Spearman's g: Links between psychometrics and biology. *Annals of the New York Academy of Sciences*, 702, 103–129.

Jensen, A.R. 1993b. Spearman's g—links between psychometrics and biology. In: Crinella, F.M. & Yu, J. (eds.), *Brain mechanisms: Papers in memory of Robert Thompson*. New York: New York Academy Sciences.

Jensen, A.R. 1997. The psychophysiology of g. In: Cooper, C. & Varma, V. (eds.) *Processes in individual differences*. London: Routledge.

Jensen, A.R. 1998. *The g factor*. New York: Praeger.

Jensen, A.R. 2006. *Clocking the mind: Mental chronometry and individual differences*. Amsterdam/London: Elsevier.

Jensen, A.R. & Munroe, E. 1974. Reaction time, movement time and intelligence. *Intelligence*, 3, 121–126.

Jinks, J.L. & Fulker, D.W. 1970. Comparison of the biometrical genetical, MAVA and classsical approaches to the analysis of human behavior. *Psychological Bulletin*, 73, 311–349.

Johnson, W. & Bouchard, T. J., Jr. 2005a. The structure of human intelligence: It is verbal, perceptual, and image rotation (VPR), not fluid and crystallized. *Intelligence*, 33, 393–416.

Johnson, W. & Bouchard, T.J., Jr. 2005b. Constructive replication of the visual-perceptual-image rotation model in Thurstone's (1941) battery of 60 tests of mental ability. *Intelligence*, 33, 417–430.

Johnson, W., Te Nijenhuis, J. & Bouchard, T.J. 2008. Still just 1 g: Consistent results from five test batteries. *Intelligence*, 36, 81–95.

Kamin, L.J. 1974. *The science and politics of IQ*. Harmondsworth: Penguin.

Kanfer, P.L., Ackerman, Y.M. & Goff, M. 1995. Personality and intelligence in industrial and organizational psychology. In: Saklofske, D.H. & Zeidner, M. (eds.), *International handbook of personality and intelligence*. New York: Plenum.

Karama, S., Colom, R., Johnson, W., Deary, I. J., Haier, R., Waber, D. P., . . . Brain Development Co-operative Group. 2011. Cortical thickness correlates of specific cognitive performance accounted for by the general factor of intelligence in healthy children aged 6 to 18. *Neuroimage*, 55, 1443–1453.

Katsanis, J. & Iacono, W.G. 1991. Clinical, neuropsychological, and brain structural correlates of smooth-pursuit eye tracking performance in chronic schizophrenia. *Journal of Abnormal Psychology*, 100, 526–534.

Kaufman, S.B., Reynolds, M.R., Liu, X., Kaufman, A.S. & McGrew, K.S. 2012. Are cognitive g and academic achievement g one and the same g? An exploration on the Woodcock-Johnson and Kaufman tests. *Intelligence*, 40, 123–138.

Kline, P. 1986. *A handbook of test construction*. London: Methuen.

Kline, P. 1991. *Intelligence: The psychometric view*. London: Routledge.

Kline, P. 2000. *The handbook of psychological testing*. New York: Routledge.

Kline, P., May, J. & Cooper, C. 1986. Correlations among elementary cognitive tasks. *British Journal of Educational Psychology*, 56, 111–118.

Koke, L.C. & Vernon, P.A. 2003. The Sternberg Triarchic Abilities Test (STAT) as a measure of academic achievement and general intelligence. *Personality and Individual Differences*, 35, 1803–1807.

Kranzler, J.H. & Jensen, A.R. 1989. Inspection time and intelligence: A meta-analysis. *Intelligence*, 13, 329–347.

Krawczyk, D.C., McClelland, M.M. & Donovan, C.M. 2011. A hierarchy for relational reasoning in the prefrontal cortex. *Cortex*, 47, 588–597.

Kremer, J. 2012. *Key concepts in sport psychology*. Los Angeles: Sage.

Kuncel, N.R., Hezlett, S.A. & Ones, D.S. 2004. Academic performance, career potential, creativity, and job performance: Can one construct predict them all? *Journal of Personality and Social Psychology*, 86, 148–161.

Larson, G.E. & Alderton, D.L. 1990. Reaction-time variability and intelligence: 'Worst performance' analysis of individual differences. *Intelligence*, 14, 309–325.

Larson, G.E., Haier, R.J., Lacasse, L. & Hazen, K. 1995. Evaluation of a "mental effort" hypothesis for correlations between cortical metabolism and intelligence. *Intelligence*, 21, 267–278.

Lawson, A.E., Banks, D.L. & Logvin, M. 2007. Self-efficacy, reasoning ability, and achievement in college biology. *Journal of Research in Science Teaching*, 44, 706–724.

Levy, P. 1992. Inspection time and its relation to intelligence: Issues of measurement and meaning. *Personality and Individual Differences*, 13, 987–1002.

Loehlin, J.C. 2004. *Latent variable models: An introduction to factor, path, and structural equation analysis* (4th ed.). Mahwah, NJ: Lawrence Erlbaum Associates Publishers.

Loehlin, J.C., Horn, J.M. & Willerman, L. 1989. Modeling IQ change: Evidence from the Texas Adoption Project. *Child Development*, 60, 993–1004.

Longstreth, L.E. 1984. Jensen's reaction time investigations: A critique. *Intelligence*, 8, 139–160.

Longstreth, L.E. 1986. The real and the unreal: A reply to Jensen & Vernon. *Intelligence*, 10, 181–191.

Lovelace, M.K. 2005. Meta-analysis of experimental research based on the Dunn and Dunn model. *Journal of Educational Research*, 98, 176–183.

Lynn, R. 1987. The intelligence of the Mongoloids: A psychometric, evolutionary and neurological theory. *Personality and Individual Differences*, 8, 813–844.

Lynn, R. 1990. The role of nutrition in secular increases in intelligence. *Personality and Individual Differences*, 11, 273–285.

Lynn, R. 1996. *Dysgenics: Genetic deterioration in modern populations*. Westport, CT: Praeger.

Lynn, R. 2001. *Eugenics: A reassessment*. Westport, CT: Praeger.

Lynn, R. 2008. *The global bell curve: Race, IQ, and inequality worldwide*. Augusta, GA, Washington Summit Publishers.

Lynn, R. & Hampson, S. 1986. Intellectual abilities of Japanese children—an assessment of 2 1/2–8 1/2-year-olds derived from the McCarthy-scales of children's abilities. *Intelligence*, 10, 41–58.

Lynn, R. & Vanhanen, T. 2002. *IQ and the wealth of nations*. Westport, CT: Praeger.

Mackintosh, N.J. 1995. Insight into intelligence. *Nature*, 377, 581–582.

Marcenaro-Gutierrez, O., Galindo-Rueda, F. & Vignoles, A. 2007. Who actually goes to university? *Empirical Economics*, 32, 333–357.

Maul, A. 2012. The validity of the Mayer-Salovey-Caruso Emotional Intelligence Test (MSCEIT) as a measure of emotional intelligence. *Emotion Review*, 4, 394–402.

May, J., Kline, P. & Cooper, C. 1987. A brief computerized form of a schematic analogy task. *British Journal of Psychology*, 78, 29–36.

Mayer, J. D., Caruso, D. R. & Salovey, P. 1999. Emotional intelligence meets traditional standards for an intelligence. *Intelligence*, 27, 267–298.

Mayer, J. D., Salovey, P. & Caruso, D. R. 2002. *Mayer–Salovey–Caruso Emotional Intelligence Test (MSCEIT) user's manual.* Toronto, ON: MHS Publishers.

McCrory, C. & Cooper, C. 2005. The relationship between three auditory inspection time tasks and general intelligence. *Personality and Individual Differences*, 38, 1835–1845.

McCrory, C. & Cooper, C. 2007. Overlap between visual inspection time tasks and general intelligence. *Learning and Individual Differences*, 17, 187–192.

McDaniel, M.A. 2005. Big-brained people are smarter: A meta-analysis of the relationship between in vivo brain volume and intelligence. *Intelligence*, 33, 337–346.

McDaniel, M.A. & Whetzel, D.L. 2005. Situational judgment test research: Informing the debate on practical intelligence theory. *Intelligence*, 33, 515–525.

McRorie, M. & Cooper, C. 2001. Neural transmission and general mental ability. *Learning and Individual Differences*, 13, 335–338.

Miller, G.W. 1970. Factors in school achievement and social class. *Journal of Educational Psychology*, 61, 260–269.

Mundy-Castle, A.C. 1958. Electrophysiological correlates of intelligence. *Journal of Personality*, 26, 184–199.

Murray, C., Pattie, A., Starr, J.M. & Deary, I.J. 2012. Does cognitive ability predict mortality in the ninth decade? The Lothian Birth Cohort 1921. *Intelligence*, 40, 490–498.

Nagoshi, C.T. & Johnson, R.C. 2005. Socioeconomic status does not moderate the familiality of cognitive abilities in the Hawaii family study of cognition. *Journal of Biosocial Science*, 37, 773–781.

Neisser, U. 1983. Components of intelligence or steps in routine procedures? *Cognition*, 15, 189–197.

Neisser, U., Boodoo, G., Bouchard, T., Boykin, A.W., Brody, N., Ceci, S.J., . . . Urbina, S. 1996. Intelligence: Knowns and unknowns. *American Psychologist*, 51, 77–101.

Nettelbeck, T. 1982. Inspection Time—an index for intelligence. *Quarterly Journal of Experimental Psychology Section A-Human Experimental Psychology*, 34, 299–312.

Nettelbeck, T., & Kirby, N. H. 1983. Measures of timed performance and intelligence. *Intelligence*, 7, 39–52.

Nettelbeck, T. & Lally, M. 1976. Inspection time and measured intelligence. *British Journal of Psychology*, 67, 17–22.

Nettelbeck, T. & Wilson, C. 2004. The Flynn effect: Smarter not faster. *Intelligence*, 32, 85–93.

Neubauer, A.C. & Fink, A. 2009. Intelligence and neural efficiency. *Neuroscience and Biobehavioral Reviews*, 33, 1004–1023.

Nunnally, J.C. 1978. *Psychometric theory.* New York: McGraw-Hill.

Oakes, J., Wells, A.S., Jones, M. & Datnow, A. 1997. Detracking: The social construction of ability, cultural politics, and resistance to reform. *Teachers College Record*, 98, 482–510.

Oberauer, K., Schulze, R., Wilhelm, O. & Suss, H. M. 2005. Working memory and intelligence - Their correlation and their relation: Comment on Ackerman, Beier, and Boyle (2005). *Psychological Bulletin*, 131, 61–65.

O'Gorman, J.G. & Lloyd, J.E.M. 1985. Is EEG a consistent measure of individual differences? *Personality and Individual Differences*, 6, 273–275.

Olsson, H., Bjorkman, C., Haag, K. & Juslin, P. 1998. Auditory inspection time: On the importance of selecting the appropriate sensory continuum. *Personality and Individual Differences*, 25, 627–634.

O'Toole, B.I. & Stankov, L. 1992. Ultimate validity of psychological-tests. *Personality and Individual Differences*, 13, 699–716.

Owen, A.M., Hampshire, A., Grahn, J.A., Stenton, R., Dajani, S., Burns, A.S., . . . Ballard, C.G. 2010. Putting brain training to the test. *Nature*, 465, 775–U6.

Pajares, F. & Kranzler, J. 1995. Self-efficacy beliefs and general mental ability in mathematical problem-solving. *Contemporary Educational Psychology*, 20, 426–443.

Pajares, F. & Miller, M.D. 1994. Role of self-efficacy and self-concept beliefs in mathematical problem solving: A path analysis. *Journal of Educational Psychology*, 86, 193–203.

Parker, D.M., Crawford, J.R. & Stephen, E. 1999. Auditory inspection time and intelligence: A new spatial localization task. *Intelligence*, 27, 131–139.

Parks, R.W., Loewenstein, D.A., Dodrill, K.L., Barker, W.W., Yoshii, F., Chang, J.Y., . . . Duara, R. 1988. Cerebral metabolic effects of a verbal fluency test: A PET scan study. *Journal of Clinical and Experimental Neuropsychology*, 10, 565–575.

Pedersen, N.L. & Lichtenstein, P. 1997. Biometric analyses of human abilities. In: Cooper, C. & Varma, V. (eds.), *Processes in individual differences*. London: Routledge.

Penke, L., Maniega, S.M., Bastin, M.E., Hernandez, M.C.V., Murray, C., Royle, N.A., . . . Deary, I.J. 2012. Brain white matter tract integrity as a neural foundation for general intelligence. *Molecular Psychiatry*, 17, 1026–1030.

Pennington, B.F., Filipek, P.A., Lefly, D., Chhabildas, R., Kennedy, D.N., Simon, J.H., . . . Defries, J.C. 2000. A twin MRI study of size variations in the human brain. *Journal of Cognitive Neuroscience*, 12, 223–232.

Petrides, K.V., Pita, R. & Kokkinaki, F. 2007. The location of trait emotional intelligence in personality factor space. *British Journal of Psychology*, 98, 273–289.

Petrill, S.A., Luo, D., Thompson, L.A. & Detterman, D.K. 1996. The independent prediction of general intelligence by elementary cognitive tasks: Genetic influences. *Behavior Genetics*, 26, 135–147.

Pietschnig, J., Voracek, M. & Formann, A.K. 2010. Mozart effect-Shmozart effect: A meta-analysis. *Intelligence*, 38, 314–323.

Pind, J., Gunnarsdottir, E.K. & Johannesson, H.S. 2003. Raven's Standard Progressive Matrices: New school age norms and a study of the test's validity. *Personality and Individual Differences*, 34, 375–386.

Plomin, R. & Asbury, K. 2005. Nature and nurture: Genetic and environmental influences on behavior. *Annals of the American Academy of Political and Social Science*, 600, 86–98.

Plomin, R., Campos, J., Corley, R., Emde, R.N., Fulker, D.W., Kagan, J., . . . Defries, J.C. 1990. Individual differences within the second year of life: The MacArthur Longitudinal Twin Study. In: Columbo, J. & Fagan, J. (eds.), *Individual differences in infancy: Reliability, stability and predictability*. Hillsdale, NJ: Lawrence Erlbaum.

Plomin, R. & Daniels, D. 1987. Why are children in the same family so different from one another? *Behavioral and Brain Science*, 10, 1–16.

Plomin, R. & Daniels, D. 2011. Why are children in the same family so different from one another? *International Journal of Epidemiology*, 40, 563–582.

Plomin, R., Defries, J.C. & Loehlin, J.C. 1977. Genotype-environment interaction and correlation in analysis of human behavior. *Psychological Bulletin*, 84, 309–322.

Plomin, R., Haworth, C.M.A., Meaburn, E.L., Price, T.S., & Davis, O.S.P. 2013. Common DNA markers can account for more than half of the genetic influence on cognitive abilities. *Psychological Science*, 24, 562–568.

Plomin, R., Kennedy, J.K.J. & Craig, I.W. 2006. Editorial: The quest for quantitative trait loci associated with intelligence. *Intelligence*, 34, 513–526.

Plomin, R. & Kovas, Y. 2005. Generalist genes and learning disabilities. *Psychological Bulletin*, 131, 592–617.

Plomin, R., Kovas, Y. & Haworth, C.M.A. 2007. Generalist genes: Genetic links between brain, mind, and education. *Mind Brain and Education*, 1, 11–19.

Plomin, R., Loehlin, J.C. & Defries, J.C. 1985. Genetic and environmental components of 'environmental' influences. *Developmental Psychology*, 21, 391–402.

Plomin, R. & McClearn, G.E. (eds.) 1993. *Nature, nurture and psychology*. Washington DC: American Psychological Association.

Plomin, R., McClearn, G.E., Skuder, P., Vignetti, S., Chorney, M.J., Kasarda, S., . . . McGuffin, P. 1995. Allelic associations between 100 DNA markers and high versus low IQ. *Intelligence*, 21, 31–48.

Plomin, R. & Petrill, S.A. 1997. Genetics and intelligence: What's new? *Intelligence*, 24, 53–77.

Polderman, T. J. C., De Geus, E. J. C., Hoekstra, R. A., Bartels, M., Van Leeuwen, M., Verhulst, F. C., . . . Boomsma, D. I. 2009. Attention problems, inhibitory control, and intelligence index overlapping genetic factors: A study in 9-, 12-, and 18-year-old twins. *Neuropsychology*, 23, 381–391.

Popper, K. R. 1959. *The logic of scientific discovery.* New York: Basic Books.

Posner, M. I. & Mitchell, R. 1967. Chronometric analysis of classification. *Psychological Review*, 74, 392–409.

Posthuma, D. & De Geus, E. J. C. 2006. Progress in the molecular-genetic study of intelligence. *Current Directions in Psychological Science*, 15, 151–155.

Posthuma, D., De Geus, E. J. C., Baare, W. F. C., Pol, H. E. H., Kahn, R. S. & Boomsma, D. I. 2002. The association between brain volume and intelligence is of genetic origin. *Nature Neuroscience*, 5, 83–84.

Press Association. 2013. Universities should target working-class white boys, minister says. *The Guardian*, January 3rd, 2013.

Rabbitt, P. M. A. 1985. Oh g Dr Jensen! Or, g-ing up cognitive psychology. *Behavioral and Brain Sciences*, 8, 238–239.

Ramey, C. T. 1992. High risk children and IQ: Altering intergenerational patterns. *Intelligence*, 16, 239–256.

Raven, J., Raven, J. C. & Court, J. H. 2003. *Manual for Raven's progressive matrices and vocabulary scales.* Oxford: Oxford Psychologists Press.

Raven, J. E., Raven, J. C. & Court, J. H. 1993. *Manual for Raven's progressive matrices and vocabulary scales. Section 1, General overview.* Oxford: Oxford Psychologists Press.

Ree, M. J. & Earles, J. A. 1991. Predicting training success—not much more than g. *Personnel Psychology*, 44, 321–332.

Reed, T. E. & Jensen, A. R. 1991. Arm nerve conduction velocity (NCV), brain NCV, reaction time and intelligence. *Intelligence*, 15, 33–47.

Rehberg, R. A. & Rosenthal, E. R. 1978. *Class and merit in the American high school: An assessment of the revisionist and meritocratic arguments.* New York: Longman.

Reynolds, M. R. & Keith, T. Z. 2007. Spearman's law of diminishing returns in hierarchical models of intelligence for children and adolescents. *Intelligence*, 35, 267–281.

Richardson, K. & Norgate, S. 2005. The equal environments assumption of classical twin studies may not hold. *British Journal of Educational Psychology*, 75, 339–350.

Rijsdijk, F. V., Boomsma, D. I. & Vernon, P. A. 1995a. Genetic-analysis of peripheral-nerve conduction-velocity in twins. *Behavior Genetics*, 25, 341–348.

Rijsdijk, F. V., Vernon, P. A. & Boomsma, D. I. 1995b. Genetic mediation of the correlation between peripheral-nerve conduction-velocity and IQ. *Behavior Genetics*, 25, 285–286.

Rindennann, H. & Neubauer, A. C. 2004. Processing speed, intelligence, creativity, and school performance: Testing of causal hypotheses using structural equation models. *Intelligence*, 32, 573–589.

Robbins, S.B., Oh, I.S., Le, H. & Button, C. 2009. Intervention effects on college performance and retention as mediated by motivational, emotional, and social control factors: Integrated meta-analytic path analyses. *Journal of Applied Psychology,* 94, 1163–1184.

Robinson, D.L. 1996. *Brain, mind, and behavior: A new perspective on human nature.* Westport, CT: Praeger.

Rode, J.C., Mooney, C.H., Arthaud-Day, M.L., Near, J.P., Rubin, R.S., Baldwin, T.T. & Bommer, W.H. 2008. An examination of the structural, discriminant, nomological, and incremental predictive validity of the MSCEIT V2.0. *Intelligence,* 36, 350–366.

Rogers, C.R. 1959. A theory of therapy, personality and interpersonal relationships, as developed in the client-centered framework. In: Koch, S. (ed.), *Psychology: A study of a science.* New York: McGraw-Hill.

Rose, S., Lewontin, R.C. & Kamin, L.J. 1984. *Not in our genes.* Harmondsworth: Penguin.

Rushton, J.P. & Ankney, C.D. 2009. Whole brain size and general mental ability: A review. *International Journal of Neuroscience,* 119, 691–731.

Rust, J. 1975. Cortical evoked potential, personality and intelligence. *Journal of Comparative and Physiological Psychology,* 89, 1220–1226.

Ryan, J.J., Sattler, J.M. & Lopez, S.J. 2000. Age effects on Wechsler adult intelligence scale-III subtests. *Archives of Clinical Neuropsychology,* 15, 311–317.

Salgado, J.F., Anderson, N., Moscoso, S., Bertua, C., De Fruyt, F. & Rolland, J.P. 2003. A meta-analytic study of general mental ability validity for different occupations in the European community. *Journal of Applied Psychology,* 88, 1068–1081.

Salthouse, T.A. 2011. Neuroanatomical substrates of age-related cognitive decline. *Psychological Bulletin,* 137, 753–784.

Saudino, K.J. & Plomin, R. 1997. Cognitive and temperamental mediators of genetic contributions to the home environment during infancy. *Merrill-Palmer Quarterly-Journal of Developmental Psychology,* 43, 1–23.

Scarr, S. & Carter-Saltzman, L. 1982. Genetics and intelligence. In: Sternberg, R.J. (ed.), *Handbook of human intelligence.* Cambridge: Cambridge University Press.

Scarr, S. & McCartney, K. 1983. How people make their own enviornments—a theory of genotype-environment effects. *Child Development,* 54, 424–435.

Schmidt, F.L. & Hunter, J. 2004. General mental ability in the world of work: Occupational attainment and job performance. *Journal of Personality and Social Psychology,* 86, 162–173.

Schmidt, F.L. & Hunter, J.E. 1998. The validity and utility of selection methods in personnel psychology: Practical and theoretical implications of 85 years of research findings. *Psychological Bulletin,* 124, 262–274.

Schmidt, F.L., Outerbridge, A.N., Hunter, J.E. & Goff, S. 1988. Joint relation of experience and ability with job-performance—test of 3 hypotheses. *Journal of Applied Psychology,* 73, 46–57.

Schmiedek, F., Oberauer, K., Wilhelm, O., Suss, H.M. & Wittmann, W.W. 2007. Individual differences in components their relations to working of reaction time distributions and memory and intelligence. *Journal of Experimental Psychology-General*, 136, 414–429.

Schulte, M.J., Ree, M.J. & Carretta, T.R. 2004. Emotional intelligence: Not much more than g and personality. *Personality and Individual Differences*, 37, 1059–1068.

Shearer, C.B. 2007. *The MIDAS: A professional manual*. Dayton, OH: Greyden Press.

Shenkin, S.D., Starr, J.M., Pattie, A., Rush, M.A., Whalley, L.J. & Deary, I.J. 2001. Birth weight and cognitive function at age 11 years: The Scottish Mental Survey 1932. *Archives of Disease in Childhood*, 85, 189–195.

Shepard, R.N. & Metzler, J. 1971. Mental rotation of three-dimensional objects. *Science*, 171, 701–703.

Sheppard, L.D. & Vernon, P.A. 2008. Intelligence and speed of information-processing: A review of 50 years of research. *Personality and Individual Differences*, 44, 535–551.

Siegler, R.S., Duncan, G.J., Davis-Kean, P.E., Duckworth, K., Claessens, A., Engel, M., . . . Chen, M.C. 2012. Early predictors of high school mathematics achievement. *Psychological Science*, 23, 691–697.

Sirin, S.R. 2005. Socioeconomic status and academic achievement: A meta-analytic review of research. *Review of Educational Research*, 75, 417–453.

Snyderman, M. & Rothman, S. 1987. Survey of expert opinion on intelligence and aptitude testing. *American Psychologist*, 42, 137–144.

Spearman, C. 1904. General intelligence objectively determined and measured. *American Journal of Psychology*, 15, 201–293.

Spinath, F.M., Spinath, B. & Plomin, R. 2008. The nature and nurture of intelligence and motivation in the origins of sex differences in elementary school achievement. *European Journal of Personality*, 22, 211–229.

Spitz, H.H. 1997. Some questions about the results of the abecedarian early intervention project cited by the APA task force on intelligence. *American Psychologist*, 52, 72–72.

Spitz, H.H. 1999. Attempts to raise intelligence. In: Anderson, M. (ed.), *The development of intelligence*. Hove: Psychology Press.

Starr, J.M., Deary, I.J., Lemmon, H. & Whalley, L.J. 2000. Mental ability age 11 years and health status age 77 years. *Age and Ageing*, 29, 523–528.

Stauffer, J.M., Ree, M.J. & Carretta, T.R. 1996. Cognitive-components tests are not much more than g: An extension of Kyllonen's analyses. *Journal of General Psychology*, 123, 193–205.

Stelmack, R.M. & Houlihan, M. 1995. Event-related potentials, personality and intelligence: Concepts, issues and evidence. In: Saklofske, D.H. & Zeidner, M. (eds.), *International handbook of personality and intelligence*. New York: Plenum.

Sternberg, R.J. 1977. *Intelligence, information processing and analogical reasoning: The componential analysis of human abilities*. Hillsdale, NJ: Erlbaum.

Sternberg, R.J. 1985. *Beyond IQ*. Cambridge: Cambridge University Press.

Sternberg, R.J. 2000. *Practical intelligence in everyday life*. Cambridge, UK/New York, NY: Cambridge University Press.

Sternberg, R.J., Ferrari, M., Clinkenbeard, P. & Grigorenko, G.L. 1996. Identification, instruction and assessment of gifted children: A construct validation of a triarchic model. *Gifted Child Quarterly*, 40, 129–137.

Sternberg, R.J. & Salter, W. 1982. Conceptions of intelligence. In: Sternberg, R.J. (ed.), *Handbook of human intelligence*. Cambridge: Cambridge University Press.

Sternberg, S. 1969. High-speed scanning in human memory. *Science*, 153, 652–654.

Stevenson, H.W. & Newman, R.S. 1986. Long-term prediction of achievement and attitudes in mathematics and reading. *Child Development*, 57, 646–659.

Stevenson, J. 1997. The genetic basis of personality. In: Cooper, C. & Varma, V. (eds.), *Processes in individual differences*. London: Routledge.

Stewart, P.W., Lonky, E., Reihman, J., Pagano, J., Gump, B.B. & Darvill, T. 2008. The relationship between prenatal PCB exposure and intelligence (IQ) in 9-year-old children. *Environmental Health Perspectives*, 116, 1416–1422.

Stieger, S., Kastner, C.K., Voracek, M., Von Stumm, S., Chamorro-Premuzic, T. & Furnham, A. 2010. Independent effects of personality and sex on self-estimated intelligence: Evidence from Austria. *Psychological Reports*, 107, 553–563.

Strenze, T. 2007. Intelligence and socioeconomic success: A meta-analytic review of longitudinal research. *Intelligence*, 35, 401–426.

Stroop, J.R. 1935. Studies of interference in serial verbal reactions. *Journal of Experimental Psychology*, 18, 643–662.

Sundet, J.M., Tambs, K., Magnus, P. & Berg, K. 1988. On the question of secular trends in the heritability of intelligence test scores: A study of Norwegian twins. *Intelligence*, 12, 47–59.

Tabachnick, B.G. & Fidell, L.S. 2007. *Using multivariate statistics*. Boston, MA/London, UK: Allyn & Bacon.

Tan, U. 1996. Correlations between nonverbal intelligence and peripheral nerve conduction velocity in right-handed subjects: Sex-related differences. *International Journal of Psychophysiology*, 22, 123–128.

Taylor, M.D., Hart, C.L., Smith, G.D., Starr, J.M., Hole, D.J., Whalley, L.J., . . . Deary, I.J. 2003. Childhood mental ability and smoking cessation in adulthood: Prospective observational study linking the Scottish Mental Survey 1932 and the Midspan studies. *Journal of Epidemiology and Community Health*, 57, 464–465.

Thatcher, R.W., North, D. & Biver, C. 2005. EEG and intelligence: Relations between EEG coherence, EEG phase delay and power. *Clinical Neurophysiology*, 116, 2129–2141.

Thienpont, K. & Verleye, G. 2004. Cognitive ability and occupational status in a British cohort. *Journal of Biosocial Science*, 36, 333–349.

Thompson, L.A. 1993. Genetic contributions to intellectual development in infancy and childhood. In: Vernon, P.A. (ed.), *Biological approaches to the study of human intelligence*. Norwood NJ: Ablex.

Thompson, L.A., Detterman, D.K. & Plomin, R. 1991. Associations between cognitive-abilities and scholastic achievement—genetic overlap but environmental differences. *Psychological Science*, 2, 158–165.

Thorndike, E.L. 1921. Intelligence and its measurement: A symposium. *Journal of Educational Psychology*, 12, 123–147, 195–216, 271–275.

Thorndike, R.L. 1985. The central role of general ability in prediction. *Multivariate Behavioral Research*, 1985, 241–254.

Thurstone, L.L. 1938. *Primary mental abilities*. Chicago: University of Chicago Press.

Tisserand, D.J. & Jolles, J. 2003. On the involvement of prefrontal networks in cognitive ageing. *Cortex*, 39, 1107–1128.

Tryon, R.C. 1940. Genetic differences in maze-learning ability in rats. *Yearbook of the National Society of Student Education*, 39, 111–119.

Turkheimer, E., Haley, A., Waldron, M., D'Onofrio, B. & Gottesman, I.I. 2003. Socioeconomic status modifies heritability of IQ in young children. *Psychological Science*, 14, 623–628.

Turkheimer, E., Harden, K. P., D'Onofrio, B. & Gottesman, I. 2009. The Scarr-Rowe interaction between measured socioeconomic status and the heritabillity of cognitive ability. In: McCartney, K. & Weinberg, R.A. (eds.) *Experience and development: A festschrift in honor of Sandra Wood Scarr*. New York: Psychology Press.

Undheim, J.O. 1981. On intelligence I: Broad ability factors in 15-year-old children and Cattell's theory of fluid and crystallised intelligence. *Scandinavian Journal of Psychology*, 22, 171–179.

Vandekerckhove, J. & Tuerlinckx, F. 2007. Fitting the Ratcliff diffusion model to experimental data. *Psychonomic Bulletin & Review*, 14, 1011–1026.

van der Sluis, S., Willemsen, G., de Geus, E. J. C., Boomsma, D. I. & Posthuma, D. 2008. Gene-environment interaction in adults' IQ scores: Measures of past and present environment. *Behavior Genetics*, 38, 348–360.

van de Vijver, F.J.R. & Brouwers, S.A. 2009. Schooling and basic aspects of intelligence: A natural quasi-experiment in Malawi. *Journal of Applied Developmental Psychology*, 30, 67–74.

van Ijzendoorn, M.H., Juffer, F. & Poelhuis, C.W.K. 2005. Adoption and cognitive development: A meta-analytic comparison of adopted and nonadopted children's IQ and school performance. *Psychological Bulletin*, 131, 301–316.

van Ravenzwaaij, D., Brown, S. & Wagenmakers, E.J. 2011. An integrated perspective on the relation between response speed and intelligence. *Cognition*, 119, 381–393.

Venkatesh, S.A. 2008. *Gang leader for a day: A rogue sociologist takes to the streets.* New York: Penguin Press.

Vernon, P.A. 1990. An overview of chronometric measures of intelligence. *School Psychology Review,* 19, 499–410.

Vernon, P.A. & Mori, M. 1992. Intelligence, reaction times and peripheral nerve conduction velocity. *Intelligence,* 16, 273–288.

Vernon, P.A., Wickett, J.C., Bazana, P. & Stelmack, R.M. 2000. The neuropsychology and psychophysiology of human intelligence. In: Sternberg. R.J. (ed.) *Handbook of intelligence.* New York: Cambridge University Press.

Vernon, P.E. 1950. *Structure of human abilities.* London: Methuen.

Vernon, P.E. 1961. *The measurement of abilities.* London: University of London Press.

Vernon, P.E. 1979. *Intelligence, heredity and environment.* San Francisco: W.J. Freeman & Co.

Vickers, D., Nettelbeck, T. & Willson, R.J. 1972. Perceptual indices of performance: The measurement of 'inspection time' and 'noise' in the visual system. *Perception,* 1, 263–295.

Visser, B.A., Ashton, M.C. & Vernon, P.A. 2006. Beyond g: Putting multiple intelligences theory to the test. *Intelligence,* 34, 487–502.

Viteles, M.S. 1930. Psychology in industry. *Psychological Bulletin,* 27, 567–635.

von Stumm, S., Chamorro-Premuzic, T. & Furnham, A. 2009. Decomposing self-estimates of intelligence: Structure and sex differences across 12 nations. *British Journal of Psychology,* 100, 429–442.

von Stumm, S., MacIntyre, S., Batty, D.G., Clark, H. & Deary, I.J. 2010. Intelligence, social class of origin, childhood behavior disturbance and education as predictors of status attainment in midlife in men: The Aberdeen Children of the 1950s study. *Intelligence,* 38, 202–211.

Wade, T., Tiggemann, M., Heath, A.C., Abraham, S. & et al. 1995. EPQ—R personality correlates of bulimia nervosa in an Australian twin population. *Personality and Individual Differences,* 18, 283–285.

Wadsworth, S.J., Corley, R.P., Hewitt, J.K., Plomin, R. & Defries, J.C. 2002. Parent-offspring resemblance for reading performance at 7, 12 and 16 years of age in the Colorado Adoption Project. *Journal of Child Psychology and Psychiatry and Allied Disciplines,* 43, 769–774.

Wagenmakers, E.J., Van Der Maas, H.L.J. & Grasman, R. 2007. An EZ-diffusion model for response time and accuracy. *Psychonomic Bulletin & Review,* 14, 3–22.

Warren, H. & Paxton, W. 2013. *Too young to fail.* London: Save The Children.

Watson, G. & Glaser, E.M. 2008. *Watson-Glaser critical thinking appraisal short form manual.* New York: Pearson.

Webb, C.A., Schwab, Z.J., Weber, M., Deldonno, S., Kipman, M., Weiner, M.R. & Killgore, W.D.S. 2013. Convergent and divergent validity of integrative versus mixed model measures of emotional intelligence. *Intelligence,* 41, 149–156.

Wechsler, D. 1939. *The measurement of adult intelligence.* Baltimore, MD: Williams & Wilkins.

Wechsler, D. 1992. *Wechsler Intelligence Scale for Children®—3rd UK Edition (WISC®-III UK).* London: Psychological Corporation.

Wechsler, D. 2010. *Manual for the Wechsler Adult Intelligence Scale—4th UK Edition (WAIS-IV UK).* London: Pearson.

Weiss, V. 1986. From memory span and mental speed towards the quantum mechanics of intelligence. *Personality and Individual Differences,* 7, 737–749.

Weiss, V. 1989. From short-term memory capacity toward the EEG resonance code. *Personality and Individual Differences,* 10, 501–508.

Whalley, L.J. & Deary, I.J. 2001. Longitudinal cohort study of childhood IQ and survival up to age 76. *BMJ: British Medical Journal,* 322 (7290).

Whalley, L.J., Starr, J.M., Athawes, R., Hunter, D., Pattie, A. & Deary, I.J. 2000. Childhood mental ability and dementia. *Neurology,* 55, 1455–1459.

White, K.R. 1982. The relation between socio-economic status and academic-achievement. *Psychological Bulletin,* 91, 461–481.

White, M. 1996. Interpreting inspection time as a measure of the speed of sensory processing. *Personality and Individual Differences,* 20, 351–363.

Whitley, E., Batty, G.D., Gale, C.R., Deary, I.J., Tynelius, P. & Rasmussen, F. 2010. Intelligence in early adulthood and subsequent risk of unintentional injury over two decades: Cohort study of 1 109 475 Swedish men. *Journal of Epidemiology and Community Health,* 64, 419–425.

Wickett, J.C. & Vernon, P.A. 1994. Peripheral-nerve conduction-velocity, reaction-time, and intelligence—an attempt to replicate Vernon and Mori (1992). *Intelligence,* 18, 127–131.

Widaman, K.F. & Carlson, J.S. 1989. Procedural effects on performance in the Hick paradigm: Bias in reaction time and movement parameters. *Intelligence,* 13, 63–85.

Wilhelm, O. 2005. Measures of emotional intelligence: Practice and standards. In: Schulze, R. & Roberts, R.D. (eds.), *The international handbook of emotional intelligence.* Gottingen, Germany: Hogrefe.

Willerman, L., Schultz, R., Neal Rutledge, J. & Bigler, E.D. 1991. In vivo brain size and intelligence. *Intelligence,* 15, 223–228.

Wilson, P. & Cooper, C. in preparation. Attention and intelligence re-visted. *Intelligence.*

Wilson, R.C. 1983. The Louisville Twin Study: Developmental synchronies in behavior. *Child Development,* 54.

Yerkes, R.M. 1919. Report of the psychology committee of the National Research Council. *Psychological Review,* 26, 83–149.

INDEX